Managing Human Resources

Second Edition

**Alan Cowling with contributors
edited by Chloë Mailer**

Edward Arnold
A division of Hodder & Stoughton
LONDON   MELBOURNE   AUCKLAND

© 1990 A. G. Cowling and C. J. B. Mailer

First published in Great Britain 1981
Second edition 1990
Reprinted 1992

British Library Cataloguing in Publication Data
Managing human resources. – 2nd ed.
1. Personnel management
I. Cowling, A. G. (Alan G.)
II. Mailer, C. J. B. (Chloe J. B.)
658.3

ISBN 0-340-52512-6

Typeset in Linotron Times with Univers by
Rowland Phototypesetting Limited, Bury St Edmunds, Suffolk
Printed and bound in Great Britain for Edward Arnold,
a division of Hodder and Stoughton Limited, Mill Road,
Dunton Green, Sevenoaks, Kent TN13 2YA by
Athenaeum Press Ltd, Newcastle upon Tyne.

Preface

Since Managing Human Resources was first published in 1981 it has been adopted on a range of management and business studies programmes, as well as finding its way on to the bookshelves of practising managers. The first edition was written primarily for line managers and students preparing for line management positions, rather than for personnel specialists. There existed then, and still exists, a sufficiency of specialist personnel texts, but too few texts addressed to the needs of managers outside as well as inside the personnel function with a major responsibility for people. The second edition has this same objective and is addressed to all who have to manage human resources within work organisations.

Since 1981 significant changes have taken place: In 1981 western economies were struggling with economic recession and rising unemployment, while the business ethos was still largely that of the 1970s, influenced by the concept that big is beautiful! In many ways 1981 marked a watershed in thinking about organisations and for the next five years private companies re-learned the message of the need to be closer to the customer and for leaner and fitter organisations. Emphasis began to be placed on enterprise cultures and in the public sector, privatisation and competitiveness. Many large centralised bureaucracies have now been slimmed down and overlarge head offices have dispersed.

As organisations have attempted to assess their competitive advantage, assessing their strengths, weaknesses, opportunities and threats they have come to reappraise the significance of their most valuable resource, the people they employ, appreciating that their strategy now required in most cases a higher calibre of human resource. There has also been the realisation that manpower costs could cripple revival and that the solution lay in lower wage costs together with higher productivity and a better motivated and trained work force. As a result in many firms wage costs per unit of output have fallen as productivity has risen and at the same time higher levels of remuneration, frequently linked to performance and value added, have been implemented.

These and other changes are reflected in this new second edition. In addition the content looks ahead to the challenges posed by the 1990s. European trends including the 1992 harmonisation proposals and the continuing economic threat from Japan and the Far East mean that human resources must be more cost effective. Demographic change, political pressures for equality of opportunity and new concepts of career and career planning that no longer assume life-time employment will also need to be taken on board by managers. In addition, research and practice are now producing new and better human resource techniques and practices. All these developments are reflected in this second edition which aims to take the effective management of human resources forward to meet the next century.

Preface to first edition

This book has been written for students of management and practising managers interested in the management of human resources, and is concerned with the policies, procedures and practices which can lead to the effective recruitment, integration and deployment of the human resources of an enterprise. It is designed as a sequel to an earlier book, R. L. Boot, A. C. Cowling and J. K. Stanworth *Behavioural Sciences for Managers*, Edward Arnold, 1977, which introduces management readers to the behavioural sciences.

Managing Human Resources has been written with a variety of potential readerships in mind. It should prove particularly useful to students taking Part 2 of the Diploma in Management Studies, Stage 2 of the Diploma in Personnel Management, and Human Resources options on MBA courses. It should also interest practising managers who find themselves unable to undertake formal courses of study but who are concerned to review the latest developments in theory and practice relevant to the management of the personnel they control. It is addressed especially to the line manager, on the assumption that line managers bear the primary responsibility for managing personnel, but includes a discussion of the role of the personnel department, and the support personnel managers can provide for line managers and the goals of the organization.

The term 'human resources' was chosen because it reflects a commendable modern emphasis in management terminology on treating employees as a valuable resource requiring expert selection and development rather than the more traditional view of employees as expendable units of labour to be indiscriminately hired and fired in the market place.

The need for this type of approach has been reinforced in recent years by the high cost of employing people and the effect of both government legislation and trade union pressures which render arbitrary dismissal an expensive procedure.

A gulf sometimes exists between theory and practice in the management of human resources, which this book attempts to overcome by decribing both practical techniques and procedures and relevant theory and research. Techniques are not decried, as is the fashion in some quarters, because the writers appreciate from first hand experience that they provide the means by which busy managers can give effect to good policies and procedures. At the same time, care has been taken to present the best techniques available, and to supply constructive criticism, where it has been felt to be relevant. The general emphasis and direction in this book is therefore a *technological* one, that is to say, it is concerned with the practical application of sound theory. It takes as its model the attention given in countries such as Germany and Japan to practical technology and the practical skills of *getting things done*. We hope that it will help readers not only to master the best procedures and practices currently available, but also to go on to forge new and instructive methods which will serve them well in the rapidly changing circumstances in which managers have to operate.

Acknowledgement is due here to the five specialist contributors each of whom we invited to participate in the book because of his or her particular expertise in what has become a very wide-ranging subject. We feel sure that this will enhance the reader's appreciation and understanding of the subject matter as well as ensuring that only the most relevant policies and practices are outlined.

Ensuing chapters in this book concentrate on such key processes as employment, training, development, manpower planning, and remuneration. Because the study of industrial relations now represents a major subject in its own right it is left for detailed treatment in a separate book. However a chapter on labour relations at *plant level* is included. Each chapter takes account of the limitations imposed by financial restraints and organizational policies at the place of work. The growing importance of legislation is reflected in the final chapter, which not only gives an overview of the manner in which legislation now has to be taken into account in the management of human resources in the UK, but also quotes many relevant legal decisions invaluable to both student and manager alike.

AGC
CJBM

Contents

Biographical notes

Alan Cowling
Alan Cowling is Reader in Personnel Management and Director of the Centre for Human Resource Management at Middlesex Polytechnic. His early industrial experience was with Cadbury Brothers and in the gas industry, and he has subsequently lectured and acted as consultant. He recently completed a term of office as Honorary Vice-President of IPM. He is co-author of *Behavioural Sciences for Managers*, second edition, published by Edward Arnold, 1988.

Chloë Mailer
Chloë Mailer is a freelance consultant and writer with practical experience of human resource management in industry. She is an Associate Advisor with the Industrial Society and a former editor of *Industrial Society*. Chloë has acted as Editorial Consultant on this publication.

Alan Anderson
Following a career in personnel management and training, in 1982 he became an independent consultant, based in Melbourn, Cambridge. He specialises in management training, development and selection. In addition, he joined Middlesex Business School in 1989 and is Head of Research Management Courses.

Brenda Barrett
Brenda Barrett is Professor of Law at Middlesex Polytechnic. She has wide experience of lecturing to managers, including safety and personnel managers. She has completed research projects, for the Health and Safety Executive, into the impact of the Health and Safety at Work Act upon management, and also, for HSE, a comparison between occupational health and safety laws on offshore installations in the UK and Norwegian sectors of the North Sea. Other research projects include a survey of the impact of the Safety Representatives and Safety Committees Regulations and comparisons between several aspects of UK and American safety laws.

Max Eggert
Reverend Max A. Eggert is a management psychologist working primarily in the field of interpersonal skills and outplacement. Max originally read theology at Kings, London, before transferring his allegiance to psychology at Birkbeck. He has an MA in Industrial Relations from the Polytechnic of Central London. Max is a Director with TDA International Consulting Group with specific responsibilities for human resources consultancy. He is also an Honorary Curate in the Diocese of Chichester.

Philip James
Philip James is a Senior Lecturer in Industrial Relations at the Middlesex Polytechnic Business School. Philip has taught at the University of Birmingham, and worked as a researcher and editor on *Industrial Relations Review and Report*. He has written extensively on industrial relations and health and safety at work.

Allan Williams
Allan Williams is Professor of Occupational Psychology at City University Business School. He has researched, consulted and published widely in the personnel and organisation development areas. He is co-author of *Changing Culture*, published by IPM.

Introduction

The importance of effective human resource management

Effective managers achieve high levels of performance with available resources. Managers supervise people; this is one of their primary tasks. They also command other resources to a varying degree, including money and physical assets. Describing people as a 'resource' is a relatively recent practice in Britain, and has encountered some resistance which is understandable since people possess far greater intrinsic worth than either money or materials. But not to recognise people as 'resource' has led in the past to less attention being paid to the task of managing people as distinct from other resources, in spite of a certain amount of lip service. Describing people as a 'resource' underlines the fact that people are just as, if not more, important than other resources, and that their management requires similar levels of care, attention and expertise. The concept however is not new. Over thirty years ago, in his classic text, *The Practice of Management*, Peter Drucker charged management with three functions: economic performance, managing managers, and managing workers and work.[1] 'Man, alone of all the resources available to man, can grow and develop' he states, and: 'It implies the consideration of human beings as a resource . . . Managers and workers together represent the human resources of an organisation.'

The role of line management

All managers have responsibility for managing their resources effectively, but most organisations give special attention to 'line managers' – those managers directly responsible for the primary business and success or failure of the enterprise. In 'for profit' companies this would encompass the functions of making, financing and selling the product or service. In complex modern and 'not for profit' organisations the distinction is sometimes harder to make. Managers in staff and

1

support functions may cover a range of activities, including specialist personnel roles, the provision of financial data and budgets. Managers directly responsible for the success or failure of the company must be given extensive control over available resources, including people. Thus they must possess or acquire the most appropriate skills and competencies, necessitating careful selection, training and appraisal, as outlined in this book.

Many managers regard the management of their subordinates as first and foremost a day to day activity concerned primarily with relations at work. It is seen as being concerned with competence in the management of interpersonal relations and the control of behaviour. (This aspect of a manager's work is of critical importance, and is addressed in the companion volume to this book. *Behavioural Sciences for Managers*,[2]). However day to day practice takes place in the context of company policies and procedures, drawn up for the good of the organisation as a whole. Human resource management, much like marketing management or financial management, is to do with policies and procedures. These policies and procedures must in turn facilitate the work of line management, with an absence of unnecessary bureaucracy.

Policy and practice

In designing policies and procedures two considerations must be borne in mind: Firstly, there is no one ideal set of policies and procedures appropriate to all organisations, and secondly, no matter how good those policies and procedures are, they will fail unless carried out and communicated by competent and inspiring managers.

Human resource policies and procedures highly appropriate for one organisation may be highly inappropriate in another. In one organisation detailed job descriptions may be appropriate and helpful; in another they may inhibit enterprise and innovation. Policies and procedures must be designed taking account of key factors such as culture technology and markets. Chapters in this book are designed to facilitate this tailor making process.

The manner of implementation is vital. For example investing large sums of money in the start-up of a new appraisal scheme wil be a waste of time and money unless staff know what they are doing, have confidence in the scheme, have received appropriate training, and continue to receive appropriate support. This may sound obvious, but it is a principle surprisingly frequently overlooked. Successful companies give close attention to both policy and practice.

Arguments for good human resource management

For too long many organisations have paid only lip service to the importance of their employees and sadly, attitude surveys conducted among employees have revealed that the claims of chief executives to value and respect them are not borne out further down the line. Managers have to be realistic and hard headed to survive and succeed, especially in today's competitive climate, and they need to be convinced of the importance of practising good human resource management. Frequently it is seen as a 'bottom line' dilemma. The direct contribution to profits of cost cutting, higher sales and innovative products can be more readily seen. Human resource management has to take a longer term view, with the benefits of improved recruitment, retention and training policies showing through indirectly, in profits in later years. But the relationship exists nonetheless and there are powerful arguments for good human resource management drawn from the best practice in UK, Europe and farther afield.

First and foremost there is the track record of successful enterprises: those which succeeded in weathering economic troughs and who have turned in good results in three years out of four. These span manufacturing, distribution and service sectors. They include household names like Marks and Spencer, ICI, IBM and Abbey National. Very few well known and successful companies have a reputation for poor human resource management. Where they have, changes for the better normally occur after a short time lapse, and frequently, a dip in performance. There exist too international comparisons of economic performance. These have become more popular with the advent of global markets and the prospect of '1992' in Europe. Books such as Peters' and Waterman's: *In Search of Excellence* have drawn attention to the time and care devoted to human resources in successful organisations in Japan, the United States, and the rest of Europe[3].

Sometimes it is changes in management style which have demonstrated a more immediate return on time and money invested in people. For example, the recent interest in 'total quality management' and 'customer satisfaction' has led to intensive programmes of training and culture changes which have shown 'bottom line' results in months rather than years.

As well as positive evidence for good human resource management, there also exist 'negative' arguments, based on necessity and the avoidance of pain. Thus it is 'necessary' to abide by legislation, and today there is far more legislation concerning employment on the statute books than ten years ago. A well informed and professional approach to these constraints is required (a point reflected in later chapters on law and employee relations). Then there are the 'negative' consequences of bad industrial relations and an alienated workforce. While the power of trade unions may have been curtailed, employee discontent can soon have an impact on profitability through poor productivity and a lack of cooperation. An alienated workforce can cost an organisation a lot of money through high levels of absenteeism, labour wastage and low levels of motivation.

There is also a moral argument for good human resource management. This is not a 'bottom line' argument, although an ethical approach to management normally earns the respect and cooperation, of employees. It is rather an argument based on social values. A liberal democracy rests on a recognition of human rights, both in politics and at the place of work. Therefore management has a duty to respect employees in both deed and work. In almost all cases nations which enjoy the highest standards of living are those where respect for individuals and groups is embedded both in the culture or the home and at the place of work.

The role of the personnel or 'human resource' department

Most medium or large organisations now employ personnel specialists, although the nature of their work and their titles can vary enormously. The Institute of Personnel Management advises that 'Personnel Management forms part of every manager's job, but it is the special concern of those employed as specialists in the management team'[4]. In the majority of organisations the personnel department is actively involved in the processes of recruitment, selection, training, employee relations, remuneration, and employee services. At the very least, a professional personnel executive should be expert and up to date in some or all of these areas, in much the same way as an accountant should have professional competence in financial matters or an engineer in a particular branch of engineering.

In the past not enough top grade executives have chosen to make their career in the personnel function, training has been inadequate, and more importantly, too many companies have reinforced the second rate image of their personnel function by drafting in people with only limited experience and providing inadequate support. Fortunately the situation is changing rapidly as organisations come to realise the importance of recruiting first class personnel executives if they are to achieve and maintain competitive advantage and quality of service.

A good personnel department should be able to perform well in a number of roles. Firstly, it should be able to give expert and up to date *advice* on day to day personnel matters, advice which is respected by managers in other departments. Thus it needs an adequate and relevant knowledge base with good social skills in relating to managers. Secondly, it should be able to advise top management on personnel issues relevant to *policy and strategy*. This means a good understanding of both policy and strategy, which in turn means that the personnel department should be knowledgeable about the nature of the business of the organisation it is involved in, including an understanding of relevant financial and legal matters. Thirdly, it should be *administratively competent*. It must be able to carry out its duties in a professional and competent manner and in a way which creates confidence in those with whom it has dealings. Fourthly, the personnel department should be able to *monitor* the execution of personnel policy throughout the organisation. Finally, 'it should', commented Len Peach when director of personnel for IBM United Kingdom, 'have a policy, planning, and research role in addition to providing personnel services such as recruiting, information and guidance to line managers on matters such as industrial relations'[5]. This contrasts with Peter Drucker's criticism of the personnel function in *The Practice of Management* that the work of the personnel department consisted of 'partly a file clerk's job, partly a housekeeping job, partly a social worker's job, and partly fire-fighting to head off union trouble, or to settle it'[6].

Finally, the personnel function has a key role in *facilitating change*. This is because today most organisations must change in order to survive. Change is primarily to do with people. As John Harvey Jones, former Chief Executive of ICI put it: 'Many of the industrial problems with which we are trying to deal in this country have to do with change: changes of value, change of methods of working, the introduction of new technology, changes in perceived career patterns and adaptation to external social values and expectations in our country. I also believe the personnel function has a particular responsibility for stimulating and making line management aware of both the theory and practical experience that can be adapted and applied to the circumstances of the organisation in which one works[7]. Personnel executives thus also require expertise and competence in applied organisational behaviour'.

These obligations on the personnel function to operate at a number of different levels require a wide range of knowledge competencies and skills. The ability to operate at an efficient day to day level, carrying out procedure and routine work in a conscientious manner, while at the same time providing creative advice at the most senior levels in the organisation, necessitate a well organised personnel department with an appropriate mix of skills. It is the same for any major functional department. In the case of the personnel function, these requirements are neatly encapsulated in the following diagram by Karen Legge which underlines the need to design personnel departments appropriate to key contingency variables influencing and constraining the organisation. Of particular importance are the dominant culture of the organisation in which it is to operate (which will influence the style of the operation), the factors which determine the organisational context (which will suggest in which directions the

Framework for the design of a personnel department

		Activity based expertise			
		Steady state activities	Innovative/ development activities	Breakdown/ crises activities	Policy/ direction activities
Expertise	Manpower planning				
	Recruitment and selection				
	Appraisal and evaluation				
	Training				
	Wage and salary administration				
	Industrial relations				
Substantive	Management development				
	Organisation development				
	Organisation design				
	Welfare				

Source: Karen Legge

personnel department may, in the future, have to change and develop) and the extent to which both suggest that the organisation is more or less differentiated[8].

This book has been written to assist all managers and management trainees as well as those in personnel function. The role of the personnel specialist has been featured because of the expert assistance he or she should be able to provide. A comprehensive survey by the Policy Studies Institute in 1984 concluded: 'personnel management has still not generally established itself as having a key part to play in all major management innovations such as the introduction of technical change', and 'we were struck by the persisting lack of professionalism in British personnel management[9]. But a more recent study by the Institute of Manpower Studies reported an increase in the size and influence of the personnel function even in recently restructured and decentralised organisations[10].

References

1 Drucker, P. F., *The Practice of Management*, Mercury Books (Heinemann), 1961.
2 Cowling, A. G. *et al.*, *Behavioural Sciences for Managers*, (second edn.) Edward Arnold, 1988.
3 Peters, J. T. and Waterman, R. H., *In Search of Excellence*, Harper and Row, 1982.
4 Institute of Personnel Management, *A Guide to the Institute*, 1978.
5 Peach, L., 'Personnel Management – Art or Science?', *Personnel Management*, IPM 1972.
6 Drucker, P. F.,*Opus cit.*, Chapter 21.
7 Harvey-Jones, J., 'How I see the Personnel Function', *Personnel Management*, IPM, 1981.
8 Legge, K., 'Contingency Theory and the personnel function', *Personnel Management*, IPM, August 1977.
9 Daniel, W., 'Four years of change for personnel', *Personnel Management*, IPM, December 1986.
10 Hirsh, W., *Manpower Policy and Practice*, Institute of Manpower Studies, Summer 1987.

1

Developing a strategy for human resources

Strategy is concerned with survival and success. Developing a strategy means taking steps to ensure that the organisation is in good shape to cope with changes in its environment, taking advantages of the opportunities which come its way, and is surviving major shocks to its system. Because it is to do with organisational capability, it is very much to do with the people who make up the organisation and their potential contribution to survival and success. Capability does not come about by chance, but by sensible forecasting, planning, and action. This applies to all kinds of organisations, whether in the private, the public, or the non-economic and mutual self-help sectors of society. Because strategy is to do with the longer term, it is frequently overlooked as organisations busy themselves with short-term tactics and reactions to day-to-day events. But a lack of attention to strategy is a sure path to eventual decline and extinction.

The need for top management commitment

Strategy has to come from the top. Top management, be they boards of directors, governing bodies, or heads of public corporations, are appointed to ensure that organisational capability is adequate for survival and success and while in the past strategic thinking has tended to focus on marketing and financial capability, far greater attention is now paid to human resource capability, particularly the calibre of management and the structure and culture of the organisation. For strategy to succeed, there has to be a high level of commitment and involvement by employees. Indeed, this was the lesson of the nineteen eighties. Strategy is not about secret plans and large quantities of paper, but about commitment and capability.

This chapter addresses the principal considerations in formulating a strategy for human resources and the key areas for strategic decision making and implementation. It aims to create a framework for the rest of the book, underlining the point that all practical decisions concerning human resources should be taken in accordance with a prior human resource strategy and it tries to progress beyond the fire-fighting mentality that has permeated too much thinking in this area. Ensuing chapters move directly into areas of practice and procedure, albeit within a strategic framework, and the book concludes with a chapter on manpower planning and control. Readers may prefer to proceed directly to the chapter on manpower planning on the grounds that planning follows logically on from strategy. It is the experience of the authors however that many readers prefer to study operational issues before returning to longer term issues. Readers of this book may not yet be in a position to formulate strategy and to draw up plans. However, all are affected by it, and most will soon be making a contribution, if they do not already do so.

Corporate strategy and human resource strategy

Corporate strategy has been described by Johnson and Scholes as '. . . the matching of the activities of an organisation to the environment in which it operates' and '. . . the matching of the organisation's activities to its resource capability'[1]. Developing a strategy for human resources is similarly a matching process, and is concerned with the manner and extent to which the stock of manpower should be varied to match predicted changes in the environment and to matching the demands of the corporate plans of the enterprise for manpower. Corporate strategy is also concerned to examine whether the corporate plans of the enterprise have to be modified because of limitations and costs relevant to the people side of the business. This requires analysis of relevant aspects of the environment as well as the existing supply of manpower and the motivation and attitudes of key groups of employees. It further requires an evaluation of the options available, selection of an appropriate strategy, and a process of implementation. This is brought out well in the model developed by Johnson and Scholes as illustrated in Figure 1.1.

The model highlights five areas where the analysis and planning of human resources is a significant element in strategic management and which are considered in some detail in this book. These are concerned with the circles in the figure labelled 'environment', 'organisation structure', 'people and systems', 'resources' and 'resource planning'.

The relevant aspect of the environment in this context is the labour market. The labour market is of strategic importance because it not only determines the supply of manpower, but also has a major impact on wage costs and the attitudes of employees. Organisation structure refers to the way in which the organisation is designed; a badly designed structure can cripple an organisation, and a well designed structure can facilitate enterprise, productivity and success. People and systems make up the organisation as a social entity. A well

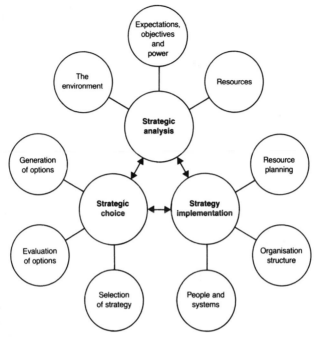

Figure 1.1   A summary model of the elements of strategic management
Source: Johnson, G. and Scholes, K. – *Exploring Corporate Strategy*, 2nd edn,
Prentice Hall 1988

motivated work force sharing appropriate attitudes and values will
demonstrate a culture committed to quality and excellence, and
people and systems will work in harmony. 'Resources' in this case
refers to human resources, in particular, the supply or existing stock of
human resources currently available to contribute to corporate objectives. And 'resource planning', in similar vein, refers to the planning of
human resources, and in particular to plans for the acquisition,
development and utilisation of people.

The first three of these areas are examined in some detail in this
chapter and the fourth and fifth are dealt with later in the final chapter
on manpower planning and control. This split reflects the current
concern of corporate planners with the first three areas, whereas
manpower planners and personnel specialists have traditionally
focussed on resources and resource planning.

A complementary model for strategic human resource planning
developed in the United States is provided by Nkomo and is illustrated
in Figure 1.2. This model brings out the contribution human resource
planning makes to environmental analysis and the need to base

operational plans and activities on a comprehensive human resource strategy.

The effects of change on strategy

Seven trends in British industry have recently been identified which are bringing about major changes and creating a need for coherent human resource strategies[2]. These are as follows:

1   Competitive restructuring. Firms are being compelled to change their organisation structures in the face of new patterns of competition.

2   Decentralisation. Firms are trying to get closer to the customer by decentralising their activities.

3   Internationalisation, including the globalisation of markets and the diminution of UK customer bases.

4   Acquisition and merger.

5   Quality improvement caused by market pressures for higher quality products and services.

6   Technological change.

7   New concepts of service provision and distribution.

While traditional personnel departments frequently do not appear equipped to handle the strategic planning required by these forces for change, there is evidence, as presented in the introduction, that new style human resource departments are making a useful contribution, in cooperation with line managers, chief executives and corporate planners. A number of success stories now exist of effective response to these changes[3]. Two concern European airlines – SAS and British Airways. In both cases human resource planning and development was a major element in the strategy and subsequent action which led to successful turnaround. In the early 1980s British Airways, by its own admission, was grossly overstaffed, morale was low and customer care took second place to internal politics and industrial relations disputes[4]. New management cut staff numbers by 23,000 and unprofitable routes and obsolete aircraft were axed. A cornerstone of the strategy for turnaround was a move to a customer orientated culture.

This required a change in behaviour by airline staff. One third of the staff, those dealing directly with the public were put through a two-day course called 'Putting people first'. Further courses were arranged to develop interpersonal skills and competencies of internal staff. Most important, the chief executive turned up in person to launch the majority of these courses.

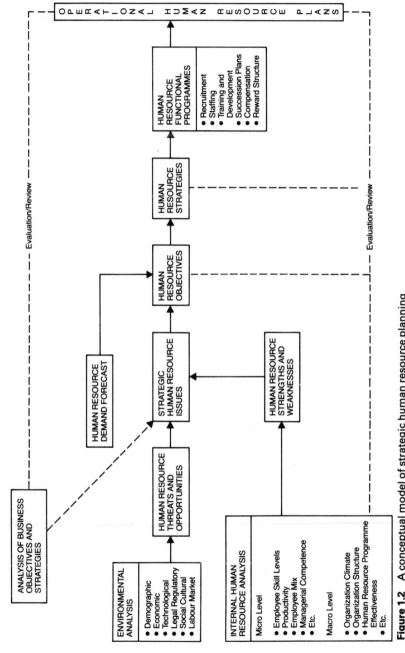

Figure 1.2 A conceptual model of strategic human resource planning
Source: Nkomo, S. M. – Strategic Planning for Human Resources, Long Range Planning, Vol. **21/1**, no. 107, Feb. 1988

A recent study in Germany identified the following factors as having been the cause of corporate failure:

- incompetent leadership
- too dominant influence of the president
- high management turnover
- loss of qualified employees
- over-estimation of financial power
- unsuccessful attempt to enter new market
- failed takeover of a company
- overhasty launching of immature new developments.

The first four lie clearly in the area of human resource management and one can reasonably argue that the other four reflect inadequate attention to strategy, resulting in poor selection and inadequate training of key personnel.

Bernard Taylor, in a review of trends in corporate planning and their implications for the 1990s, concludes that: 'To survive and grow the Western company has to achieve a higher level of performance all round: a reduction in unit costs, a higher productivity, improved quality and better customer service. Also faster new product development, the introduction of new information technologies and more effective marketing'. As a result he says 'New personnel policies have become a special concern of top management:

- segmented organisation structures which divide businesses into smaller autonomous units;
- entrepreneurial managers who are held accountable for profit and growth targets;
- employee communication and training programmes aimed at making the company culture more explicit;
- multi-skilled personnel who are able to do a range of jobs;
- profit-sharing and share ownership schemes available for all levels and;
- performance-related pay and bonuses aimed at fostering team-work and commitment.'

As already indicated, three aspects of corporate strategic analysis and implementation deserve special treatment in a chapter on human resource strategy. They are:

1   labour market analysis,

2 organisation structures,

3 culture and organisation change.

1 Labour market analysis

The external labour market represents the potential *supply* of manpower to the organisation. It also represents the potential *demand* for manpower by competing organisations. It is therefore also concerned with the *price* and *quality* of manpower, which in turn is reflected in *costs* of employment. The supply of, the demand for, and the costs of labour can all be critical to the future of an organisation. The information proceeding from an analysis of the labour market will not only be useful for strategic planning but will greatly assist in the effective recruitment, labour relations and remuneration policies. A potential shortage of young recruits, a skills shortage, or escalating wage costs all represent a threat to the successful execution of strategy.

Areas of current interest to planners include demographic change, skills shortages and labour costs. Demographic trends are also of interest to market planners, who foresee changes in market demand as the age structure of the population changes. These trends are of particular concern to employment departments faced with a rapid decline in the number of school and college leavers entering the labour market. Figure 1.3 highlights this predicted drop in 16–19 year olds in the UK and stabilisation of the labour force during the 1990s. This trend is reflected over most of Europe. A recent survey by the National Economic Development Office and the Training Commission showed that only one in seven employers was well informed about these trends[5]. Of the projected increase of 900,000 in the labour force by 1995 more than four in five net additions will be women, many returning to work after raising families.

The need to plan recruitment and training in the context of demographic trends is highlighted in a recent headline from a national newspaper 'Nine nurses trained to fill 500 vital intensive care jobs'[6]. Organisational capability has been severely constrained in this case, leading to an inability to staff children's intensive care units throughout the UK. A series of short term decisions about the pay, recruitment and training of nurses at a time when school leavers have been in greater supply has left the service in a critical state which will be exacerbated by demographic change. This change also increases demand for nursing skills because it leads to an ageing population.

Skills shortages are a subject of concern to many employers, in spite of the pool of unemployed. Shortages range from qualified engineers and accountants to skilled craftsmen and recent college graduates. Such shortages threaten corporate plans. Human resource planners

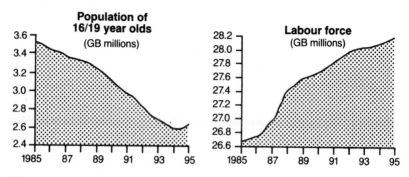

Figure 1.3   Labour force projection from 1985–1995

have first to identify the likely supply of, and demand for those skills in the labour market. One director of human resources in a rapidly expanding computer manufacturing company in trying to anticipate 1992 and its impact on the labour market and skills shortages comments '. . . we'll have to ask what is the manpower story, and look at demographics, the competition, our results, the attractiveness of our conditions. We'll do it in stages. Over the next couple of years, with 1992 coming, that will have an influence on easing mobility in Europe. Standardisation of things like social security, health care, may or may not contribute. But the demographics – that bothers me'[7]. It is likewise predicted that many employers will face an acute shortage of graduates after 1992'[8].

Vocational training is unsatisfactory in Britain. For example, engineering sector craft and technician qualifications in Britain rose from 27,000 in 1975 to 30,000 in 1987. In the same period, however, the increases in France and Germany were from 66,000 to 98,000 and from 103,000 to 134,000 respectively[9].

An imaginative approach to coping with skill shortages at shop floor level by a strategy which combined manpower planning, career structures, annual appraisal and objective setting is provided by the case study shown in Fig 1.4 opposite.

2   Organisation structures

That 'structure follows strategy' is now a cliché of corporate planners. This rests on the principle that having decided on your strategy, you are in a position to design a structure to ensure that it is carried out. While life is rarely that simple, the importance attached to good organisational design has increased in recent years, reflecting the pace of change in the environment. Old fashioned organisation structures based on hierarchy, functional specialisation, and bureaucratic procedures cannot keep pace with contemporary demands.

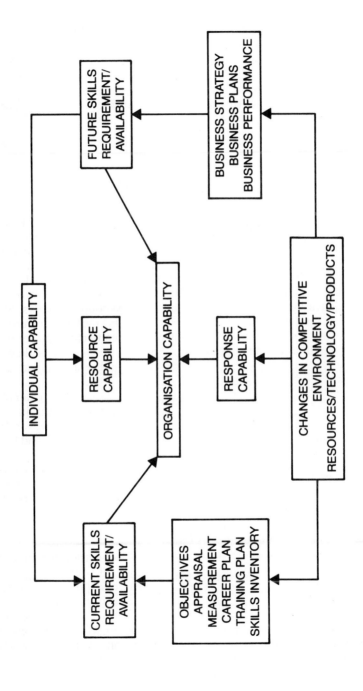

Figure 1.4 Case study – The changing role of the shop floor operator: ICL's strategy

In designing or modifying organisation structure, attention has to be paid both to the formal design of the structure and to *styles* of management. This is because organisations consist of people, and gaining commitment and cooperation is of paramount importance.

Decisions about structure are primarily about the size of operating units, spans of control, reporting relationships and number of levels in the hierarchy. Recent trends have been towards what Peters and Waterman describe as 'simple form, lean staff', representing a swing away from complex reporting relationships and overlarge head offices, to simpler decentralised structures[10].

A typology of basic structures runs as follows:

(a)   *Simple structure*   Employees report directly to the head of the concern, with little or no division of managerial responsibility.

(b)   *Functional structure*   Employees are grouped by functional specialism, with functional heads reporting to a chief executive. This is the most commonly found type of structure in traditional businesses.

(c)   *Divisional structure*   Employees are grouped in divisions, each division comprising a group of homogeneous products. Within each division employees are normally grouped on a functional basis. Activities of divisions are coordinated and regulated by head office.

(d)   *Holding company structure*   The organisation operates as a number of businesses, frequently with their own names and with a high degree of autonomy. Each business is owned by, and reports to, a holding company and board of directors.

(e)   *Matrix structures*   There are a number of different forms of matrix structure, but the essential element is a matrix of responsibility and authority, with functional specialists 'loaned' for periods of time to programme or project directors, who then have 'line' authority over these resources. In another variation, managers may have a matrix of reporting relationships while continuing to occupy their traditional offices, for example to the head of their divisional unit, to a functional head, and to a regional or head office director as well.

(f)   *Adhocracy*   This is not so much a structure as an absence of structure. Normally used for a short period of transition, when the organisation operates on an informal basis.

In deciding the most appropriate form of structure from this typology a number of considerations must be taken into account. These include:

- *Size* The larger the size, the greater the pressure to move to a divisional or holding structure.

- *Markets* The more complex and turbulent the markets the greater the need to adopt a decentralised flexible structure.

- *Coordination and speed of response* The greater the need for coordination and speed of response, the stronger the case for project style matrix structure.

The nature of the environment in which the organisation is operating is the key variable in determining structure. This is brought out in Table 1.1 on p. 20.

A key issue in organisation design is decentralisation. Structures can be operated in a more or less decentralised manner. While divisionalised forms lend themselves to decentralisation, it is possible for a divisionalised structure to be operated in a highly bureaucratic and autocratic manner, with all key decisions being taken at the centre. The evidence from a number of studies is that there exists a strong trend to decentralisation of operating decisions, while financial reporting and control may have become more centralised[11]. This process has been influenced by the IT (information technology) 'revolution', which enables a much faster transmission of information for decision making purposes.

Another key issue is the dominant culture of senior management. There needs to exist a degree of congruence between the beliefs and attitudes of management and structure. Culture and culture change is examined in more detail in the next section, but their impact upon structure and vice versa is sufficiently important to include here. This is brought out by Miles and Snow's typology of dominant cultures and their impact on structure, illustrated in Table 1.2[12]. Thus *Defenders* who aim for a secure and stable niche in the market will prefer stability, efficiency and functional structures. *Prospectors* keen on the exploitation of new products and markets will prefer flexible and decentralised structures. *Analysers* who aim to match new ventures to the present shape of the business will place emphasis on coordinating structures and intensive planning.

3 Culture and organisation change

Too frequently in the past personnel management has been characterised by bureaucratic devices and techniques, developed and operated in order to keep things running efficiently and smoothly and on an even keel.

Selection, training and pay were seen as the application of administrative procedures with which to reinforce the status quo, and this assisted in running 'a tight ship'.

Table 1.1   Four core environments and their structures

	SIMPLE	COMPLEX
STATIC	1. Low perceived uncertainty Environment: Small number of factors and components in the environment: these factors and components are somewhat similar to one another, remain basically the same, and are not changing. Structure: High complexity, high formalisation, and centralisation. Examples: Lawrence and Lorsch's container firms and Woodward's massproduction manufacturing firms.	2. Moderately low perceived uncertainty Environment: Large number of factors and components in the environment; these factors and components are not similar to one another but remain basically the same. Structure: High complexity, high formalisation, and decentralisation. Examples: Hospitals, universities.
DYNAMIC	3. Moderately high perceived uncertainty Environment: Small number of factors and components in the environment; these factors are somewhat similar to one another, and they are in a continual process of change. Structure: Low complexity, low formalisation, and centralisation. Examples: Entrepreneurial firms, where the chief executive maintains tight, personal control.	4. High perceived uncertainty Environment: Large number of factors and components in the environment; these factors and components are not similar to one another and they are in a continual process of change. Structure: Low complexity, low formalisation, and decentralisation. Examples: Lawrence and Lorsch's plastic firms, NASA, electronic firms.

Source: Adapted from Robert Duncan, 'What is the Right Organisation Structure?' *Organization Dynamics.* Winter 1979, p. 63; and Henry Mintzberg. *The Structuring of Organizations* (Englewood Cliffs, N. J.: Prentice-Hall, 1979), p. 286.

Administrative procedures have their right and proper place, but organisations now face more turbulent environments and the emphasis has to be on coping with change rather than maintaining stability. In cases where *strategic planning* points to a need for implementing organisational change, this will in turn require culture change as people in the organisation attempt to move to a new set of values and attitudes to work, and to new ways of behaving. This trend has recently been associated with increased international competition, a greater attention to customers and quality of product or service and a pursuit of excellence. All three of these themes were embodied in the book *In Search of Excellence* by Peters and Waterman, which was instrumental in reviving an interest in culture among business executives, as well as leading to further studies and reports[13]. The nature of their approaches is brought out in Figure 1.5.

Table 1.2 Strategy-structure typologies

STRATEGY	GOAL	STRUCTURAL CHARACTERISTICS
Defender	Stability and efficiency	Tendency toward functional structure with extensive division of labour and high degree of formalisation
		Centralised control and complex vertical information systems
		Simple coordination mechanisms and conflict resolved through hierarchical channels
Prospector	Flexibility	Tendency toward product structure with low division of labour and low degree of formalisation
		Decentralised control and simple horizontal information systems
		Complex coordination mechanisms and conflict resolved through integrators
Analyser	Stability and flexibility	Tendency toward a loose structure combining both functional and product structures
		Moderately centralised control
		Extremely complex and expensive coordination mechanisms: some conflict resolution through product managers, some through normal hierarchical channels

Source: Adapted from Raymond E. Miles, Charles C. Snow, Alan D. Meyer, and Henry J. Coleman, Jr., 'Organizational Strategy, Structure, and Process,' *Academy of Management Review*, July 1978, pp. 552, 554, 556.

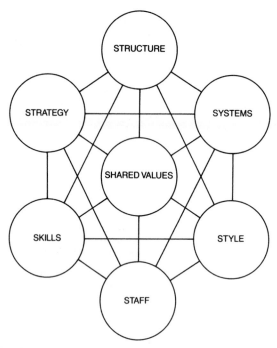

Figure 1.5   McKinsey 7-S framework

This quest for excellence in American corporations was launched in response to the perceived threat of competition from Japan and led to the recognition that the so called soft Ss of – Skills, Staff, Style, and Shared Values – were just as important as the so called hard Ss of Strategy, Structure and Systems. Shared values were seen as the essential key in moving to an organisation where all employees were devoted to the pursuit of excellence in relation to company goals.

It is quite one thing to recognise the significance of culture and values, but quite another to change it in countries such as the UK where there has frequently been distrust between management and employees. Social psychology teaches us that attitudes are hard to change. But social psychology also teaches us that attitudes are more easily changed through peer group pressures, than by confrontation or overt attempts at indoctrination or manipulation. Because values can be taken to refer to deepseated beliefs about the moral order and right and wrong, it is probably more appropriate to refer to attitudes in the context of culture change at work. Here one is concerned to change the attitudes and behaviour of employees in their work situations, for example, both to adopt the attitude that quality is important, and to behave as if quality was important. In one sense, management is primarily concerned with behaviour, and is not concerned with cognitive processes that may or may not be taking place.

Attempting to change culture is a long and expensive business with major implications for the future of the organisation. This is of course why it ranks as a strategic level decision. Typical objectives of culture change programmes in the UK are increased productivity, greater customer satisfaction, better quality, better sense of corporate identity, higher profits, better return on assets and enhanced competitiveness. Typical new culture patterns aimed for include greater customer orientation, participative management styles, open behaviour, greater participation, greater innovativeness, corporate loyalty, and a learning culture[14].

Two popular definitions of culture indicate the simplicity yet complexity of the concept. 'The way things are done around here' reflects the average manager's instinctive recognition of a new culture when he or she moves to a new organisation. 'Culture is that pattern of basic assumptions that a given group has invented, discovered, or developed in learning to cope with its problems of external adaptation and internal integration, that has worked well enough to be considered valid, and therefore, to be taught to new members as the correct way, to perceive, think, and feel in relation to these problems' is the rather more complex definition provided by Edgar Schein[15]. Deal and Kennedy consider that 'Values are the bedrock of any Corporate Culture'[16]. Values express the philosophy of a company and provide guidelines for behaviour. They place great emphasis, based on American studies, on three aspects of culture critical to culture change, namely:

- *Heroes* Heroes are managers with vision, persistence, and commitment who embody the new style values and motivate others.

- *Rites and rituals* Rituals reinforce socially acceptable behaviour, and rites assist in socialising newcomers (a point long recognised in army regimental tradition).

- *Cultural networks* These are the communication networks, formal and informal, that pass messages and which reinforce a particular culture and set of values.

British experience in successful culture change is more prosaic and largely encompasses traditional personnel practices. These include the use of selective redundancy, recruitment and selection of new types of employees, individual and group discussion, conferences, group problem solving, social events, financial rewards, new appraisal procedures and new budgetting systems. This process is facilitated by a strategy led approach, acceptance of the need to change, top level commitment, the impetus of a crisis or new ownership, training and visionary leadership[17]. Further aspects of culture are examined in Chapter 7 in the context of organisation development.

References

1   Johnson, G. and Scholes, K., *Exploring Corporate Strategy* (2nd edn), Prentice Hall, 1988.
2   Hendry, C., Pettigrew, A. and Sparrow, P., 'Changing Pattern of Human Resource Management', *Personnel Management*, November 1988.
3   Cowling, A. and Evans A., 'Organisation Planning and the Role of the Personnel Department', *Personnel Review*, **14**, no. 4, 1985.
4   Marshall, C., 'Two Wings and a Prayer', *The Times*, 17 September 1988.
5   Young People and the Labour Market: A Challenge for the 1990's. NEDO, 1988.
6   Sherman, J., *The Times*, 22 February 1988.
7   Ferguson, A., 'Compaq's Personnel Solution', *Management Today*, May 1988.
8   Pearson, R. and Pike, G., The Graduate Labour Market in the 1990's, *IMS Report*, No. 167.
9   Crafts, N., 'Economical Comment', *Management Today*, April 1988.
10 Peters, T. and Waterman, R. H., *In Search of Excellence* Harper and Row, 1983.
11 Cowling, A. and Evans, A., *Ibid.*
12 Miles, R. E. *et al.*, 'Organisational Strategy, Structure and Process', *Academy of Management Review*, July 1978.
13 Peters, T. and Waterman, R. H., *Ibid.*
14 Dobson, P., Walters, M. and Williams, A., 'Changing Organisational Culture', Paper presented to IPM Annual Conference, October 1988.
15 Schein, E., 'Suppose we took Culture Seriously', *Academy of Management OD Newsletter*, Summer 1984.
16 Deal, R. E. and Kennedy, A. A., *Corporate Culture*, Addison Wesley, 1982.
17 Dobson, P., *et al.*, *Ibid.*

2

Matching people and jobs

Strategic planning looks at the opportunities and threats facing the organisation; manpower planning ensures that human resources will be available when required. Managers contribute to both these processes, and benefit long term from the results. But for most managers a more immediate priority is matching people and jobs. This chapter provides guidelines on this process and outlines sensible and psychologically sound practices and procedures. At the heart of the process is the widely used technique of job analysis which provides the basis for many of the techniques used in human resource management and is therefore examined at this early stage in the book. The process must not rest there however because jobs are being constantly modified. These modifications need to take account of human capabilities as well as technological and commercial considerations. Matching the worker to the job has to be complemented by matching the job to the worker. Today this is a continuous process.

What is job analysis?

Job analysis is the systematic study and analysis of the tasks that together make up a job of work. Information about jobs and tasks is essential to managers involved in:

- planning work loads
- deciding better ways of doing jobs
- selecting and training people for jobs
- determining appropriate levels of pay, and
- reorganising departments and work groups

When undertaking job analysis the following stages should be tackled in a systematic manner.

1   Check on existing sources of information about jobs. Job analysis can be costly in time and money and duplication should be avoided.

Therefore, first check whether relevant job studies have already been carried out by personnel from management services, employment, training or wage administration departments and make use of any records and information that may be available.

2   Decide on the best method of obtaining first hand information about the job. Possible sources of information include direct observation of the job, doing the job oneself, and interviewing the job holder and the supervisor. Where the time cycle is short, as with unskilled and semiskilled jobs, direct observation of the job is recommended. As the time cycle increases and greater discretion is exercised, greater reliance has to be placed on obtaining information from the job holder or holders.

3   Collect information in a systematic manner. The nature and detail of the information collected must be tailored to the objective of the exercise. For example, analysing a job for the purpose of setting up a skills training programme as described in Chapter 5, will require a detailed analysis of skill elements in the job, such as perceptual cues, which are unlikely to be relevant to job analysis for wage administration purposes.

When collecting information ask questions about the job that probe into pertinent aspects: questions which start with such key words as what, why, how, who, when and where. Also observe the guidelines to interviewing provided in Chapter 4. Six checks as a practical aid to systematic and comprehensive job analysis are provided in Table 2.1. Remember to enquire into difficulties job holders may have been experiencing in carrying out their tasks, and any unpleasant features. Distasteful features of jobs are easily overlooked but must be taken into account if problems in recruitment, training and retention are to be overcome. Remember too that a job which may appear dull and uninspiring to you may be of great importance to its occupant, so avoid wounding the feelings of job holders. There does exist a natural tendency for job holders to inflate the importance of their own jobs. Discrepancies between the descriptions of jobs provided by job holders and by their supervisors arise surprisingly often, and need to be reconciled.

For purposes such as training it is also important to establish how a job can best be done (examined in Chapter 5). Consider enlisting the services of a work study or management services department.

Job descriptions

Following job analysis, a job description may be drawn up as a permanent record of the key features of the job and as an aid to recruitment and training. But first, a word of warning: Job descriptions

Table 2.1   Check list for systematic job analysis

Check One – *The key words approach*
What is done
When is it done
Why is it done
Where is it done
How is it done

Check Two – *Responsibilities*
Responsibility for subordinates
Responsibility for machinery, equipment and materials
Responsibility for money

Check Three – *Working relationships*
Relationships with superiors
Relationships with colleagues
Relationships with other departments
Relationships with the public

Chek Four – *Job requirements*
Required standard of performance and results
Required skills and experience
Required intelligence
Required education and training
Required physique and health
Required motivation and social skills

Check Five – *Working conditions*
Physical conditions and surroundings
Social conditions and the working group
Economic conditions including pay

Check Six – *Check up*
Check back with the job holder
Check back with his superior

take time, cost money to produce and traditionally describe the current requirements of a job. Because of this, many organisations do not invest resources in detailed job descriptions. It is noteable, for example, that many Japanese companies do not make great use of job descriptions. This is because they place heavy emphasis on job flexibility. Such companies will use job analysis in say, a job improvement programme or a quality circle, but do not employ individuals just to carry out one specific job.

Nonetheless, written job descriptions are useful in many circumstances. They are useful for example, in organisations where jobs do not change rapidly and the emphasis is on efficient administration and a tidy hierarchical order. But care must be taken that job descriptions do not bring about an inability to respond to change. They are useful in providing information to applicants for employment, the grading of jobs in a job evaluation exercise, and the comparison of jobs in a labour market survey of rates of pay involving several different companies.

Record of information

A job description, according to the BIM should be '. . . a report which outlines the duties, responsibilities and conditions applicable to the job under review. It is essentially a description of the job itself, and not of the individual who is performing the job'[1]. The results should therefore give a clear, concise and readily understandable picture of the job. When wording a job description it is good practice to describe the duties in short crisp statements that start with a verb, and convey the essence of the task. An example is shown in Table 2.2. Where appropriate, a note concerning pay, grading, conditions and reporting relationships should be added.

Table 2.2   Job descriptions – an example

Job title   *Buying Department Manager*
Job grade   *10*
Responsible to   *Contracts Managers*

A. Summary of main responsibilities and activities

☐ Has overall responsibility for procurement of contracts for both direct orders and sub-contracts, including negotiating terms and conditions with suppliers, initiating enquiries, analysing quotations etc., with detailed involvement in very large or complex orders.

☐ Liaises with Estimating and Engineering Departments for technical and cost information; makes recommendations on selection of suppliers.

☐ Responsible for preparation of shipping and packaging for 'Freight on Board' Contracts.

☐ Arranges storage of materials for delayed contracts.

☐ Responsible for inspection and the expediting of orders to ensure that materials, plant and equipment meet the specifications for the job and are available when required. Issues inspection and test reports to the client.

☐ Authorises payment to suppliers and sub-contractors.

☐ Negotiates increased costs with suppliers in association with Contracts Manager.

B. Specific responsibilities

1. Staff
     ☐ *Direct:* Responsible for Senior Buyer, Buyer, Assistant Buyer, Senior Expeditor.
     ☐ *Indirect:* Responsible for (selection, training, development, and appraisal of) all buying and inspection staff in liaison with Contracts Manager.

2. *Assets*
   □ Recommends selection of suppliers and equipment.

3. *Planning*
   □ Plans allocation and organisation of work in contract Buying and Expedition Department.
   □ Provides advice to Contracts Manager during contract planning.

4. *Technical decisions*
   □ Recommends selection of suppliers and sub-contractors on the basis of commercial (rather than technical) considerations.

5. *Financial*
   □ Responsible for negotiating terms and conditions with suppliers and sub-contractors, up to £150,000.
   □ Ensures all orders are executed within Estimators' Budget.
   □ Recommends authorisation of final payments to suppliers and sub-contractors.

6. *Confidential information*
   □ Prices, discounts, profit margins and similar commercial information.

7. *Degree of supervision*
   □ Works within the broad directives of Contracts Manager.
   Reports monthly on deviations in terms of cost, time, quality etc.

8. *Contacts*
   □ Liaises with Head Office Staff e.g. Contracts Manager, Project Engineer, Design Engineers and Estimates for requisitions, specification and prices.
   □ Supplier and sub-contractors
   □ Clients (occasional)
   □ Site staff

9. *Working conditions*
   □ Head Office based; fortnightly visits to suppliers.
   □ Pace of work is often high, working with strict time pressures; involves overall responsibility for a large number of contracts simultaneously.

Job analysis and organisation change

Because managers have in the past been heavily influenced by the 'Scientific Management's school of thought, traditional approaches to job analysis invariably assumed that jobs of work should be stable and structured. 'Scientific Management'advocated organisation structures based upon conventional organisation charts, functional specialisation, and a hierarchy of positions with fixed roles, positions, and reporting relationships. Research as well as practical experience has demonstrated however that there is no one ideal type of organisation structure, and further that enterprises operating in a dynamic environment where markets, technology and social norms are changing fast, need to adopt a flexible approach as outlined in the previous chapter[2]. The implication for job analysis is that traditional job descriptions are appropriate to stable circumstances and correspondingly bureaucratic types of organisation structure, but that a more 'organic' approach is needed in dynamic situations.

This does not do away with the need for job analysis in an organic or less rigidly structured type of organisation, because individuals and jobs still have to be matched. But it does mean that in this situation job descriptions need to be kept brief, and to focus on the objectives of the job rather than detailing historical methods of completing tasks. This point will be taken up again in the context of 'management by objectives' in Chapter 6.

Job descriptions should be written in order to get results, not to stifle creativity. Roger Plachy has made this point well in writing for American managers. 'Job descriptions have been used for their "contractual" purposes: If you do these things, I will pay you. Job descriptions have not been viewed as a method of education, an opportunity to help employees understand why and how the organisation works . . . Let us give employees a sense of purpose and participation in the organisation'[3]. Therefore job descriptions must emphasise the purpose of the job and the results which are expected. The language should include 'action' verbs, and emphasise the importance of initiative and the need to respond to change.

New approaches to managerial job descriptions

Conventional methods of job analysis and job description may not do full justice to the complexities and demands of senior management positions, and a more dynamic approach is called for that makes use of the behavioural sciences. In the UK Rosemary Stewart has successfully developed and applied such an approach. In an earlier study she used daily diaries to record how managers spent their time[4]. The result was a profile analysis which came up with the following as typical profiles:

Group 1   *The Emissaries*
Managers who spent most of their time away from the office e.g. sales managers.

Group 2   *The Writers*
Managers who spent much of their time reading, writing and calculating e.g. payroll and computer managers.

Group 3   *The Discussers*
Managers who spent most of their time with other managers e.g. production engineers and personnel managers.

Group 4   *The Troubleshooters*
Managers who spent a lot of time directly managing subordinates and inspecting work.

Group 5   *The Committee-men*
Managers who spent up to half their time in 'multiple discussion', usually in committee e.g. production managers in charge.

She found that most managers jobs contained aspects of all five factors, but tended to polarise in one particular direction. Further work by Rosemary Stewart[5] analysed management jobs under the headings of 'Constraints', 'Demands', and 'Choices', and has produced modified job profiles. In the USA Mintzberg[6] has usefully analysed the work of managers by focussing upon interpersonal roles, informational roles, and decision roles. While further work needs to be done on the application of role theory to managerial job descriptions, the importance of this approach has now been established, and job analysis of managerial positions should include an investigation of job roles.

There is considerable interest at the present time in the concept of 'competence' as applied to managerial work. Managers are seen as requiring a set of competencies if they are to fulfil their roles adequately. As the debate centres on management development, the nature of these so called competencies and their measurement and development are dealt with later in Chapter 6 in the context of management development.

Assessing the individual

So far we have concentrated on job content, but matching people and jobs also requires a framework for assessing people in relation to job content. Such a framework or plan must adequately describe human attributes relevant to the work situation, in a manner which is psychologically sound and at the same time uses language that makes sense to line management.

The seven-point plan

The best known person profile plan in the UK is the '7 Point Plan' devised by Alex Rodger and widely publicised by the National Institute of Industrial Psychology[7]. The seven 'points' are Physique, Attainments, General Intelligence, Special Aptitude, Interests, Disposition, and Circumstances.

The five-fold grading system

This plan devised by John Munro Fraser[8], has also been widely applied with particular relevance in employment interviewing. It concentrates on the factors of 'First Impression', 'Qualifications', 'Abilities', 'Motivation' and 'Adjustment'.

The vital factors

Whatever scheme is used when matching people to jobs, managers must take account of six basic factors. These are presented briefly here, and then examined in greater detail in the next chapter.

Physical attributes

Jobs vary greatly in their physical demands. Some manual jobs require continuous physical effort and considerable strength and dexterity. Some executive positions require a physique that will stand up to stress, long hours, and much travel. Engineering apprentices must not suffer from colour blindness. Policemen have to demonstrate an impressive physical appearance, and so on.

Mental attributes

In addition to the general intelligence assessed by conventional intelligence tests, jobs may require persons with creative ability, numerical ability and verbal ability.

Education and qualifications

Some jobs demand particular qualifications, such as degrees, diplomas and certificates of education. Many professions now require higher education and appropriate professional qualifications. It is important not to specify qualifications higher than those really required, as over-qualified employees become easily dissatisfied with their jobs.

Experience training and skill

Education and qualifications do not necessarily result in the acquisition of practical skills. Skill is the demonstrable ability to cope at an appropriate level of competence with the demands made by a task or set of tasks. A trade union card is not a guarantee of a skill, nor a college degree a guarantee of competence. Skills are mainly acquired through training and experience.

Personality

Personality problems all too frequently prevent well qualified and skilled employees from producing good results. Key factors are motivation and social adjustment.

Special circumstances

Some jobs make special demands over and above those already listed. They may, for example, only be undertaken by persons of particular sex or age or social group. Satisfactory person profile plans must not only cover the essential demands made by a job, but do it in such a way that the factors are susceptible to measurement and reasonably precise description.

Measurement and grading of people and jobs

Matching people and jobs should be based as far as possible on systematic measurement and grading. Measuring human attributes can present a challenge because the precise definitions and forms of measurement used in the physical sciences are frequently not appropriate to the behavioural sciences. Human 'qualities' are difficult to define and are frequently not susceptible to direct observation and measurement. 'Motivation' for example is generally agreed to be a key factor at the place of work, but is difficult to define and measure in a precise manner.

For certain human attributes objective tests have been developed and we examine these in the next chapter. A practical compromise however has been found in the development of grading schemes linked to person profile plans and comparative scales.

Comparative scales

In every day life a variety of measurements, comparisons and descriptions are incorporated into the discussion and assessment of people's abilities which range from the objective to the subjective. Physical measurements such as temperature, height and weight are nicely precise and objective. But for most purposes we make use of personal judgements, such as 'he is a good worker' or 'she is a slow worker', termed 'nominal' scales. Whilst nominal judgements may be based on fleeting and highly subjective impressions, they can also be based upon careful observation and wide experience. Such judgements can be converted into useful comparative scales, termed 'ordinal' scales, where people are put into rank order.

Ordinal scales add the concept 'greater than' to the concept 'different from' used in nominal scales. Nominal scales cannot be dealt with arithmetically because they are not quantitative. Ordinal scales however do permit a limited degree of mathematical calculation, although we still cannot add multiply and subtract comparative judgements. Thus we can sensibly say that person 'A' is more intelligent than person 'B', and that person 'A' is as intelligent as the top ten per cent of a sample of persons, but we cannot therefore say that 'A' is twice as intelligent as 'B'.

Further precision is added by using an 'interval' scale, that is a scale which gives information about distances between adjacent points, as well as about their order. Temperature scales represent interval scales. Where possible it is useful to turn measurements and judgements of human attributes into interval scales or, failing that, into simple grading systems. Assessment is also aided by use of standards of comparison. The information that 'A' earns one hundred pounds a week, or that 'A' is more intelligent than 'B' calls for some kind of yardstick to show whether one hundred pounds is a relatively low or high wage, or whether 'A' and 'B' are more or less intelligent than others in the population.

Statistical analysis, particularly sampling techniques, and our knowledge of the manner in which human attributes are distributed in the population, are of great assistance in drawing up standards for comparison, and in devising grading systems and interval scales. The best known and most widely used are based on the so called 'normal curve of distribution'.

The normal curve of distribution

Many human attributes e.g. height, weight, intelligence and manual dexterity, are distributed 'normally' throughout the population, with a large proportion of people tending to be somewhere near to 'average'. When measurements from a large random sample of the population are plotted on a scattergram, the result will tend to look like the curve represented on Figure 2.1.

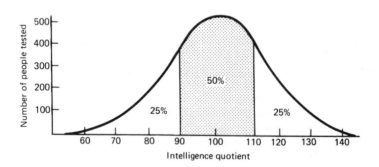

Figure 2.1 Normal distribution curve for general intelligence. The illustration shows Intelligence Quotient as measured by an intelligence test on large random sample of the population but it might just as well have shown height, weight, or a special aptitude. Note that half the population falls within quite a narrow band of ability.

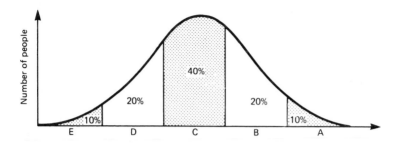

Figure 2.2 Grading scheme based on curve of distribution (A/E scale)

Provided a statistically valid sample has been used, useful statements about individual measurements appearing within the distribution can be made. These include statements concerning the 'average' (i.e. the arithmetic mean, median, or mode), the 'range' (the spread from highest to lowest measurement) and the 'standard deviation'.

This type of distribution provides us with the basis for interval scales and grading systems. Thus the IQ scores on Figure 2.1 can be used as an interval scale. For practical purposes a fivefold grading scheme, resembling many used by managers in their day to day work e.g. in appraisal systems, can be imposed on the distribution. This is illustrated in Figure 2.2. By convention the top ten per cent are graded as 'A', the next twenty per cent as 'B' and so on. (See also Table 3.1 in Chapter 3.) If this system is used to match people and jobs an important element of precision is achieved.

Instead of talking vaguely about 'average' or 'good' and 'bad' employees and aptitudes, managers are now able to refer to a particular grade as percentage.

Naturally this system has its limitations, and these should be clearly recognised. The problems of definitions and measurement have already been alluded to, and insufficient data is available concerning the distribution of many human attributes. But where scales can be constructed and used in conjunction with the type of systematic person profile plan already described, managers are able to progress from simple intuition or guesswork to a much firmer basis in matching people and jobs. Further ways of measuring human abilities are examined in the next chapter.

Job specifications

Drawing up a job specification represents the final stage in job analysis directed towards finding individuals to match job requirements, and avoiding square pegs in round holes. A job specification is a highly specific description of the type or types of person who would perform successfully in a particular job of work. It should outline in precise fashion the characteristics of such persons using a person profile plan, and where applicable, a grading system. It is good practice to lay down

Table 2.3   Job specification using Six Factor Plan:
Job title: Buying Department Manager

A. **Physical attributes**
Minimum
Good health record. Few absences from work. Tidy appearance. No significant disabilities.
Desirable
Excellent health record. Smart appearance. Creates good impression on others. Capable of working for long hours under pressure.

B. **Mental attributes**
Minimum
Top 30% (AB Grade) for general intelligence, verbal ability and numerical ability.
Desirable
Top 10% (A Grade) for general intelligence, verbal ability and numerical ability.

C. **Education and qualifications**
Minimum
4 GCSE subjects, including Maths and English at grade C or above
Desirable
Higher National Certificate in either Business Studies or Engineering. Membership of Institute of Purchasing and Supply. Diploma in Management Studies.

D. **Experience training and skill**
Minimum
5 years' experience in purchasing, including responsibility for contracts of up to £100 000. Two years' experience of supervising a small office or section. Ability to write good reports and to understand basic financial information.
Desirable
10 years' experience in purchasing, including responsibility for contracts up to £150 000. Successful record of supervising qualified staff. Good social skills. Successful completion of a reputable management training course. Ability to plan organise, co-ordinate and control work under pressure.

E. **Personality**
Minimum
Motivated to achieve middle management status. Stable personality. Career record shows ability to adjust to normal social circumstances.
Desirable
Motivated to achieve senior management status. Mature and stable personality. Socially well adjusted. Able to communicate at all levels.

F. **Special circumstances**
Minimum
Aged between 28 and 55 years. Able to work overtime and at weekends.
Desirable
Aged between 32 and 50 years. Willing to work long hours when required, and to transfer to other locations in the UK.

---

both the minimum and desirable characteristics sought, recognising that the ideal type of worker may not be available. Table 2.3 provides an example of a job specification based on the job described in Table 2.2 on page 28. Equipped with job description and a job specification, a manager is able to tackle recruitment, training, allocation of pay grades and appraisals in a systematic fashion.

Many organisations are looking again at their job specifications in the light of demographic change and skill shortages. Given the drop in the number of school leavers and the shortages of trained manpower, recruitment age bands are being broadened, and fresh attention is being paid to minority ethnic groups, and part time workers. This point is taken up again in the next chapter in the context of recruitment. Apart from moral and political issues, many organisations have failed to optimise their sources of recruitment because they have not based their job specifications on a genuine analysis of the qualities really required to perform well in a job, and have suffered because of their prejudices.

Fitting jobs to people

While managers have generally recognised that jobs sometimes have to be adapted to individuals, especially where someone of unusual talent is concerned, emphasis has traditionally been placed on fitting people to jobs, rather than fitting jobs to people. However, recent economic technological and social pressures have led to measures that adapt jobs to suit the average employee. These pressures include:

- the need for greater efficiency and productivity from all categories of employee,

- shortages in labour markets and high labour turnover creating difficulties in the recruitment of employees to match existing job specifications,

- social change reinforced by legal and political pressures.

The contribution of ergonomics

Ergonomics is concerned with '. . . the study of the relations between man and his occupation, equipment and environment, and particularly the application of anatomical, physiological and psychological knowledge to the problems arising therefrom[9]. Modern ergonomics considers person and machine as interacting parts of the same system. This is illustrated in Figure 2.3. A three stage approach is recommended, consisting of:

System analysis

The person-machine system should be analysed for the definition of its goals and the functions necessary to achieve these goals, using such criteria as cost, safety and performance.

Work station analysis

From considerations of the person in terms of age, size, intelligence, training and so on the analysis should move onto his or her interaction with the machine and subsequently to interaction with the workspace, covering items such as position of tables, chairs and controls, and using the basic criteria of posture, reach, safety, efficiency and comfort. Finally, consideration should be given to the working environment including heating, lighting, ventilation and social interaction.

Evaluation

Any new system should be subjected to trial, evaluation, and any necessary corrections.

Examples of the practical application of ergonomics can be seen in the improved layout of control panels in petrochemical plants and power stations, better office furniture, and more efficient instrument panels in modern automobiles and machine tools[10].

Work restructuring

A further response to labour market problems and social change has been the restructuring of work to create greater variety and participation.

The most significant developments have included:

1 *Job enlargement*   Greater variety may be added to a job without altering the level of skill needed.

2 *Job rotation*   Workers are trained in several different jobs which they take turns to work upon.

3 *Job enrichment*   Workers are given greater responsibility and discretion in carrying out their tasks.

4 *Group autonomy*   Groups of workers are given training in a set of interdependent tasks comprising a number of jobs, and then take on collective responsibility for their completion.

Most work on job redesign programmes has been undertaken in Scandinavia and Northern Europe, where improvements in produc-

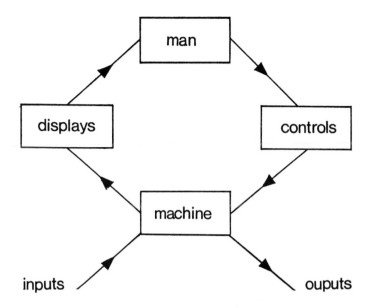

Figure 2.3   Man-machine system

tivity and labour relations have generally been demonstrated[11, 12]. Less initiative has been shown in the United States and in the UK. However, several successful job redesign programmes have been undertaken in the UK. One example is provided by the United Biscuits Company in Liverpool[13]. In this case, the technology of biscuit production inhibited radical changes in the physical aspects of work. Emphasis was therefore put on forming work groups, recognising flexibility within each group and involving employees through group meetings in issues such as safety, hygiene costs, quality and control information.

One of the forces for change is the pursuit of quality and excellence at work. The pressure of Japanese competition and the expectation of customers has led to the adoption of total quality programmes, where all employees are expected to contribute to the elimination of defects and to improved customer care. This is frequently included in the type of strategic initiative and culture change programme described in the previous chapter. From the perspective of improving the match between people and jobs its relevance lies in reminding managers that employees themselves can make an enormous contribution to the design of work and work procedures. The modern manager is expected to achieve the successful involvement of his subordinates in a manner rarely demanded of his predecessors.

The impact of information technology

Developments in information technology are resulting in new ways of working in all sectors of the economy, from the use of robots on production lines to the electronic office. Two features of this process, which promise in time to revolutionise the design of work, are worth noting here.

The advent of the electronic office and the increase in VDU operations can lead to many complaints by employees. Badly designed work stations can cause intolerable strain. Increased keyboard operations, as in word processing, have brought about strain injuries, including backache, eyestrain and headaches. These problems can be overcome by the application of ergonomics, and a number of recommendations for better practice have been made[14].

Expert systems are being developed to improve the match between people and jobs. Expert systems are computer programs which contain knowledge about particular fields of human activity and experience which, through linkages and rules built into the system design, can help to solve real problems. These developments are still at an early stage, but will make an increasing impact on the management of human resources in the future[15].

References

1   British Institute of Management, *Job evaluation*, Management Publications Ltd., 1970.
2   Cowling, A. G. *et al.*, *Behavioural sciences for managers*, Ch. 6, Edward Arnold, 1988.
3   Plachy, R. J., 'Writing Job Descriptions that get Results', *Personnel*, October 1987.
4   Stewart, R., *Managers and their jobs*, Macmillan, 1967.
5   Stewart, R., *Contrasts in management*, McGraw Hill, 1976.
6   Mintzberg, H., *The nature of managerial work*, Harper 1973.
7   Rodger, A., *The seven point plan*, National Institute of Industrial Psychology, 1968.
8   Munro-Fraser, J., *Handbook of employment interviewing*, MacDonald Evans, 1978.
9   Singleton, T., 'Psychological aspects of man-machine systems', *Psychology at work*, P. B. Warr (Ed.) Penguin, 1971.
10 Murphy, J. W. and Shackel, B., 'Are we sitting comfortably' *Personnel Management*, August, 1970.
11 Cooper, R., *Job motivation and job design*, Institute of Personnel Management, 1974.
12 Gyllenhammer, P., *People at work*, Addison Wesley, 1978.
13 Bailey, J., 'Moulding work to people', *Industrial Society*, May/June 1978.
14 Damodaran, L. *et al.*, *Designing Systems for People.*, NCC/Loughborough 1980.
15 Green, H., 'Matching People to Jobs: an expert system approach', *Personnel Management*, September 1987.

3

Recruitment and selection

Replenishing their stock of human resources is a critical activity in most organisations. Recruitment and selection practices have an impact in both the short and long term on the capability of the enterprise. In the short term the selection of high calibre senior managers can have a rapid impact on corporate capability. However, this is only possible if the work force itself possesses the capability to rise to new challenges, and creating a competent and committed work force is a longer term proposition. The importance of good recruitment and selection has been highlighted in the recent past as the focus in labour relations has shifted from collective bargaining to human resource development and recruitment.

The responsibility for recruitment and selection, as in all good human resource practices, is shared between line management and the personnel function. The personnel department should be competent to advise on the best and most modern techniques and practices, and to provide a professional support and monitoring service, while line management must be involved in the final decisions as to who does or does not work in their departments. This means that line management must receive training and advice in selection matters, particularly in interviewing. Too many bad employment decisions can still be put down to untrained line managers recruiting staff on the basis of a badly conducted interview. Interviewing is such an important subject it is given special treatment in the next chapter.

It is worth reflecting for a moment on the potential costs and benefits of recruitment and selection. The decision to employ someone is an important decision both for the organisation and that individual. The costs of employing someone can be looked at from three perspectives. The first is the cost of recruitment and selection, involving as it does the costs of advertising, testing, interviewing and placement, which in itself can run into several thousand pounds or more. The second is the employment costs which accrue once that individual has started work.

These costs are considerably more than just direct wage costs, involving as they do indirect benefits plus the costs of office or factory space plus equipment and support services. Furthermore, these costs can no longer be treated as simple variable costs, because labour can no longer be hired and fired in an indiscriminate manner. Rather these are quasi-fixed costs and the decision to employ an individual is tantamout to an investment decision by the organisation. Additionally, there is the potential cost of a bad decision. Whether at management or shop floor level, the employment of someone who turns out to be a 'rotten apple' can have a marked impact upon morale and the competence of the organisation. Eyebrows have been raised at the time and money devoted by Japanese firms in the UK to the recruitment and selection of manual workers and yet it has paid handsome dividends. The costs of poor recruitment and selection decisions can cripple an organisation, but the benefits of good recruitment and selection show through in enhanced capability, higher quality decisions and better customer service.

The two terms recruitment and selection refer to complementary processes in employment. Recruitment is the more general term, and refers to the process of confirming the need to employ fresh staff, locating where potential recruits exists, and attracting appropriate applications for employment. Selection takes place once an appropriate short list has been drawn up. While more attention has traditionally been paid to selection than recruitment, particularly by occupational psychologists, there are times when recruitment has a higher priority. This applies particularly when there are skill shortages or, as at the present time, when demographic change means that the labour market can turn into a sellers market. The most sophisticated selection procedures are of little use if there are no suitable candidates for employment. This is one reason why labour markets and recruitment now feature in strategic planning, as outlined in Chapter 1.

The process of recruitment

Recruitment describes the process and various stages of searching for suitable candidates to fill vacancies in the work force. Three initial conditions however must be fulfilled before this search begins:

1 confirmation of the need to fill the vacancy;
2 reference to the manpower plans to check on the overall situation;
3 completion of appropriate job analyses and specifications.

Vacancies usually arise because of the departure of existing employees ('labour turnover'), but may also come about because a new position has been created. In either case it is important to check whether internal reorganisation or temporary staff can make recruitment superfluous. To avoid the process being continuously initiated without questioning, many organisations operate a system of job requisitions, which have to be countersigned by a senior executive.

The search for suitable candidates to fill a *confirmed* vacancy should begin within the organisation. This practice is good for morale, assures employees of avenues for promotion, and ensures that existing talent is not overlooked. Frequently agreement is reached with trade unions to advertise all vacancies internally prior to, or at the same time, as they are advertised externally. Care must be taken that this practice is not taken too far, hindering the recruitment of talent from outside. It is largely a matter of getting the balance right so that the organisation continues to thrive and prosper, in the interests of all concerned.

External services in recruitment

A wide variety of bodies, both public and private, provide a service to the recruiter. In the UK free service is offered by the Department of Employment through its Job Centres for manual and clerical staff, although the suitability of candidates referred to employers varies considerably from region to region. Some professional and trade associations also offer a free service concerning their own members.

Private agencies generally charge a commercial fee based on the salary offered. They frequently specialise in office, technical, or professional and managerial staff. (The services offered range from advertising and initial search for suitable candidates, to interviewing, testing, checking references and final selection.) While all agencies claim to investigate the credentials of the candidates they supply, it is good practice to check on this. A few management recruitment agencies and consultants specialise in searching for executives with special talents (by making a personal approach to individuals) who may not respond to press advertisements. This practice of 'head-hunting' is naturally subject to debate because it causes apparently contented executives to change employment.

The decision on whether or not to use outside agencies must turn on the availability of existing personnel services within the organisation, and the cost of the exercise in relation to the benefits likely to accrue. In general those employers who know what they are looking for and take the trouble to check on the calibre of recruits obtain a better service from outside agencies than those who do not.

Labour market 'intelligence'

The labour market represents the supply of existing or potential recruits to the labour force. The most efficient selection methods are of little use if an adequate supply does not exist within the labour market. It is therefore important for management to have a good intelligence service concerning the numbers and quality of candidates likely to seek work in the labour market in relation to the skills employed by the enterprise, and the pay and conditions which will equate demand and supply. In most organisations it is the responsibility of the personnel department to provide such information (advice on planning the labour supply is provided in Chapter 12 and on establishing competitive rates of pay in Chapter 8).

Competitive rates of pay however are not sufficient to guarantee an adequate supply of candidates. Successful recruitment also depends on the image the enterprise has created as an employer. An employer's image does not rest so much on smart advertising and public relations, as on the reputation established over a number of years on the manner in which it has managed its human resources.

Advertising vacancies

For certain levels of vacancy, the traditional notice at factory or office gates may well produce suitable candidates, but more usually space has to be taken in newspapers and periodicals. More ingenious methods can be resorted to, such as radio commercials or television advertisements, but as this is costly, much depends on the type of vacancy. It is generally advisable to employ the services of a reputable recruitment advertisement agency. Their services are usually cost-effective, because the basic fee is deducted from media charges. In general advertising in the national press is a costly business; advertising campaigns can cost thousands of pounds. In order to achieve value for money, the following set of guidelines should be observed[1].

1   Study the job specification to extract relevant information.

2   Decide on the target population e.g. accountants located in SE England, or skilled fitters in a local urban area.

3   Select media which will give good results. Most newspapers will provide a breakdown of their readership, classified by socio-economic group. Journals may be cheaper than newspapers, and be read by a more precisely defined target population, e.g. electrical engineering trade journals. Journals however possess the drawback of a slow response and long time intervals between issues.

4   Determine the best selling points of the job, and select which ones to feature in the advertisement. These might include salary, nature of the job, or location.

5   Consider the desired response, and plan accordingly. It may be best to ask applicants to write, telephone, call, or attend a special interview centre.

6 Tailor the job description in the advertisement to achieve the desired response.

Too loose or glamorous a description can lead to an embarrassingly large response and is one of the hallmarks of an unsatisfactory job advertisement. Except in special cases, the final result should include in suitably concise form: job title, description of the company, job description and person specification, remuneration and benefits, and the instructions for application. The personnel department in a large organisation should carry out a continuous review of all recruitment advertising, and be in a position to present data on costs and the response generated by different media[2].

The effective application form

The primary purpose of an application form is to aid good selection. The secondary purpose is to provide personal information when and if the applicant commences employment, but in a way that this does not inhibit the recruitment process. The form should encompass:

1 personal details – name, address, age, next of kin, etc.,

2 education, training, qualifications, and skills,

3 career history to date,

4 health record,

5 extra-mural interests.

Application forms are useful even where handwritten letters of application are received because they can provide a systematic record of information, as well as complementing gaps left in letters of application.

For senior staff an extensive and carefully constructed application form can be devised (sometimes referred to as a 'biographical information' form or 'blank'). Its success is based on the well-substantiated generalisation that how a person will behave in the future is best predicted by how he or she has behaved in the past, a point taken up again in the next chapter on interviewing. It is a relatively cheap selection method. Research has shown this to be a useful tool for predicting future employment behaviour. Studies at Standard Oil of New Jersey, for example, established its usefulness in predicting employment behaviour of both skilled craftsmen and managers[3].

Drawing up the short list

The objective of recruitment should be to produce a short list of candidates who are worth interviewing. On occasion, the demand for particular skills will exceed the supply rendering short lists inappropriate. Where a degree of choice does exist, information on the application forms should be matched against the job specification, and applications sorted into three categories of 'probable', 'possible', and 'unsuitable'. Short lists can then be made up from the first two files, and unsuitable applicants politely declined. It is very important that at all points in the recruitment process unsuitable candidates are notified to this effect courteously and promptly. Sloppy inattention to this aspect of the process does nothing to enhance the reputation of the organisation in general or the employment manager in particular.

Selection

Selection represents the final stage of decision-making in the recruitment process. A wide range of techniques are available to assist managers carrying out selection including interviews, tests and references. (Interviewing is considered in the next chapter.)

As the primary objective in selection is to employ satisfactory workers, selection methods should predict with reasonable accuracy and consistency which applicants are likely to prove satisfactory. Like any management process it has also to be subject to financial and social restraints. The four key criteria which all selection methods should satisfy are: *validity*, *reliability*, *cost-effectiveness*, and *acceptability* which are considered briefly in turn.

Validity

Validity is the measure or judgement of the extent to which a selection device accurately predicts subsequent performance on the job. Formal selection tests normally permit a degree of objective measurement, although some forms of selection, particularly interviewing, rely rather more heavily on subjective judgement.

Proper measurement is at very least a two-stage process, requiring measurement of the applicant's performance during the selection procedure and subsequently of performance on the job. Neither is easy, and measurement of work performance can be particularly difficult. Some jobs lend themselves far more readily to performance measurement than others, especially where there is an observable physical output from the job, as in some factory or office work. Jobs with a large discretionary element, including managerial or research type jobs, are difficult to measure. This problem is referred to by occupational psychologists as the criterion problem. Then there exist such considerations as the time at which the measurements should be taken, quality of work, impact upon co-workers and length of service. Difficult though it may be, a degree of validation must be carried out by the organisation to ensure that its money is being well spent on its selection methods[4].

Four approaches to validation have been found to be particularly useful.

1 *Face validity* Is there an apparent relationship between what is being tested at selection stage, and the content of the job? This is a common sense approach, and requires a judgement as to whether the selection device bears a suitable resemblance to the intended work. Important though it is, this is rarely sufficient by itself. Objective measurement may show that the judgement as to face validity was incorrect.

2 *Content validity* This is a more rigorous application of face validity, involving a detailed examination of the content of the job as well as the content of the selection test to see if there is a match. Again it is not a sufficient form of validation in itself.

3 *Concurrent validity* The selection device can be given to existing employees, where the level of their work performance is already known. Their performance on the test can then be correlated with their performance at work to see if a significant correspondence exists. While this permits objective measurement, it can suffer from a number of limitations. It may be hard to persuade existing employees to undergo selection tests, stimulating trade union opposition, and the sample of existing employees may not match the sample of job applicants.

4 *Predictive validity* This requires measurement both during selection and during subsequent work performance. A correlation between the two can then be calculated. This is intrinsically the most satisfactory form of validity measurement. However it too suffers from limitations. Firstly, there are the practical problems of measurement already referred to. Secondly, there is the uncertainty as to how those applicants who were rejected might have performed if selected. Thirdly, there is the time and expense involved in such longitudinal studies. Predictive validity is illustrated by the diagrams in Figure 3.1, showing scattergrams in which selection performance has been plotted against work performance, giving a range of possible correlations.

The statistical relationship between predictor and criteria is provided by calculating the coefficient of correlation. Approximate correlations are shown in Figure 3.1 illustrating how correlations can vary from zero (no correlation) to one (perfect correlation) depending on the relationship between predicted and actual work performance. When this data has been obtained, a scattergram can be used as a

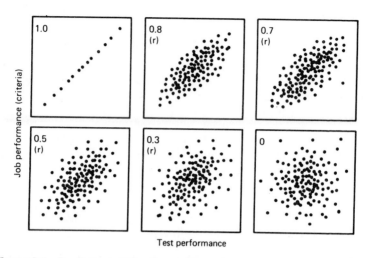

Figure 3.1   Predictive validity. Scattergrams showing possible relationships between test and job performance with correlations ranging from 0 to 1

practical aid in making decisions concerning the cut off point in selection i.e. the minimum score or grade at which applicants will be considered for employment. This is illustrated by Figure 3.2. Four possible test scores, $T_1 - T_4$ are indicated.

(a)   With T_1 as the cut off point a high proportion of applicants will be offered employment, with the bulk unlikely to achieve satisfactory levels of performance.

(b)   When T_4 is taken as the cut off point, few applicants will be accepted but all will achieve satisfactory levels of performance. Here many potentially good workers having been rejected, the cost per recruit will be appreciably higher than at T_1. T_2 and T_3 represent intermediate positions. Candidates X and Y are shown here as reaching equal levels of work performance.

(c)   At T_1, both candidates X and Y will be accepted. But at $T_2 - T_4$ only X will be accepted. Factors to be considered when deciding appropriate cut off points for selection include *number of recruits desired, number of applicants, financial resources available*[5], and the social and legal problems likely to arise when employing a proportion of potentially unsuccessful candidates.

Reliability

Reliability is a measure of the consistency with which a predictor continues to predict performance with the same degree of success. If a selection method is going to be used time and time again it is important to have confidence in its continuing validity. The three most widely used methods of assessing reliability are:

1 *Test-retest method* groups of subjects are given the same test again after a time interval, and the results are compared.

2 *Split-halves method* the test is divided into halves; scores gained in one half are compared with the scores gained in the other half.

3 *Equivalent form method* two different but equivalent forms of the test are administered, and the scores compared.

Because employment circumstances change, it is important to check on the reliability of selection methods from time to time. It has been found that an employment method valid for some years may lose its validity in altered circumstances as the calibre of applicants changes.

Cost effectiveness

Selection costs money, including the frequently invalid and unreliable methods practised in many organisations. Money invested in improved selection methods generally achieves a good 'pay off' in terms of better recruits and greater labour stability. However there comes a time when diminishing returns set in. Furthermore budgets may place a constraint on improving selection methods. This means that money

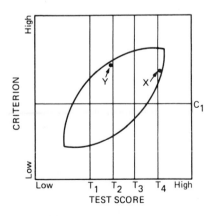

Figure 3.2 Use of different cut off points for selection

may not be available, or could possibly be invested with even greater benefit elsewhere e.g. in improved training. Selection methods therefore need to be costed (relevant costs are considered under training costs in Chapter 5. See also reference[5]). It will be found in most organisations that existing selection procedures can be improved at relatively small cost, and with beneficial results (bearing in mind that a bad interview costs as much as a good interview).

Acceptability

Selection methods may exhibit all the virtues of validity, reliability and cost effectiveness and yet still not be acceptable. This may be because of legislation (e.g. on the grounds of racial discrimination), on the attitudes of senior managers to applicants (e.g. antipathy to personality tests), or the moral principles of the manager responsible for selection. For example, a lie detector might produce useful results, but would it be acceptable in most organisations?

Selection tests

Selection tests are used by nearly all employers, although this is frequently not recognised. In fact any attempt to predict future behaviour on the basis of behaviour manifested at the time of application is a form of test. Thus the judgement that a weak handshake indicates a weak personality represents a test and a prediction. All managers concerned with employment must try to ensure that the most appropriate forms of selection are used. These may include formal tests in addition to interviews. Formal tests fall into two categories, namely aptitude and attainment. *Aptitude tests* aim to assess potential; *attainment tests* verify skills already acquired. There are also various forms of personality test.

Aptitude tests

Aptitude tests cover mental and psychomotor abilities and a range of less significant abilities. Some tests are in the form of test 'batteries' designed to cover a range of aptitudes.

Mental ability or 'intelligence' tests

These tests have a long history of scientific investigation. Intelligence can manifest itself in a variety of forms, including general reasoning ability, verbal comprehension, numerical ability, creative ability, and the ability to understand spatial relationships[6]. Such tests are especially useful when employing young people, where there is no

Which of the six numbered figures fits into the vacant square? (Insert the number in the square)

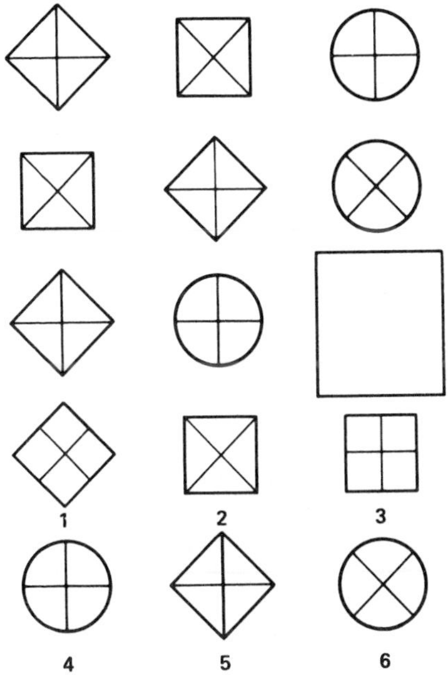

Figure 3.3 Example of mental ability test question using symbols

career record and few academic qualifications. Of course while possession of formal academic qualifications generally indicates above average levels of intelligence, their absence does not necessarily imply an absence of intelligence (academic qualifications also reflect other factors, such as motivation, self discipline, and quality of teaching).

General reasoning ability is the ability to reason in a logical manner, deducing the correct answers from the information provided. There is evidence that it is reflected in all forms of mental ability testing. General reasoning ability is required in most technical and professional tasks that require the exercise of discretion by the job holder. In order to isolate it from verbal and numerical ability, questions are frequently presented in symbolic form, as in Figure 3.3.

Verbal comprehension is the ability to understand the meaning of words and their relationships with each other, a faculty pertinent to many occupations. Curiously a large proportion of the population is more competent at solving problems couched in words rather than numbers. Examples of the kind of questions likely to be found in a test of verbal comprehension are:

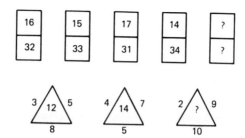

Figure 3.4 Examples of numerical ability test questions

1   Underline the odd-man-out: house, igloo, bungalow, office, hut.
2   Insert the word missing from the brackets:
    fee (tip) end
    dance (. . .) sphere

Numerical ability is the ability to be fast and accurate in making numerical calculations of an arithmetical type. This aptitude is required in technical and commercial departments. Examples are provided in Figure 3.4.

Spatial ability is the ability to perceive fixed geometric relations among figures and to be able to visualise their manipulation in space. Engineering and design work makes demands on this aptitude. Examples are provided by Figure 3.5.

Creative ability is widely recognised as important to success in many occupations e.g. advertising and research, but has proved difficult to

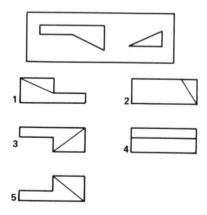

Figure 3.5 Example of spatial aptitute test question (Question – which figure would result if the two pieces in the picture were put together?)

test. Most intelligence tests emphasise 'convergent' thinking, that is to say they present problems that have logically defined and 'correct' answers. Creativity may require 'divergent' thinking including the ability to think of a range of possible solutions to a problem. For the population as a whole the research evidence is that scores on conventional intelligence tests tend to be positively correlated with scores on creativity tests, but within the top 10% there appears little relationship between intelligence and creativity. Some who score well on intelligence tests score badly on creativity. This ability may be a reflection of personality as well as intelligence, and is not easily susceptible to testing[7].

The term IQ or Intelligence Quotient, is often used synonymously with general intelligence and mental ability. It was originally a measure developed to indicate the intelligence manifested by a child relative to other children in the population, and was calculated as a ratio of mental age (MA) to chronological age (CA).

$$IQ = \frac{MA}{CA} \times 100$$

More recently the most widely used method, based on the Stanford Binet tests, has been to assign an IQ value of 100 to the mean score for each age group, with a standard deviation of 16. For example, a child whose score on the test falls one standard deviation below the mean for his or her age receives IQ of 84. However today, the term IQ is frequently used to describe adult intelligence using a scale based on the distribution of intelligence in the general population, as illustrated by Table 3.1.

Psychomotor aptitude

Manual tasks require psychomotor aptitudes including skilled and semi-skilled industrial jobs and professional work such as dentistry and

Table 3.1 Distribution of intelligence quotients on the Stanford-Binet test battery

IQ	Verbal description	Percent in each group
Above 139	Very superior	1
120–139	Superior	11
110–119	High average	18
90–109	Average	46
80–89	Low average	15
70–79	Borderline	6
Below 70	Mentally retarded	3
		100

surgery. These include manual dexterity, finger dexterity, hand-eye co-ordination, and finger-wrist dexterity. For industrial jobs it is the manual and finger dexterities which are most likely to contribute to success, but tasks like piloting a plane demand a variety of complex psychomotor aptitudes. Whilst these aptitudes may seem at first sight to be easy to identify, in practice it has been difficult to establish tests that are valid for a wide range of manual occupations. Probably the best known test is the Purdue Pegboard, designed to test finger dexterity, in which metal pins have to be inserted into rows of holes in a wooden board[8].

Combination aptitude tests

Combination aptitude tests combine a number of different but related aptitudes in a vocationally orientated test. The most widely used are mechanical and clerical tests. Mechanical tests, as might be set for applicants for craft apprenticeships, usually assess dexterity, perceptual speed, and spatial visualisation. Clerical aptitude tests, as might be given to applicants for clerical positions, usually cover computation, spelling, comprehension, and the ability to follow directions correctly.

Attainment tests

Attainment tests are tests of skills already attained or achieved, and which are directly relevant to the jobs in question. They are therefore also known as 'achievement' and 'performance' tests. An example is the typewriting and dictation tests frequently given to applicants for secretarial vacancies. They possess considerable advantage over aptitude tests because of their direct connection with the tasks to be performed, and are to be preferred where available. Unfortunately it is frequently not feasible to ask applicants to carry out a range of actual tasks in an employment situation; managers cannot be asked to 'manage' for 30 minutes, nor can skilled maintenance workers be asked to demonstrate their full repertoire of skills and diagnostic abilities.

Trainability testing represents an interesting new development. A trainability test comprises the detailed instruction of a job applicant in a piece of work which is part of the job being applied for. Applicants then have to perform the task without any further assistance while under scrutiny from the instructor. Each test is designed for a particular job, taking the crucial elements in that job. It has been used with considerable success for selecting manual workers in the clothing industry[9].

Personality tests

Judgements about people are continually being made on the basis of observation. Personality tests represent an attempt to place this process on a scientific basis. In an endeavour to achieve greater objectivity these tests are frequently administered as 'paper and pencil' tests. Such tests are more properly described as 'question-naires', with no 'right' or 'wrong' answers. The candidate is usually asked how he or she feels about or would react to different situations. A number of obvious limitations exist to the practical application of such tests, apart from the healthy scepticism they usually arouse. One is the problem of establishing in a valid and reliable manner traits and personality profiles from the answers, and a second concerns the ensuing problem of establishing whether one set of traits is likely to correlate more highly with success on the job than another.

Probably the best known attempt to profile human traits describing personality is provided by the work of Cattell. Sixteen traits or 'personality factors' have been isolated using factor analysis and

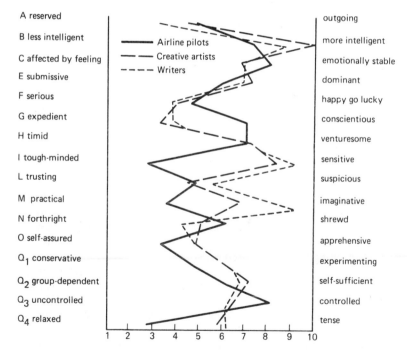

Figure 3.6 Personality profiles – Personality profiles for 3 professions based on Cattell's 16 personality factors

combined into a '16 PF' questionnaire. 'Yes' or 'no' answers are required for more than 180 questions, and the results assessed to give corresponding personality profiles. This is illustrated by Figure 3.6 which shows average test scores for a group of airline pilots, artists, and writers. As is to be expected, the pilots profile differs markedly from the artists and writers[10].

Norms on the 16 PF test are available for a variety of occupations, including accountants, advertisers, engineering apprentices, business executives, and chemists[11].

Two dimensions found in most factor-analytic studies of personality are *introversion-extraversion* and *stability-instability*. The first measures how far an individual is turned inward towards self or outward to the external world. The second refers to the emotions, measuring whether an individual is calm, well-adjusted and reliable, or moody, anxious, temperamental and unreliable. Some personality tests are based principally on these two factors[12].

A personality test especially developed for use in the UK for selection purposes and validated with the cooperation of British employers is the OPQ or Occupational Personality Questionnaire[13]. The 'Concept' model of this questionnaire has scales covering the following dimensions:

1 *Relationships with people* Factors assessed are 'persuasive', 'controlling', 'independent', 'outgoing', 'affiliative', 'socially confident', 'modest', 'democratic' and 'caring'.

2 *Thinking style* Factors assessed are 'practical', 'traditional', 'forward planning', 'data rational', 'artistic', 'change orientated', 'conceptual', 'innovative', 'detail conscious' and 'conscientious'.

3 *Feelings and emotions* Factors assessed are 'relaxed', 'worrying', 'tough minded', 'emotional control', 'optimistic', 'crictical action', 'competitive', 'achieving', 'decisive'.

Another widely used personality questionnaire is the Myers-Briggs Type indicator, developed in America and based on Jung's theory of types. It contains four scales: introversion/extroversion; sensing/intuition; thinking/feeling; and judging/perceptive. It is used primarily for counselling but can be used for selection.

This is probably due to the dynamic interaction between personality and situation, leading to variations in behaviour in different situations, only partly attributable to measurements of traits. To understand behaviour, we need to know how the characteristics of the individual interact with those of the situation. Attempts to predict behaviour in an employment situation require a consideration of personality in relation to conditions likely to be experienced, discussed in the next chapter on interviewing. 'A good tester' advised Stewart[14] 'will consider a test result . . . not as a ceiling above which the person can progress, but as a base-line of ability which there is no excuse for sinking below'.

Some of the less reliable forms of personality test provide tempting answers to management's quest for quick and easy answers to selection problems. Handwriting for example can be regarded as an expression of personality (as can many other personal characteristics) but scientific evidence of its validity and reliability as a predictor is not yet available.

Testing group behaviour

A popular approach to predicting behaviour among personnel executives responsible for executive selection is the group behaviour test, sometimes termed 'leaderless group discussion'. Here a small group of candidates undertake a task, such as discussing a case study of solving a simulated business situation. Throughout the exercise they are observed and their behaviour and interactions analysed to see whether they exhibit what is regarded as behaviour appropriate to the vacant position. This type of exercise has apparent content validity, although it is open to question whether behaviour in the test situation will be reproduced in the 'real life' situation. There is nonetheless some evidence that with adequate training (and training is important) of observers this type of assessment improves the chances of successful selection[15, 16]. Observers ratings tend to concentrate on the factors of individual prominence (including confidence, initiative, aggressiveness and striving for recognition), contribution to goals (efficiency, cooperation and adaptability) and sociability.

Assessment and assessment centres

A number of large employers have developed special assessment centres, both to aid in the selection of applicants and to assess internal candidates for promotion. Best known in the UK are the War Office Selection Boards ('WOSBIES') developed during the Second World War to select soldiers for officer training. These lasted two to three days, and comprised a variety of selection methods, including interviewing, testing and leaderless group situations. Subsequent studies demonstrated a significant improvement in selection standards compared with earlier methods based on manufactured interviews. This approach has been followed in recent years in Britain by the Civil Service Selection Board and by a number of large commercial enterprises both in UK and in the United States[17]. (Assessment centres are discussed in greater detail in Chapter 6.)

The practical application of selection methods

In addition to selecting valid, reliable, cost effective, and acceptable selection methods, management has to ensure that selection is carried out by persons with adequate training and using sound and sensible practices. If tests are being used, they should be administered by trained testers in the manner laid down by the agency supplying the tests. It is also important to ensure that applicants are treated with kindness, consideration, and firmness. Tests should only be obtained from reliable sources. In the UK these include the National Foundation for Educational Research and University departments of Occupational Psychology.

Biographical data (information about an individual's past history) is generally a good predictor of job performance. A systematic way of utilising this fact is to apply so called 'bio-data' selection procedures. Such factors as past behaviour, attitudes, interests and demographic background are given a mathematical weight to produce a 'score' for each individual. Personal history factors which are found to give the best prediction of future job success receive the most weight in the scoring process. In the UK this approach is generally used for pre-selection screening rather than final selection[18].

Surveys of selection methods in the UK raise serious questions about the validity and reliability of current practice. For example, an investigation by the Institute of Manpower Studies found that the three most frequently used selection methods were interviews, cvs and references[19]. When asked why these methods were used without the support of more objective techniques most employers were unaware of research findings or firmly believed that subjective judgements were reliable.

By now it should be clear that the basic goal in selection should be an all round assessment of candidates using a number of different sources of information, rather than a decision based on just one criterion. Unskilled and semi skilled factory and office workers' assessment should also be based on application forms, structured interviews, references and, if the situation warrants, attainment, trainability, or aptitude tests.

Employers, who are desperate for labour which keeps production going may be tempted into employing workers just 'because they are warm and have two arms and legs'. However, these employers soon suffer from high labour wastage, low productivity, and low morale.

Medical tests

Medical tests prior to employment are only required by law in special cases, including the employment of minors, certain dangerous industries, and where food is to be handled. Many large organisations insist however on medical examination, frequently by their own medical department. The important point to note in the context of selection is that company doctors and nurses should be encouraged to act as members of the selection team. Ideally they should be trained in occupational medicine and be conversant with working conditions and job descriptions. There exists a tendency in Britain for applicants to be turned down for health reasons which bear little relationship to success on the job[20], a point taken up again in Chapter 9 on employee welfare.

Taking up references

Used with discretion this is a sensible practice in most employment situations. It permits a check on the career history contained in the application form, and provides reassurance that the applicant has not blotted his or her copy book elsewhere. Basic points to bear in mind are that references should be:

1 taken up only with the applicant's consent
2 processed promptly and with confidentiality
3 checked over the telephone if in doubt

References should be treated with caution. Sometimes deliberately misleading references are made. They should be considered in the context of the other information gleaned during selection.

Discrimination, equal opportunities and monitoring selection methods

In recent years the question of possible cultural bias in tests and selection methods generally has been raised by minority ethnic groups. While it is difficult to produce a selection method that can be proved to be 'culture fair', it must be borne in mind that the whole process of selection tends to be subjective and the inclusion of properly validated tests, in conjunction with job descriptions, introduces a degree of impartiality and objectivity which should be generally welcomed and encouraged.

The Equal Opportunities Commission in the UK has published a code of practice which includes the following recommendations on the use of tests:

1 if selection tests are used, they should be specifically related to job and/or career requirements and should measure an individual's actual or inherent ability to do or train for the work or career, and

2 tests should be reviewed regularly to ensure that they remain relevant and free from any unjustifiable bias, either in content or scoring mechanism.

The Institute of Personnel Management has likewise produced a code on occupational testing which advocates monitoring and provides re-assessment of selection and test procedures[21]. Legal aspects of employment are examined further in Chapter 11.

References

1 Cameron, K. and Allen, J., 'Applications are invited', *Industrial Society*, May 1973.
2 Stainer, G., 'Esso's cost-effective job ads', *Personnel Management*, IPM, **1**, no. 8, July 1968.
3 Bass, B. M., *Man, work and organisation*, pp. 298–9, Allen and Bacon, 1972.
4 Livy, B. and Vant, J., 'Formula for selecting roughnecks and rousabouts', *Personnel Management*, Feb. 1979.
5 Dunnett, M. D., *Personnel Selection and placement*, pp. 174–183, Tavistock Publications Ltd., 1966.
6 Eysenck, H. J., *Know your own I.Q.*, Penguin, 1962.
7 Hilgard, E. R. Atkinson, R. L. and Atkinson, R. C., *Introduction to psychology*, Ch. 12, Harcourt Brace Jovanovich Inc., 1979.
8 Bass, B. M. and Barratt, G. Y., *op. cit.*, Ch. 9.
9 Downs, S., 'Trainability Testing', *Personnel Management*, August 1984.
10 Cattell, R. B., 'Personality pinned down', *Personality Today*, July 1983.
11 Cattell, R. B., 'Personality assessment', *Recruitment Handbook* (2nd edn), pp. 130–4, Ungerson B., (Ed.) Gower Press 1975.
12 Eysenck, H. J. and Eysenck, B. B. G., *The Eysenck personality inventory*, University of London Press, 1963.
13 IDS Study no. 341, 'Psychological Assessment', *Incomes Data Services*, July 1985.
14 Stewart, V. and Stewart, A., 'How to spot the high fliers', *Personnel Management*, September 1979.
15 Kaess, W. A., Witryol, S. L., and Nolan, R. E., 'Reliability, sex differences, and the validity of leaderless group discussion techniques', *Journal of Applied Psychology*, 1961.
16 Bass, B. M., 'The leaderless group discussion', *Psychological Bulletin*, **51**, no. 5, 1954.
17 Stevens, C., 'Assessment Centres: the British experience', *Personnel Management*, July 1985.
18 'Biodata – from past to future perfect', *Personnel Management*, 1958.
19 Bevan, S. and Fryatt J., 'Employee Selection in the UK': *IMS Report* no. 160, Institute of Manpower Studies December, 1988.
20 Todd, J., 'Dismiss the doctors who can lose you a job', *The Sunday Times*, 2 Sept., 1975.
21 'Code on Occupational Testing', IPM, 1988.

4

Interviewing in practice

Interviewing plays an important role in the process of good management. It is a widespread method of receiving and giving information, involving social skills as well as the other management competencies of planning, organising, motivating and controlling. The majority of interviews take place in one-to-one situations, although groups may be involved, and may be more or less formalised. Most managers consider that they are good at interviewing. The weight of evidence is that, unfortunately, most managers are not good at interviewing! Fortunately, this situation can be rectified in most cases. This chapter concentrates on the type of interviewing relevant to the key employment processes of selection, appraisal, grievance and counselling. It provides pointers to the way in which managers can enhance their skills and achieve better results.

Successful interviewing requires skill, and skill cannot be learnt just by acquiring knowledge. Knowledge however is an essential ingredient in the practice of high order skills. Doctors, dentists, professional footballers, skilled machinists and interviewers all require a considerable amount of knowledge. Research into interviewing and the observations of successful interviewers provides us with guidelines applicable in the great majority of situations. This chapter initially sets out guidelines to good interviewing practice; it then examines a number of specific interviewing situations, and relevant research and techniques.

General guidelines to good interviewing

While no two interviews are or should be exactly the same, the following guidelines should be observed in the majority of interview situations, and variations developed only after careful consideration.

Clarify the aims and objectives of the interview Consider such questions as 'What is to be achieved by this interview?' and 'Is there possible conflict between objectives?' An appraisal interview, for example, should not be used at one and the same time to advise a

subordinate of a salary review, and to generate a relaxed and constructive discussion of general progress.

*Collect and study the necessary information and paperwork before the
interview*   An employment interview, for example, requires a study of
the job specification and application form. Before conducting any
disciplinary interview it is essential to *establish* the facts of the case.

Inform the interviewer in a manner appropriate to the occasion   For
most interview situations this means informing the interviewee in such
a way as to put him or her at ease beforehand. There are a few
exceptions of course as with disciplinary interviews for example. But to
summon an operator from the factory floor for an interview without
explaining its purpose is likely to get the interview off to a bad start, as
well as being discourteous.

Plan the sequence of the interview   An inexperienced interviewer
should write down the items to be covered, in advance. In this way
important matters will not be overlooked and continuity in the interview will be facilitated.

Prepare the layout of the room   Should the interview be conducted
from behind a desk, or in a more informal and relaxed manner?

Ensure there will be no interruptions   Interruptions, of any kind, can
destroy rapport between interviewer and interviewee and generally
impair good communications.

Open the interview in a friendly but controlled manner   Broadly this
means opening the interview in a way which puts the interviewee at
ease. This can be done by commencing with a brief discussion of a
neutral topic – even the weather will sometimes do! Employment
interviews particularly require presence of mind here because interviewees are generally strangers, and need careful handling during the
opening few minutes.

*Ask open-ended questions which require more than 'yes' or 'no' for an
answer*   This will encourage the interviewee to talk and to explain. A
major purpose of most interviews is to obtain information.

Do not express personal judgements   A clever interviewee can exploit
personal judgements to his or her advantage, and attempt to manipu-
late the interviewer.

Maintain continuity in the discussion   Avoid awkward pauses, unless
these are used deliberately, as this disconcerts both parties.

Encourage interviewees to extend useful statements   If an interviewee
pauses when more information is required, encourage him or her to
continue with friendly gestures, expressions of interest, and repetition
of his or her last few words.

Do not make promises you cannot fulfil   It is tempting to try to placate
interviewees by promises of action, but a manager who makes a habit
of this without delivering the goods undermines his or her own
reputation.

Listen with interest   In a majority of interviews the interviewee should be talking for more than half the allotted time; good interviewing still depends on attentive listening.

Observe non verbal behaviour   An interviewee will frequently indicate his or her feelings by face and body movements, (examined later in this chapter).

Avoid personal bias and prejudice   Recognise your own weaknesses, biases, and personal preferences, and keep them under control. (One employment manager in a well-known confectionery firm had an abhorrence of bow ties, and wisely used to ask his assistant to deputise for him when the applicant arrived wearing one!)

Beware of a 'halo' effect   We are all inclined to favour interviewees who make statements of opinion with which we sympathise, and vice versa. This clouds judgement.

Make any notes in an open manner   If it is necessary to take notes, do not do it in a way that interrupts the flow of conversation, or upsets the interviewee. Don't forget however interviewees may be adept at reading your handwriting! Detailed notes are best left until after the interview has ended.

Probe and follow up points made by the interviewee   Novice interviewers are frequently reluctant to probe when further information is required. A skilled interviewer combines tact and persistence.

Ensure a satisfactory hearing   Leave the person being interviewed with the feeling that he or she was given every chance to speak out.

Conclude the interview with firmness, tact and courtesy   Develop a repertoire of useful concluding phrases such as 'you will be hearing from us shortly' and 'I have enjoyed this discussion and will follow up the points for action we have agreed upon', to be used as appropriate.

Allow time for recollection   Schedule a few minutes after the conclusion of an interview to complete your notes and come to a balanced judgement.

Specific interviews and counselling

The selection interview

Interviewing is widely used for selection. There is evidence that it could be used far more effectively than appears to be the rule.

Shortcomings and limitations   In a classic investigation Scott[1] arranged for six interviewers each to interview 36 applicants for sales positions. Interviewers subsequently placed the interviewees in rank order from most to least suitable. For 28 applicants interviewers could not agree whether they belonged in the top or bottom half of the distribution. Studies based on the University of McGill in Canada in the nineteen fifties investigated selection interviews conducted by businessmen[2]. The most important finding was that interviewers reached a decision on whether to accept or reject applicants in the first few minutes of the interview, indicating that interviewers came to snap judgements, and that interviews lasting longer than five minutes were generally a waste of time. If the application form and the appearance of the applicant did not impress the interviewer, then the applicant stood little chance of acceptance.

In 1965 Ulrich and Trumbo reviewed research findings on the selection interview, and concluded that other methods of selection were generally to be preferred[3]. Research by the Life Insurance Agency Management Association, USA has demonstrated the strong effect of unfavourable information on interviewers[4]. Only a few items of unfavourable information appeared sufficient to create a strongly negative impression on the interviewer, whereas favourable impressions are created much less rapidly. Hakel Dobmeyer and Dunnette studied interviews by Certified Public Accountants in the USA for students seeking accountancy jobs[5]. They found that decisions were made on the basis of scholastic standing rather than business experience and interests. Judgements were also affected by the sequence of interviews; if a manager interviewed a candidate who was in fact just average after interviewing three or four inferior candidates, the average one received a favourable rating.

Evidence like this has led many psychologists to suggest the abandonment of selection interviews and the substitution of tests. However, there is also evidence in favour of selection interviewing – provided it is conducted by trained interviewers, and in conjunction with biographical information, job descriptions, and test results. In the War Office Selection Board studies (referred to in the previous chapter) it was found that assessment centres that included tests and exercises as well as interviews achieved greater success than the previous system of interviews by untrained senior staff[6]. A review by Mayfield found that structured interviews i.e. interviews following a pattern, yielded fairly consistent ratings of the same persons by different interviewers[7]. Reeb studied interviews for the Israeli defence services by non psychologists who had received a few months of relevant training and showed that assessments contributed usefully to prediction of success on military service[8]. Studies in the UK defence services have shown that some interviewers are better than others at spotting good applicants subsequent to training[9]. The life insurance (LIAMA) study referred to earlier, found that structural interviews produced agreement among interviewers on suitability of candidates.

Some critics of selection interviewing overlook the other purposes which interviews satisfy. A selection interview should be a two-way exercise and should permit the applicant to satisfy himself or herself about the work and conditions. Few organisations would wish to offer employment to persons they have not had a chance to look at, and few applicants would wish to take up employment without a visit to the place of employment and the opportunity to ask questions.

In addition to the general guidelines already provided, the following points should also be borne in mind by the selection interviewer.

1 Prior to the interview, compare the job specification with the information on the application form. Plan the interview around the elucidation of further information about critical aspects of the applicant's career history.

2 Structure the interview to cover the key areas listed in Chapter 2, especially education, qualifications, experience, training, skills, motivation, social adjustment and any special circumstances.

3 Pay attention to the impact the candidate is likely to make on others, including appearance, manner and bearing[10].

4 Check subsequently on whether your predictions concerning applicants offered employment are borne out (but this medicine can be hard to swallow!).

A number of selection interview are conducted by more than one person. In some cases, applicants are interviewed initially in the personnel department and if suitable are passed on to a departmental manager for a second interview. The two major purposes of these second interviews are to check on the technical experience and skills of the applicant, and to give the parties an opportunity to consider whether they are mutually acceptable. On other occasions an interview may be conducted jointly by the personnel officer and department representative. This practice may be more economical of time, but it is more difficult for two interviewers to reach rapport with a candidate.

An amusing final point on the selection interview is provided by the findings of a survey into secretarial and clerical recruitment by a large private employment agency in London[11]. The investigators invited a cross-section of executives – ranging from chairperson and managing director to office managers and junior executives – to complete questionnaires giving their impressions of recent interviews. They then asked a cross-section of candidates the same questions. 86% of the 660 employers interviewed claimed they started interviews punctually, while only 42% of the 830 candidates agreed with this statement. Only 20% of employers admitted to interruptions during the interview, compared to 75% of interviewees. 84% of employers claimed they outlined job specifications, while only 64% of candidates supported this. 93% of employers claimed to achieve a relaxed atmosphere, whereas only 49% of applicants experienced this and so on. Whether or not these employers were actually following correct interviewing procedures, they were clearly failing to communicate this fact to their candidates!

A study by Dougherty *et al.* in an American oil company of three employment interviewers found that one interviewer was consistently selecting successful candidates who performed well in their jobs, whilst the predictions of the other two were little better than chance[12]. Similar results had been found earlier by Heneman[13]. This possibility has been overlooked in the majority of research studies into interviewing. Too many studies have used pooled data concerning heterogeneous subgroups of interviewers, and their findings have also suffered from other methodological faults[14]. This regrettably has led to a negative approach to interviewing that has not helped managers wishing to increase their competence and to improve the quality of their selection decisions. These findings just referred to remind us once again that not all managers can become good interviewers. After all, we would not expect all managers to be able to become good scientists or good artists or good accountants. But as with all skills most managers can become better interviewers, and a few will achieve excellence.

Panel interviews are more popular in the public sector. This type of interview means that the candidate can be faced with three or more interviewers. Too often these interviews are conducted in an unstructured manner, and research concerning the validity of the panel of interview is not reassuring. Group pressures begin to assert themselves, and decisions are made on the basis of political influence within the groups, rather than an objective evaluation of the candidates. Such panel interviews frequently take place to satisfy internal pressure groups and to create an impression that selection is being done on an open and above board basis. There is evidence however that panel interviews can achieve better levels of validity and reliability. Research by Campion *et al.* showed a very adequate level of correlation with panel interviewers, between prediction and performance. When the questions asked were based on job analysis, the same questions were asked of each candidate, and answers were scored using a rating scale[15]. Special attention was paid throughout to job relatedness, fairness, and scrupulous documentation.

The grievance interview

The following comment by Elizabeth Sidney and Margaret Brown provides the manager with a useful starting point here: 'The manager who can listen to his staff, who is prepared to understand their point of view before he does anything else, finds that this action alone is often enough to dispel frustration and to release the speaker's own abilities to handle the problem'[16].

As well as the general guidelines provided earlier, the following points have particular relevance when conducting grievance interviews.

1   If there exists a formal grievance procedure ensure that it is complied with. (Grievance procedures are considered in Chapter 9 in the context of industrial relations.)

2   Allow plenty of time initially for the interviewee to put his/her case and blow off steam.

3   Take care not to become emotionally involved. Emotional involvement prevents clear thinking and provokes fruitless argument.

4   Aim to get a coherent story. An emotionally disturbed employee may not give a clear account to begin with; careful questioning may be required.

5   Remember that there are least two sides to every dispute.

6   Do not promise action which you cannot carry out.

Counselling

A manager who is concerned with the development and well being of his staff will have to provide counsel from time to time. The following points are helpful in what may well be difficult situations: (adopted from Beveridge)[17].

1   Help the employee to envisage a constructive approach to his or her own situation. Ask questions which help the employee to make his or her own evaluation. In the long run it is the employee who must be responsible for his or her own actions.

2   Provide appropriate information. As a manager you may have access to useful information.

3   Work out with the employee an appropriate course of action.

4   Ensure follow up.

In many organisations specialist departments e.g. personnel and welfare exist to provide help in counselling, (see also Chapter 9).

The appraisal interview

This is considered in Chapter 6 in which we discuss appraisal systems and practices. (For a fuller examination of social skills and the manager see Behavioural Sciences for Managers, 2nd edn Ch. 5. *opus cit.*)

Interviewing as a social skill

All skilled workers display competence. They can make relatively difficult tasks look easy. They know when to make the right decisions. In the hands of a potter, a lump of clay on the wheel grows into a thing of beauty. A skilled toolmaker will produce a piece of metal shaped with fine precision. Socially skilled managers display competence to a greater or lesser degree in handling other people. The main hurdle to competence is that people are far more complicated to handle than clay or metal. We are fortunate here in the knowledge gained over recent years concerning the nature of social skills which now exists to help managers develop their own social skills.

Success as a skilled performer in most walks of life requires the presence of a number of factors. These include basic aptitude, physical and mental abilities, know-how, practice, experience, appropriate facilities and circumstances, motivation to succeed – and feedback or knowledge of results. While all these factors are essential to success as an interviewer, the last of these is frequently the hardest to acquire. More repetition does not develop skill. We would not expect someone to develop expertise as a golfer if they *never* knew where they had hit the ball! Skill requires knowledge of results. Yet many managers who conduct interviews do not obtain knowledge of results. Their interviewees never stand up at the conclusion of the interview and criticise or praise the interview unless they have received specialist training. They are rarely observed by another interviewer with considerable expertise or corrected when they make mistakes. It is largely this factor

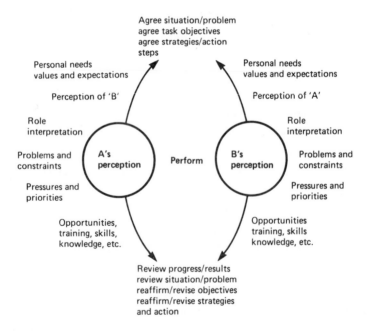

Figure 4.1   The reality of the interview

that accounts for the poor standard of social skill displayed by many interviewers. Twenty years experience as an interviewer does not of itself produce a good interviewer.

Social skills represent a more complex situation than manual skills, because the subject is a human being who is in turn attempting to cope with the interviewer. Interviewees possess intelligence and motivation, and possibly their own repertoire of social skills. This situation is illustrated by Figure 4.1 (see opposite). Another essential ingredient for skill is a heightened sense of perception relative to the task. A skilled performer is able to see more in a situation than an unskilled performer. A skilled footballer sees more possibilities on a football field than an unskilled player. This heightened perception is in a sense the fruit of a highly developed skill. Thus the skilled interviewer will perceive more concerning the interviewee than an unskilled interviewer. Sidney, Brown and Argyle[18] refer to three important components of social skill.

1 *Perceptual sensitivy*
   The ability to perceive accurately the emotional states and interpersonal attitudes of others.
2 *Skill at synchronising*
   The ability to deal rapidly and easily with a variety of interaction styles used by others.
3 *Poise*
   The skilled interactor is poised and at ease in social situations.

The need for training

Our understanding of social skills in relation to interviewing underlines the need for appropriate training in interviewing skills. Research quoted earlier in this chapter indicated the unsatisfactory results achieved by untrained interviewers. Training to achieve success as a skilled interviewer requires the development of perception, synchronisation, and poise, through a programme that provides feedback to the interviewer as to how well he or she is performing, and assists him or her to do better. Training devices such as CCTV, one-way mirrors, and the presence of a counsellor in interviewing situations can be of assistance. But adequate skill is not going to be developed on a one-day course. More extensive training and self development are needed, a point taken up again in Chapter 6.

Considerable interest has been aroused in recent years in so-called 'body language', the way in which we communicate with each other through body movements rather than through words. The use of eyes and eye contact is a method we are probably familiar with, and eye contact is important during an interview[19]. Other more obvious signs include physical tension, sweating, anxious features and nervous movements of the hands and legs. The experiments by Argyle found that if verbal and non-verbal cues expressing attitudes such as friendliness, hostility, inferiority and superiority were combined, the non-verbal cues have a far more powerful effect than the verbal. To indicate that you like someone it is more effective to smile, look, sit side-by-side, and adopt the appropriate tone of voice, than to use words. The perceptive interviewer will be aware of non-verbal cues during an interview, and in turn will be manifesting non-verbal behaviour demonstrating both poise and confidence and encouraging the interviewee to respond appropriately.

References

1   Scott, W. D., 'The scientific selection of salesmen', *Advertising and Selling*, **25**, no. 5/6, pp. 94–96, 1915.
2   Webster, E. C., 'Decision making in the employment interview', Industrial Relations Centre, McGill University, Montreal, 1964.
3   Ulrich, L. and Trumbo, D., 'The selection interview since 1949', *Psychological Bulletin*, **63**, pp. 100–116, 1965.
4   Carlson, R. E. *et al.*, 'Improvements in the selection interview' *Personnel Journal*, **50**, no. 4, pp. 268–275, 1971.
5   Hakel, M. D., Dobmeyer, T. W. and Dunnette, M. W., 'Relative importance of three content dimensions in overall suitability ratings of job applicants resumés', *Journal of Applied Psychology*, **54**, no. 1, pp. 65–71, 1970.
6   Vernon, P. E., *The structure of human abilities*, University of London Press, 1950.
7   Mayfield, E. W., 'The selection interview: a re-evaluation of published research', *Personnel Psychology*, **17**, pp. 239–260, 1964.
8   Reeb, M., 'Structured interviews for predicting military adjustment', *Occupational Psychology*, **43**, 1969.
9   Wagner, R., 'The employment interview: a critical summary', *Personnel Psychology*, **2**, 1949.
10 Munro Fraser, J., Handbook of employment interviewing (5th ed.), Macdonald & Evans, 1978.
11 Allen, R., 'What actually happens when you go for a job', *The Times*, 16 May 1975.
12 Dougherty, T. W., Ebert, R. J. and Callender, J. C., 'Policy capturing in the employment interview', *Journal of Applied Psychology*, **71**, 1986.
13 Heneman, H. *et al.*, 'Interviewer validity as a function of interview structure, biographical data, and interviewee order', *Journal of Applied Psychology*, **60**, 1975.
14 Dreker, G. F., Ash, R. A. and Hancock, P., 'The role of traditional research design in underestimating the validity of the employment interview', *Personnel Psychology*, **41**, no. 2, 1988.
15 Campion, M. A., Pursell, E. D. and Brown, B. K., 'Structured Interviewing: raising the psychometric properties of the employment interview', *Personnel Psychology*, **41**, no. 1, 1988.

16 Sidney, E. and Brown, M., *The skills of interviewing*, Tavistock Publications, 1961.

17 Beveridge, W. E., *Problem solving interviews*, Allen and Unwin, 1968.

18 Sidney, E., Brown, M. and Argyle, M., *Skills with people*, Hutchinson, 1973.

19 Argyle, M., *The psychology of interpersonal behaviour*, Pelican, 1967.

5

Training and learning

Training aims to change behaviour at the workplace in order to stimulate efficiency and higher performance standards. It is concerned with work-based learning. In turn, learning is seen as a form of behavioural change.

Training has been usefully defined as: . . . 'the systematic development of the attitude knowledge and skill behaviour pattern required by an individual in order to perform adequately a given task or job'[1].

One of the themes running through this chapter is that the responsibility for training at the workplace rests not only with both line and staff managers, but also with the learner or trainee. Although the chapter will focus on the workplace roles of manager and trainee, the inputs of other agents will also be kept in mind[2].

It is best if both trainer and trainee understand the process of learning. Consequently, this chapter will consider: the rationale for training; linking learning with training; training models and cycles; management training roles and the role of the learner. It will also cover the organisational needs as well as the self developmental needs of individuals. Further, the authority and task relationships of 'who does what' between different types of trainer is addressed once the systematic learning model has been developed. Finally, a self developmental vision with emphasis on the learner's role, needs and wants is advocated.

The rationale for training

What are the benefits of training? From the organisational point of view training can make work more efficient. Reduced learning times, more effective work methods and more skilled applications of given tasks as well better means of working can flow from training. More positive attitudes towards the organisation and the customer can be inculcated through training. The application of knowledge and skills, or specific techniques such as negotiation, make for greater efficiency. At the top of the learning pyramid, judgement and decision-making, if not creativity and lateral thinking, can be stimulated by training. Accidents may be prevented and reduced by safety training; the market planners may have greater insights; the accountants may make shrewder investment appraisals; the production people may have less scrap and wastage; the personnel department may have less labour turnover owing to helpful induction and job learning programmes. This may mean greater profitability all round and it may result in a more effective organisation. It is however a considerable jump in logic, from individual and group improvement in efficiency to organisation-wide effectiveness, and the relationship between training and effective organisations needs more rigorous research.

Some writers on organisational effectiveness[3] place training centre stage as one of the indicators of greater profitability. The impact of training at individual and group level is undisputed as a useful mechanism for increasing efficiency; either way, training is primarily justified as a means of increasing task or job performance. At the same time, training is only one human resource discipline and there can be an inter-changeability of human resource management, from selection through to conflict management, to salary administration and incentive schemes. Again, performance may be improved by non-human resource factors such as machines, methods, tools, equipment or plant, but if the problem is perceived as a human resource issue and the manifestations of that problem concern shortfalls in skill, attitudes or knowledge, it is likely to be a training problem with an appropriate training solution.

Improved performance is not the only end product of training. The task or job objective, *increased performance*, is only achieved through individual and group ability, and above else, effort and commitment. The learner's self fulfilment at the place of work may be heightened by the results of training, by for example, pride in doing a good job, an awareness of one's competence and earning the respect of others for that competence[4]. Such competence through training can also make the individual more marketable.

The process of undergoing learning through training may be equally important to the individual. For instance, attendance at a seminar on transactional analysis[5] will necessitate self-learning about the learner's own approach to people and to given scenarios before moving to the next phase of analysing social interactions. 'Learning how to learn' rather than recalling a list of principles may be more transferable back to the place of work and may help adaptability to non-routine problem solving. Hence there are individual payoffs from training. At the same time, so far as selling training is concerned, personal consultancy experience shows that managers are concerned with the immediate task rather than more esoteric benefits to people. Without commitment on the learner's part however, training is a fruitless and costly exercise.

Linking learning with training

The acquisition and use of skills, knowledge and attitudes in such a way that behaviour is modified forms the basis of learning and of training. Learning theories can be quite complex and very diverse with distinct paradigms[6]. Much of the content and method of the learning theories have been based on the psychologist's laboratory. There is a gap between the studying of learning and the practice of training. The psychologist's emphasis on animals with a view to predictive validity contrasts with the more pragmatic, less controlled, environment of the trainer who is more concerned with observing behaviour emanating from some learning experience. The psychologist in the laboratory deals with a limited number of variables to test hypotheses in a rigorous fashion; the trainer tends to be more of a practitioner rather than researcher, or a more applied researcher[7]; he tends to dilute scientific aims and methodologies in a more practical work environment. Both the psychologist in the lab and the training officer in the training centre share the fact that learning itself is not observable and we have to infer that it has taken place by observing changes in behaviour.

Common themes shared by both psychologist and applied trainer do provide us with a useful framework. They agree for example that motivation goes to the core of learning. Extrinsic motivation, independent of the task, may include praise, sound peer relationships, a feeling of belonging to a group and an awareness of contributing to the overall job. Intrinsic motivation, within the task, such as pride in the work, a feeling of accomplishment of a set of tasks can be used by the trainer in a staged learning approach. Ultimately, wherever the source of motivation is coming from is not the issue: the individual needs to be convinced of the need for training for without such commitment, learning will be at best a very slow process.

Knowledge of results and feedback on performance allow the repetition of known (successful) responses and adjustment of inadequate responses. It should make the task more interesting and feed the self-motivation of the learner.

This is related to a reward vision. The desired response is rewarded with praise for example, and it may stimulate a repetition of that behaviour. In the world of work, and outside work, there ought to be little mileage in a punishment-oriented approach to learning. The focus ought to be on rewarding not punishing.

People learn at different rates. This may be caused by a failure in communication between trainer/line manager and learner, an inability to follow directions, the personality/background of the learner and tutor, differences in age and intellectual ability; motivation, and the learning environment whether from a noisy workshop in a textile factory to a hotel suite for executive seminars. Above all else, learning is affected by individual differences.

The rate of learning may be affected also by learning curves. Progress tends not to be steady. If we were to plot learning progress on a graph, the curve tends to rise steeply, levels off, rises, and levels. This plateau, or level, is partly a response to fatigue, which may be more marked in the older worker, as well as a period of assimilation and reorganising of old/new ideas. Individuals studying for examinations or formal assessments need to be aware of learning curves as do course designers and instructors.

Learning by doing rather than listening, practice, and constant repetition in a 'safe' learning environment are particularly important for skill acquisition as well as for coping with boredom and stimulating motivation.

Complex subject matter may need to be broken down into segments or into a 'part-learning' format. For example, an electrical engineering input for a technician serving some form of traineeship takes years rather than days. 'Whole learning' would be required if the task is simple or complete: the example of learning mathematical or statistical formulae comes to mind.

Ultimately the learning needs to be dovetailed into the job. *'Off the job'* learning, physically removed from the place of work, may result in more effective learning in systematic fashion with fewer obstructions to learning, although transfer back to the workplace can be more difficult. *'On the job'* training, at the place of work, has suffered in the past from being unsystematic and ad hoc with 'sitting by Nellie' predominating at the expense of formalised learning with key objectives. However it does facilitate transfer to the job and, provided that it is systematic has a lot to offer. Unfortunately, although it is popular in UK industry, the resultant learning is quite random in places and unsystematic overall. To summarise, learning theories and the application of learning principles are the cornerstone of training – whether 'on' or 'off' the job. Thus far, much has been made of the term systematic; it is now time to turn to the systematic model or cycle of training which gives a useful approach to the application of learning at the workplace.

Training models and cycles

Some form of framework or point of reference is required by both trainer (line or staff manager) and by the trainee. The systematic approach provides a straight-forward framework (see Fig. 5.1).

It is mechanistic however, with the cycle apparently going only in a clockwise direction. Further, it assumes that the phases are distinct with little overlap between stages and little feedback from each stage.

This systematic approach has variations upon the theme. The focus

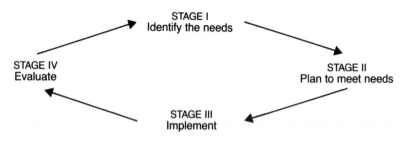

Figure 5.1 The systematic training cycle

of early training models tended to be on Stage I, the needs analysis. It is divided into 'macro' needs at organisational level and 'micro' needs at job level. Programme design and evaluation/feedback phases complete the model.

In themselves however, these types of models are inadequate. There has to be an area of 'pre-assessment'[9] where the training solution is treated as one possibility only of the human resource options. Resources and limitations of resources must be noted. An external environmental scan is a requisite format to incorporate into the macro needs analysis (see Chapter 1). Perhaps most important of all, the evaluation needs to be in-built into every phase as well as being seen as a distinct unit on its own[11]. For example, in the organisational needs analysis, the evaluation, if in-built, could cover availability of objectives, acceptability and potential evaluators.

The ASDICE model

Recent mainstream models tend to follow earlier models with distinct phases or stages, and with 'pre-assessment' not really being enlarged upon, and with evaluation placed in a different box or category rather than running through the whole model. The ASDICE model is a good example of this approach[11]. It has six distinct phases with 'sub systems' within the phases with an emphasis on design and development.

Briefly the ASDICE model shows:

1 Assessment of training needs.

2 Specification of training objectives.

3 Design of training programme.

4 Instruction of methods selection.

5 Conduct of training.

6 Evaluation of training programme.

To take the analysis further, this section will highlight needs, pro-gramme design/development, implementation and evaluation. These are the most critical aspects alongside the physical implementation phase or learning, emanating from the specific analysis. Again, regret-tably evaluation is treated as a separate 'box' – it should run through each phase – and it is assumed that a training problem does exist.

Training needs analysis

This is a method of 'gap' analysis. It is the difference, or gap, between actual and required performance. The inherent assumption, which must be tested, is that the shortfall in performance is caused by deficiencies in knowledge or skills or attitude.

Early models tended to operate on two levels of need: organis-ational and job. In effect, models can operate at sub-organisation level, from profit or cost centre to department, as well as from group and individual to job levels. In many ways, this is the core of the training system, for without an objective needs analysis, the system is built on shifting sands. For our own purposes, the focus will be on techniques or 'how to do it', but first there should be a brief examina-tion of 'levels' at which training needs may operate.

The text book approach may give a prescriptive view of organis-ational analysis, job analysis and person analysis. In reality, costs and other resource constraints may determine a more specific intervention-ist strategy rather than the blanket, and costly, coverage. Either way, accurate learning objectives derived from real needs should underpin blanket or ad hoc strategies.

The blanket approach can be used and specific intervention strategies can be derived as required from a wider perspective. The mission of the organisation, the environmental scan, the marrying up with internal strengths and weaknesses of the organisation can deter-mine macro needs to combat hostile environments or to maximise internal personnel strengths. Strategy at functional level has a knock-on effect to the human resource/manpower plan. This is covered in the manpower planning chapter (Chapter 12). However there is a need for a training plan covering priority training requirements to be drawn up from the combination of business and operational plans as well as a manpower/human resource plan. For example, the stock of labour, available skills and competencies and shortfalls in skills can be ident-ified from the human resource/manpower plan. It needs to be allied to the Corporate Plan with new product innovation, research develop-ment and operational changes, technological changes, investment/plant/machinery alterations and marketing initiatives. The reconcili-ation of supply and demand of skills, knowledge and attitudes is the core of this process.

The next two levels of analysis can be classified as 'operation' and man or (person) analysis. The operation analysis is job centred. The job is described, analysed and criteria of performance built into the specification. The final category is at individual level. This can encompass groups as well, undertaking similar tasks. Job knowledge, quality specifications and faults analysis combine to give an 'experienced worker standard' as the criteria for measurement[12].

How to determine training needs

General surveys of managers and employees can identify issues that need further investigation. Organisational-wide surveys can attempt to fuse corporate planning with human resource/manpower planning requirements. Discussions with individuals and observation of work by skilled analysts can highlight problems. Non-training indices, such as labour turnover, absence records, safety problems and grievance/disciplinary issues may highlight requirement for further 'training' investigation. Job/skill analysis, questionnaires, interviews and diaries showing critical incidents as well as formal assessment centres, and performance appraisal sessions can highlight job and individual training needs. The problem in practice is often, not how to analyse the needs, but the criteria or judgement on what constitutes a priority need.

Programme design and development

This is derived from actual priority training needs. The subject matter needs to reflect the needs analysis. Resources from physical location, money, staffing, abilities of tutors and line managers as trainers, and the use of external assistance have to be taken into consideration. The trainees, their level of expertise, prior knowledge and level of expected commitment should be added to the design criteria. Learning objectives should be derived from the training needs, and effective principles of learning must permeate the whole of the design phase.

The terminal objectives or end product of training can be expressed in behavioural terminology. For example, 'by the end of the negotiating seminar, the trainee will:

1 understand proven principles of negotiation;

2 construct a plan of campaign and develop settlement ranges in the plan;

3 avoid the most common errors;

4 refine existing negotiating skills'

They must be clear, as specific as possible, quantified as necessary, and activity-oriented.

Once the aim and objectives are clarified the method needs to be considered. There is a spectrum of different learning objectives: from the tangible 'how to use a special drawing pen on technical draughtsmanship' to the more abstract such as the implementation of a 'social skills workshop for middle managers'[13]. The link should be made between objective and method. Learning objectives range from knowledge, skill, use of knowledge and skill, social skills and interpersonal skills, to self-awareness/understanding. The progression of methods relates to these objectives with the textbook, lecture, audio tape, television, algorithm, case studies, role playing, simulation groups and experiences to give increasing feedback to participants.

The CRAMP[14] approach provides an alternative relationship between objectives and methods. It highlights the type of learning involved. A design algorithm is used depending upon the actual learning type. It is more skills-based and geared to operator or technical training but it can be useful elsewhere. 'C' type learning is essentially comprehension or understanding; 'R' type is reflex learning involving skilled movements such as operating a lathe; 'A' type learning is attitude development; 'M' type learning is memorisation or knowing what to do in a given situation; finally, 'P' type learning is procedural learning where a handbook would suffice rather than commitment to memory.

For example, the college student wishes to understand the subject matter (C learning). Comprehension implies the ability to transfer to a wide variety of applications. The student is accustomed to this field of knowledge. Hence lectures, tutorials and text books are deemed to be the way to process this knowledge.

The intrinsic merits of each method from lecturing to role playing cannot be covered in a single chapter. The merits or otherwise of the aids to training programmes can be found elsewhere[15]. Learning principles and specific learning objectives derived from the needs analysis being translated into the learning/resource environment of the organisation provide the keys to programme design and developments.

Programme implementation

We have now reached the implementation stage which is derived from the needs analysis and design/development stages. Given the subject matter, it is useful to ask relevant questions rather than to give instructions on how to carry it through.

The relationship between 'on' and 'off' the job training needs to be examined. Is there use in a 'half way house' with some simulated workshop for technicians or aeroplane cockpit for pilots? What are the limits of 'off the job' learning? Do external courses really meet our needs? Can we buy in ready-made packages for our needs? What is the cost of external consultants? How do they supplement our existing skills of our training departments? How can we measure on the job training? Can we designate 'line' training managers or do we need to develop all managers in 'training the trainer' programmes? Some attempt to codify these issues and to give some answers is given elsewhere by the author[16].

Evaluation

Evaluation attempts to measure the overall cost benefit of the course or programme. Validation, part of this process, attempts to measure how far the course or programme meets its specific objectives.

A classical approach to evaluation which is quite useful and has been used by a leading nationalised industry can be summarised as follows[17]:

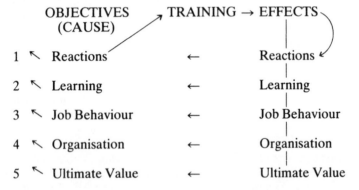

Reaction occurs at the end of the programme and later after a short period on the job. Questionnaires, interviews or discussion methods are used to assess this.

Learning occurs not only at the end of the programme but is ongoing throughout the formal period of training. Of course, control of non-learning variables is difficult at this stage.

Tests, written and practical, can be combined with critique sessions.

Job behaviour is more difficult to quantify. This should occur some 3–6 months after the learning event. Observation, self assessment, questionnaires, interviews and performance appraisals can be used.

The next level attempts to link individual learning with performance, and ultimately with the achievement of organisational objectives. Methods concentrate on research into organisational effectiveness. The ultimate value takes on a metaphysical orientation in this context.

An alternative approach is to develop the initial definition of evaluation with some sort of cost-benefit analysis. The costing side is reasonably easy to legislate for *off the job* training. Materials, trainers' time, trainees' time, buildings/training centre, fixed costs, admin. support, 'publicity' material, the cost of external courses and advisors can be included in a good budgetary system – so long as accurate training records are maintained[18]. Again such a record system is critical to the real costings of *on the job* training and may facilitate the systematic approach to *on the job* training.

The allocation of costs and budgets between line managers and staff trainers requires fine tuning. Cost effective measures comparing one programme with, say another at a business school or centre, may give a comparative analysis on the cost side. The cost benefit measurement asks: do the benefits outweigh the costs of the training? Again the benefits side seems to be difficult to quantify unless some human asset – accounting type of technique is applied to the evaluation system[19].

A different method is to move away from the focus on learning objectives and the various levels of learning[20]. Instead a 'total systems' approach can be adopted with eleven steps to evaluation, from external influences to pre-course activities as well as the 'norm' of training activity, reaction and learning. This is an interesting method but the benefits at the place of work are more difficult to quantify, particularly as other non-training variables enter the scene and as the time-span between formal learning and working is lengthened. This does not mean that evaluation is impossible – only that it is difficult to undertake. The more radical visions of evaluation have much to offer.

To summarise, the concept and the benefits have been examined and the value of the systematic cycle noted. Discussion has centred on the actual process of the training model, particularly on needs analysis, design and evaluation, with a brief input on implementation. How we organise this training and the resultant roles now needs to be addressed.

The role of the trainer

The training practitioner, who is a manager, may have various roles including: administrator, consultant, designer and instructor. Most of the research on roles takes the practitioner as a full-time trainer as its model. Little attempt has been made to examine the line manager's input, and the perspectives of other 'clients' towards the training practitioner's role seem to be undervalued, if not under-researched. These points are important, as training is usually shared between staff training specialists and line managers, and the basis of roles involve an interaction with, and an expectation of/from others. While accepting these limits, research on roles has been quite fruitful.

Some of the most illuminating work has been carried out by Petti-grew and Reason[21]. They attempt to place training roles in the context of a given culture, or organisational 'personality', the person under-taking the role and the role itself. Five categories are highlighted: the *provider*, the *manager*, the *change agent*, the *passive provider* and the *role in transition*. A brief note on each should suffice.

The *provider* improves performance and is involved with mainten-ance rather than change. He has a concrete and practical focus. Variations include the *cultural* operator who identifies with the mores of the organisation; the *individual contributor* giving a unique and personal influence; and the *role performer* who is an admin-type who tends to get bogged down in the bureaucracy.

The *training managers* coordinate resources. They can be authority figures as well. Their role is geared to influence and power games using training policies and procedures to advance their departmental (and own) objectives.

The *change agent* attempts to alter the culture of the organisation (See Chapter 7 on Organisation Development and change). These internal consultants have high personal credibility and are often outside the mainstream of the organisation. The *passive providers*, often found in large numbers, either await *clients*, have little political *feel* or write voluminous reports, doing endless routine work at the expense of the potentially more rewarding, non-routine work.

The *role in transition* possesses a more radical vision with more contextual awareness and more political *feel*. He is moving more towards an advisory capacity, not quite the change agent, but certainly not just a provider – passive or otherwise.

Clearly there are mixed roles here, some with political clout, and others awaiting people to buy their 'goods'. There is no ideal model. Greater professionalism, with trained trainers having political awareness and sensitivity with a desire to innovate must be the way forward.

The role of the learner

Finally to come full cycle, training is essentially learning and the organisation has a major input into the process of learning. The individual also has a role. In particular, individuals must attempt to develop themselves. Many non-managerial jobs do not allow the individual to grow or to flourish and many managerial jobs do not bring out the full potential of individuals. Pedler and Boydell's views are highly relevant: self discipline, learning about oneself, being prepared for some self sacrifice, and conscious work on one's own self must be the hallmark of the developing individual[22].

Achieving a balance

Of course, the self developer will benefit from help in various forms from the organisation: commitment from the top to the concept of training; application of the principles of learning; a systematic approach, based on a needs analysis as well as a programme, designed developed and evaluated on the basis of these needs. These are all necessary commitments from the organisation.

At the same time, there is a need to marry up organisational commitment with a positive motivation towards training by the individual, thus humanising the systematic approach outlined earlier in this chapter. The work of Carl Rogers[23] is relevant to our understanding of this process. He argues for a free environment to facilitate learning. Themes from his work are:

1   The subject matter to be learned must be perceived as being relevant to the needs of the individual.

2   Attempts to change the learner's self perceptions will be seen as threatening, and may be resisted.

3   To reduce such resistance, external threats should be minimised and steps taken to foster a 'safe' environment.

4   'Learning by doing' should be encouraged.

5   Responsible participation by the student in the learning process should be encouraged since this will facilitate learning.

6   Self-initiated learning involving the whole person of the learner-feelings as well as intellect – is the most lasting and pervasive; hence self development is centre stage.

7   Self evaluation is of primary importance; evaluation by others plays a secondary role.

Both the trainer and trainee need to balance the structured approach derived from the systematic method (or cycle) with the humanistic principles of training and learning associated with the more radical vision of Carl Rogers to achieve successful results.

References

1   Department of Employment, *Glossary of training terms*, HMSO, 1971.
2   An excellent 'macro' introduction to the environment of training is given by Richardson, J. J. and Stringer Joan, K., 'The Politics of Change with Special Reference to the Politics of Industrial Training Policy 1964–1980', *Industrial and Commercial Training*, Feb. 1981.
3   Campbell, J. P., 'On the Nature of Organisational Effectiveness' in P. S.

Goodman *et al.*, *New Perspectiveness on Organisational Effectiveness*, San Francisco: Jossey Bass, 1977, pp. 36–41.

4   A phenomenological perspective is epitomised by the work of Maslow. For example see Maslow A, 'A theory of human motivation', *Psychological Review*, 1943, **50**, no. 4.

5   Berne, E., *Transactional Analysis in psychotherapy, a systematic individual and social psychiatry*, New York, Random House, 1961.

6   A comparison of the views of Mednick, S. A., *Learning*, Prentice Hall, 1964 and Lewis, D. J., *Scientific Principles of Psychology*, Prentice Hall, 1961, can be quite illuminating on these different perspectives.

7   Bennett, R., 'Using Research in Training', *J. of European Industrial Training*, **3**, no. 5, 1979, pp. 1–32.

8   Sloman, M., 'On the Job Training – a costly poor relation', *Personnel Management*, February 1989.

9   Kenney, J. and Reid, M., *Training Interventions*, IPM, London 1988.

10   Donnelly, E., 'The Training Model: Time for a Change?' Industrial Commercial Training, May/June 1987.

11   Torrington, D. and Chapman, J., *Personnel Management*, 2nd edn, Englewood Cliffs, Prentice Hall, 1983, (1979 Prev. edn).

12   EITB Research Report no. 2, 'The analysis and training of certain engineering craft occupations', shows limits of over-mechanistic approach.

13   Long, C. G. L., A Theoretical Model for Method Selection, *Industrial Training Inter.*, **4**(11), 1969, pp. 475–8.

14   Illustrated in *CRAMP 'Package'* by Cambridge-based Industrial Training Research Unit, ITRU Res. Paper TRI.

15   Laird, D., *Approaches to Training and Development*, Philippines, Addison Wesley, 1978.

16   The writer has just completed a text, *The Management of the Training Process in the Organisation*, which highlights these issues.

17   Hamblin, A. C., *Evaluation and Control of Training*, London, McGraw Hill, 1974.

18   The importance of a good record system for costing and evaluation purpose cannot be underestimated. See 'Training records: An aid to sound company training', *PPITB Training Guide*, no. 7, undated.

19   For example see, *Cost Benefit Aspects of Manpower Retraining*, HMSO, 1970.

20   Morris, M., *The Evaluation of Training*, ICT, March/April 1984.

21   Pettigrew, A. M. and Reason, P. W., 'Alternative Interpretations of the Training Officer Role – A Research Study in the Chemical Industry', Chem. and Allied Products ITB.

22   Pedler, M. *et al.*, *A Managers Guide to Self Development*, London, McGraw Hill, 1978.

23   C. Rogers, *Freedom to Learn*, Colombus (Ohio), Merrill, 1969, and *Freedom to Learn for the 80's*, Columbus, Merrill, 1983.

6

The appraisal and development of managers

All employees should make a contribution to the goals of the organisation that employs them. This contribution should be regularly and systematically assessed. But it is managers who are primarily responsible for the achievement of corporate goals, and who exercise the greatest discretion in their work. Thus the appraisal of managers is a key issue. The earlier chapter on 'developing a strategy for human resources' indicates the attention now being paid to management development by successful and dynamic organisations. Management development has to be relevant and purposeful, it must therefore be preceded by an appraisal of what further development needs to take place. Appraisal also contributes in other important ways to human resource management, but because of its close interdependence with development the two topics are examined together in this chapter.

Appraisal and development are very much part and parcel of the work of line managers. Managers both appraise and are appraised, develop others, and are developed themselves. Appraisal and development should not be procedures imposed by 'central personnel' department, but should be welcomed as a means by which managers can manage in a more effective manner. Managers who do not appraise and develop their staff are managers in name but not in substance.

Appraisal

A good appraisal scheme places on a sound foundation the judgements which managers continually make about their subordinates. Its principal objective should be an improvement in performance. Appraisal can also make a contribution to the following organisational objectives:

1 Systematic evaluation of individual training needs.

2 Encouragement and reward of individual effort.

3 Communication to staff of their standing and progress.

4   Supply of data about staff capabilities essential to manpower planning.

5   Provision of objective information for promotion purposes and succession planning.

6   Regular review and revision of job descriptions and work objectives.

In spite of their potential benefits, appraisal schemes are no general panacea for poor management or fundamental weaknesses in the organisation. Experience and research indicate that the following constraints must be faced realistically from the outset:

1   *Bureaucracy*   Too much emphasis on form filling and too little attention to the real needs of line management have undermined confidence in appraisal schemes in the past.

2   *Cynicism*   A lack of follow up to appraisal can re-inforce the natural cynicism of many employees.

3   *Trade union hostility*   Some trade union leaders actively support appraisal schemes, provided they are consulted in advance. Others, particularly in the public sector, can be hostile and obstructive, seeing it as a potential threat to their own power.

4   *Lack of confidence*   This can be a genuine concern on the part of managers, and can arise from either a lack of training in appraisal, or a lack of confidence in the integrity of top management. In a widely quoted study of appraisal in the United States, Douglas McGregor concluded that '. . . Managers are uncomfortable when they are put in the position of playing God'[1].

All these challanges can be overcome. The following outlines ways of putting appraisal on a sound foundation: Key issues in appraisal are 'what is to be appraised?', 'how should people be appraised', and 'when should people be appraised?'. The first of these concerns whether it is primarily personality or performance which should be appraised.

Personality or performance?

On the grounds that in personality lies the key to success or failure at work, a large number of appraisal schemes have been developed which require appraisers to evaluate the personality traits of subordinates. Despite their popularity in the past such schemes have experienced a number of serious difficulties which call into question this type of approach. These difficulties stem from the subjective nature of judgements about personality, the difficulties inherent in discussing with subordinates aspects of their own personality, the near impossibility of mature adults changing their personality following an appraisal, and the fact that high levels of work performance are sometimes achieved by individuals possessing noticeable personality defects.

In consequence, in recent years there has been a trend towards the assessment of an individual's performance and results rather than the individual's personality. This has been stimulated by a widespread feeling that it is performance not personality which really matters in the pursuit of business objectives. This trend has been further boosted by the management by objectives movement linked to evidence that appraisal schemes which focus on results avoid a number of personality traits still popular in many organisations.

A recent study in the UK found that 82% of employers operate performance based appraisal schemes[2]. However, an analysis of appraisal forms found that 29% still included personality trait rating. It is of course possible to cover both performance and personality on the same form, provided a clear distinction is maintained.

Measurement in appraisal

Not only does the question of what is to be appraised pose problems, but so too does the form of measurement to be used. As we noted in Chapter 2, measuring human behaviour presents numerous difficulties. The most popular solution has been to use some form of rating scale. In appraisal schemes this has traditionally taken the form of a rating scale, usually based on a continuum from 'unsatisfactory' to 'excellent'. This is illustrated in Table 6.1, taken from a personality trait based appraisal scheme.

If rating scales are used by a large number of line managers, an acceptable degree of validity and reliability can only be achieved if the factors themselves are clearly defined, understood, and interpreted in the same way by all participants. Terms such as 'satisfactory' and 'average' must be given uniform interpretation. This is clearly a tall order, and the research evidence is not encouraging, although many of the faults stem in practice from lack of training. Rating scales of this type also tempt busy managers to take the easy way out, and to tick all subordinates as 'satisfactory' or 'good' irrespective of their actual performance.

In order to counteract this, and to force managers to do their homework, a number of techniques have been tried, including the following:

1 *Discontinuous rating scales*   Instead of scales being based on a simple continuum, they incorporate brief descriptions of good and not-so-good behaviour. These statements are placed in a discontinuous sequence, and the manager has to tick the most

Table 6.1   Traditional appraisal report form

Appraisal: In relation to work over the preceding 12 months, place a tick in the appropriate boxes below. *Do not tick against any item which is not strictly relevant to the responsibilities of the job.*

	A	B	C	D	E		Definitions
Performance (output and quality)							
Relations with colleagues and others							A. Excellent
Powers of expression							B. More than fully meets the standard for the position.
Initiative							
Judgement							
Original thought							C. Fully meets the standard for the position.
Reaction to pressure							
Powers of leadership							D. Not fully up to standard required.
Ability to delegate, co-ordinate and direct							
Development of subordinates							E. Unsatisfactory.
Overall rating							*month year*

give comments where considered necessary.

appropriate one. This deters him from simply ticking down the central column.

2   *Paired comparison*   All subordinates must be compared in turn with all their colleagues, and rated as better, the same as, or worse in performance. The results are then added up to give a league table.

3   *Rank order*   All subordinates are placed in rank order, from best to worst, by the supervisor, based on the supervisor's estimation of their performance.

4   *Forced distribution*   Subordinates have to be placed in accordance with a statistical distribution covering the department. Usually this takes the form of nominating the best 10%, the next best 20%, the middle 40%, and so on, using a normal curve of distribution as described in Chapter 2.

5 *Forced choice* Groups of statements describing performance, usually four in number ('tetrads') are included on the appraisal form. Tetrads are so designed that two statements appear favourable and two unfavourable. The supervisor must indicate which statement is most descriptive of the person, and which is least descriptive. Scoring is carried out subsequently in the personnel department.

While all these methods put pressure on managers to be more objective in the assessments, they are relatively expensive and time consuming, and inhibit discussion in the appraisal interview. Managers may also resent being pressurised in this manner. In consequence many organisations prefer to use results-orientated schemes which transfer the measurement from personality to work results, and encourage greater participation by managers and subordinates.

Results-orientated appraisal

Results orientated appraisal schemes are currently the most popular type among large organisations in the UK. They have been heavily influenced by the recent popularity of management by objectives (MBO) schemes, and continue to thrive despite the waning in popularity of formal MBO schemes – MBO in its full sense represents a philosophy of management and is not simply an attempt to quantify management goals. Peter Drucker preferred to use the term 'Management by objectives and self control'[3]. It is this emphasis on self control which marks it out from crude target-setting, and which makes it so relevant to modern management development and appraisal schemes.

In orthodox versions of MBO the process of setting objectives commences at the top of the organisation, usually with the board of directors. A corporate plan is drawn up which sets out objectives for the enterprise and its major functions. Different levels of management are then required to make their contributions to corporate objectives. A middle manager would typically be invited to set out 'key result areas' for his department, and to discuss and agree them with his superior. Key result areas must be limited in number, capable of measurement (i.e. quantified) and given dates for review and completion[4]. An example of this process is provided in Table 6.2.

After agreeing objectives with the subordinate, a manager is under an obligation to assist the subordinate to achieve these objectives and to ensure the necessary training and resources available. Progress in achieving objectives is subsequently reviewed at appropriate times throughout the year. While actual practice is a great deal more complex than this simple exposition may have suggested, the advantages which have been claimed for appraisal and management development schemes based on target setting and joint review of performance include the following:

- Appraisal and appraisal interviews focus on work performance, which most staff feel competent and willing to discuss, rather than personality traits.
- Appraisal is not a once a year undertaking, but a continuous process.
- Appraisal and management development can be effectively integrated, because development plans are directly related to work performance.
- Managers can directly observe the benefits of appraisal and training.
- Subordinates feel involved in the process, and are thereby motivated to improve their performance.

In spite of the potential benefits of results-orientated type schemes, the outcome has not always lived up to the promise. Sometimes this has been the fault of poor management and administration, where it has been introduced in an autocratic fashion, or where a general climate of distrust has prevailed, or when too much emphasis on paperwork and form filling has 'buried' the scheme. Also where little real scope for discretion exists and political interference is common, as in some parts of the public sector, success can be hard to achieve. In a survey of appraisal schemes in the UK, Williams concluded that 'In some companies it appeared that where long-term objectives were either too grandiose or vague they were either ignored or sacrificed in order to concentrate on easily identifiable short-term goals . . . some of the targets reflected 'fire fighting' situations . . . If MBO and other formalised approaches to managing are to succeed, it is the philosophy which must predominate not the paperwork'[5].

A serious limitation to appraisal based solely on target-setting is that success in a job is no guarantee of success in a more senior position. Defenders of MBO argue that improving current work performances must have priority over predicting promotion potential for a small minority. However this limitation can be overcome by supplementing results-orientated schemes with soundly based appraisal of potential. Two methods of appraising potential which can claim a higher degree of validity and reliability than the traditional supervisor's assessment of personality traits are the use of assessment centres and behaviourally anchored rating scales (BARS).

A further warning on the potential dangers of basing appraisal too slavishly on MBO is based on research in the United States. Kane and Freeman found that managers 'fudge' their work unit objectives in favour of their superiors' views when they know that the objectives will be used as a basis of their appraisals[6]. They argue that performance

Table 6.2 Management by objectives – excerpt from a results-orientated scheme

Aim	Objectives	Control
1. Market research To investigate the potential within the catering market for XYZ services.	a) In the short-term to report to director within 3 months of appointment on the current market situation. b) In the long-term to develop an Information System that will keep him up to date on market trends. This system should be established within 6 months and fully operational within the year. c) To provide 6 reports to director on market trends.	a) Agreement with director on current market situation at 3 monthly meeting. b) Any action based on Market research listed under 2–5 below achieves acceptable financial success.

2. Forward planning
 	
To produce short, medium and long term plans (Sales Targets) for Sales Force within the constraints of company policy and the nature of the market to be developed.
	a) Within 6 months of appointment to provide Sales Forecasts, based on market research data and historical data, covering the next 2 years.
	b) Within 1 year of appointment to provide Sales Forecasts covering the next 5 years.
	c) Provide 1 year Sales Forecasts for each Region in January of each year.
	d) Confirm feasibility of servicing forecasts with director both prior to publication and at regular meetings.
		a) Sales achieved are not less than forecast over any two year period:
		  i. In total
		  ii. By Region.
		b) Market research information concerning competitors positions shows that competitive position is being maintained.

appraisal must restrict its focus to the effectiveness with which job incumbents have carried out the functions that their jobs comprise, whereas MBO should focus on work-unit objectives and restrict its role to planning. They see performance appraisal and MBO as two useful activities that must work in concert, but cannot work in combination.

Assessment centres

A typical assessment centre offers a two or three day programme designed to assess as objectively as possible the management potential of suitable candidates. Some of the techniques used were described in Chapter 3. These include interviews, paper and pencil tests, practical exercises and group selection. Large organisations can afford to operate their own centres, but independent centres offer a service to smaller companies. Contemporary assessment centres owe much to work undertaken on improving officer selection in the UK during the Second World War, notably by the War Office Selection Boards (the so called 'Wosbies', frequently held in large and remote country houses). This approach was subsequently adopted by Civil Service Selection Boards and a few large commercial undertakings. In the United States assessment centres have been adopted enthusiastically by a number of large companies. A major evaluation of the use of assessment centres in ITT (the 'Bell Telephone Study')[7] came to the conclusion that:

1 Assessment centres made a useful contribution to appraisal;

2 Assessments correlated fairly well with later advancement and salary progress;

3 Each exercise in the programme made a contribution to overall assessment;

4 Simulation exercises played the largest part in overall assessment; followed by mental ability tests, and with personality questionnaires playing the smallest part.

In the UK IBM have extended the use of assessment centres to provide feedback and counselling to participants, with the aim of developing as well as assessing staff, and in recognition of this have changed the name to 'Personal Development Programmes'. They comment that 'Participation in the programme is regarded as developmental in itself, but its prime purpose is to clarify the participant's developmental needs which the individual can then discuss with his own management, and agree a plan of action'[8].

This approach is now widespread. Stevens commented recently in a review of British practice that 'The practical integration of assessment centre techniques into the company's activities has moved naturally from criterion-based interviews into the area of feedback. This trend has increasingly been welcomed as a basis for the personal development plans of employees[9].

Assessment centres are however expensive. A typical assessment centre exercise involves twelve participants and six assessors. Assessors are drawn from a pool of senior managers who have received at least three days of training. Additional costs are represented in the development of the procedures, the operating costs of the centre, and the need for follow up.

However no quick cheap short cuts have yet been found to achieving the objectives of comprehensive assessment, prediction, and feedback. While each of the specific components of the assessment procedure has some value in its own right, such as psychometric tests, the full benefit can only be achieved by multiple assessment methods. The cost of assessment centres must therefore be considered in relation to the benefits gained from the subsequent contribution of higher calibre managers[10].

Behaviour scales

Behaviour scales are a rating device based on sets of statements about employee behaviour. These statements describe behaviour which may or may not contribute to more effective work. Supervisors are asked to indicate which statements on the specially devised form most accurately describe subordinates' behaviour. In one version subordinates are involved by drawing up the statements themselves; they then check them out with colleagues, and subsequently discuss them with their superior. In this way they can find out whether their own behaviour matches up to 'desired' behaviour.

A sophisticated version of this approach is represented by 'Behaviourally Anchored Rating Scales' (BARS). Statements about work behaviour are used to create scales, which are then extensively tested to see whether they are relevant and precise. In certain forms statements about behaviour are integrated statements about results in an attempt to get the best of both worlds. This approach is time consuming, and although a number of claims for success have been made, more development and evaluation is needed[11]. An example is provided in Table 6.3.

Guarding against bias

Judgements about subordinates are inevitably subject to bias and personal feelings, and it is therefore important to insert checks and balances into a scheme if it is to gain the confidence of staff. One method of doing this is the so called 'grandfather' method, where it is not only the immediate supervisor but also the next level of management who sign the appraisal. Some schemes operate an appeal system, whereby subordinates can indicate disagreement with an appraisal and appeal to a special panel. Sometimes third parties sit in on appraisal interviews to see that fair play is done. But the best guarantee against bias is provided by the choice of a good system, and the effective selection and training of managers.

Self assessment

A recent trend has been to involve staff in the appraisal process by asking them to assess themselves prior to a discussion with their superior. In a results-orientated scheme, for example, they may be asked to fill in a form prior to interview, stating whether they have achieved their objectives in the past year, where they feel their

Table 6.3 An example of a behaviourally anchored rating scale

Behaviour rating scale of department manager in supervising sales personnel.

	9	
		Conducts a full day's sales clinic with new sales personnel and thereby develops them into top sales people in the department.
	8	
Gives his sales personnel confidence and a strong sense of responsibility by delegating many important jobs to them.		
	7	
		Never fails to conduct training meetings with his people weekly at a scheduled hour and to convey to them exactly what he expects.
	6	
Exhibits courtesy and respect toward his sales personnel.		
	5	
		Reminds sales personnel to wait on customers instead of conversing with each other.
	4	
Criticises store standards in front of his own people, thereby risking their developing poor attitudes.	3	
		Orders subordinates to come in even though she/he called in to say she/he was ill.
Goes back on a promise to an individual whom he had told could transfer back into a previous department if she/he didn't like the new one.		
	2	
		Makes promises to an individual about her/his salary being based on department sales even when he knew such a practice was against company policy.
	1	

(Adapted from John P. Campbell, Marvin D. Dunnette, Richard D. Arvey and Lowell V. Hellervik, 'The Development and Evaluation of Behaviourally Based Rating Scales' *Journal of Applied Psychology* **57**, pp. 15–22 (1973).

strengths and weaknesses lie and where they feel they need further training and development. This form is then used as a basis for discussion at the appraisal interview. An example is provided in Table 6.4.

There is evidence supporting the use of this approach in organisations where there already exists a climate of trust between managers and subordinates. Such involvement can lead to greater commitment, a feeling of fairness, and improved results. Where mutual trust does not exist however self assessment can be perceived by subordinates as a potential 'suicide kit', in which they are asked to provide the rope with which they are to be hanged; in such a situation subordinates will be reluctant to provide more than defensive statements about work performance. It is worth repeating that appraisal schemes cannot provide a panacea for fundamental weaknesses in an organisation.

Merit rating

Merit rating represents a traditional form of appraisal of manual workers, linked to 'merit payments', where subordinates are rated under a number of simple headings, such as 'output', 'quality of work'

Table 6.4 A self development review form

Name:

Job title:

Unit:

This form has been given to you for completion to help promote and guide a discussion between you and your manager which has been arranged for .... at .... The purpose of the discussion is to review your work activities over the last ... months so that you may have a clear understanding of the requirements of your job and to agree what training and development, if any, can help you to maintain your strengths and overcome any difficulties you have had or may encounter. After the discussion you may give the form to your manager, retain it or destroy it, as you wish.

1. Do you fully understand the requirements of your job? If not, what aspects are not clear?

2. What were your most important achievements in the period under review?

3. Which of the responsibilities on your job description have you carried out most successfully?

4. Which of the responsibilities on your job description have you carried out least successfully?

---

and 'timekeeping'. It is rarely used today in this crude form because of its unpopularity with supervisors, workers, and unions, and a lack of supporting evidence. Such schemes are frequently more trouble to operate than they are worth.

However, many managements continue to favour the establishment of a direct connection between pay and performance. This remains a hotly debated issue in relation to appraisal, and is examined further in the next section and again in Chapter 8.

Pay versus development in appraisal

Should performance appraisal be linked to the review of pay? There is no clear cut answer, and a number of factors need to be taken into account before making a decision. Training specialists generally advocate separation of the two processes, in case the subject's concern over pay should inhibit useful discussion of work performance and personal development. For example, Williams concluded that '. . . the introduction of salary reviews into a discussion where the primary task is to talk through the many implications of improving effectiveness means that money rather than performance will become the predominant issue'[12]. On the other hand both practical experience and research in the behavioural sciences indicate that money can motivate in a powerful manner in certain situations. Based on extensive research in the behavioural sciences Lawler concluded 'The more important pay is, the more power it has to motivate behaviour. Increasing the importance of pay will therefore increase its power to motivate[13].

A number of compromises have been attempted by organisations in an effort to cope with this dilemma. Some have chosen to separate in time the annual pay review from the performance appraisal. However it is usually apparent to all concerned that there still exists some relationship between performance review, pay, and promotion. Some results-based appraisal schemes provide for a more or less continuous review of performance as circumstances warrant, thus cutting the direct link with the annual pay review.

The converse also operates in some companies, where the pay of managers is very much performance related, and where, if a manager meets a previously agreed target, the previously stipulated bonus becomes payable. Performance related salary structures are examined in Chapter 8.

Appraisal interviewing

Not all appraisal schemes include an interview, but where it is included it is frequently handled badly. A bad appraisal interview can be counter-productive. Successful appraisal interviewing requires considerable skill, and the points made earlier in Chapter 4 about the necessity for relevant aptitude, knowledge and training apply with some force in this context. Essential ingredients for successful appraisal interviewing include a sound appraisal system, adequate training of appraisers, and the willing co-operation of subordinates.

A classic study of appraisal interviewing conducted in the General Electric company in the United States, led to the following broad conclusions[14].

1   Where emphasis in the appraisal interview was laid on criticism, work performance subsequently tended to show some deterioration;

2   Where emphasis was laid on praise, work performance tended to show neither deterioration nor improvement;

3   Where emphasis was laid on goal setting, some improvement was noticeable.

Conclusions such as these provide support for results-orientated appraisal interviews. Later research in the UK by Beveridge indicated that criticism could sometimes be helpful – provided it was directed towards performance and not the subordinate himself[15]. A study within the British Civil Service where appraisers had the benefit of a two-day training course provides evidence for training and a participative problem-solving approach to the appraisal interview[16]. Further evidence of the benefits of training in appraisal interviewing comes from a study with Fisons UK[17].

The advice of Fletcher and Williams concerning appraisal interviewing should be followed in most instances '. . . keep the emphasis on the performance of the job itself and, where there are problems or deficiencies in this, set goals relating to these for the individual to achieve, rather than fall back on general exhortations to improve'[18].

Management development

The selection and development of managers represents one of the most important activities in an organisation. Some would say it is the most important activity, because the success of an organisation is directly affected by the calibre of its management.

Systematic development ensures that managers maintain their ability to manage successfully. Given the importance of this process, it is surprising how little attention is paid to management development in many organisations in Britain. Almost half of America's top companies give their manager more than five days off-the-job training each year, as do many large companies in Germany and France. In Britain, by contrast, managers receive an average of only one day's training a year, and over half of all companies make no provision for management training[19]. 80% of the three and a half million supervisors and managers in UK have no qualifications directly related to management[20].

This chapter focusses on the development of managers as individuals. Management development must however take place within the context of strategic and manpower planning, and efforts to increase the effectiveness of the organisation as a whole. Thus the chapter should be read in conjunction with the ensuing chapter on organisation development, which places management development in its organisational context.

The nature of managerial work

Effective management development programmes need to rest on an adequate understanding of the nature of managerial work. In fact surprisingly little useful research has been conducted into the nature of managerial work. All too frequently management development programmes have been organised by relatively junior training executives on the basis of custom and practice or the recent whims of fashion. Traditional definitions of managerial work, such as 'working with people' or 'planning, organising, coordinating and controlling resources' are misleading generalisations, and provide an unsatisfactory basis for spending large sums of money on attempts to alter the behaviour of an organisation's most precious resource.

What both research and practical experience do clearly indicate is that managerial work is not homogeneous. Managerial work varies both within and between organisations and cultures. Comment was made in Chapter 2 on the work of Rosemary Stewart and Mintzberg on analysing managerial roles[21, 22]. Their conclusions support this point. Table 6.5 is based on Mintzberg's findings and underlines the need to tailor management development programmes to the roles represented in different management jobs. It also is necessary to recognise that a manager's *effectiveness* in a particular job is constrained by a number of contingent variables that include the personality of the manager and his superior, the authority and power at his disposal, and the extent to which a bureaucratic or organic organisation structure prevails. (For a fuller treatment of relevant aspects of organisation, see *Behavioural Sciences for Managers*, Chs. 7 and 8)[23].

Adequate job analysis relevant to management training needs must be carried out in advance of the establishment of a management training programme.

Diagnosing management training needs

The orthodox methods of job analysis outlined in Chapters 2 and 5 provide a starting point for diagnosing the training needs of managers. In addition a range of more sophisticated techniques should be used, including the following.

1 *Appraisal* Appraisal schemes as described in the first part of this chapter can and should provide vital information on training and development needs.

2 Self report questionnaires Managers can be asked to report directly on their own training needs, aided by a questionnaire.

3 *Content analysis* Training needs can be revealed by an examination of the contents of relevant departmental documents and reports. These will give a clue to successes and failures and the appropriate measures that need to be taken. Clearly suitable discretion must be exercised concerning confidential documents.

4 *Diary method* Managers can be encouraged to keep a diary of their activities which will highlight crucial features of their work.

Table 6.5 The manager's roles

The following statement about the roles, or sets of behaviour belonging to a manager's position, is useful in drawing attention to several facets of the manager's job. The content and relative importance of each facet will vary with the type of organisation and its function but the roles are interdependent.

Interpersonal roles

Figurehead:
symbolic head, ceremonial, status maintenance.
Leader:
responsible for motivation and integration of subordinates' activities.
Liaison:
developing and maintaining network of outside contacts and informers.

Information roles
Monitor:
seeking and receiving information to develop full understanding of organisation and its environment. (Internal, external, analysis, trends, ideas)
Disseminator:
of factual and value information within the organisation.
Spokesman:
transmitting information to outsiders.

Decision roles
Entrepreneur:
initiating and supervising change in his organisation.
Disturbance handler:
Trouble shooter responsible for correcting action to cope with problems.
Resource allocator:
scheduling, authorising and programming subordinates' work.
Negotiator:
representing the organisation at major negotiations.

Source: H. Mintzberg, *The Nature of Managerial Work*, Harper and Row, 1973.)

Diaries can be either general, covering all aspects of the work, or instead concentrate on special features established in advance as being of special significance. Skilled assistance should be available from the training manager.

5 *Attitude surveys*   Attitude surveys provide an indication of training needs. One method found to be of particular use is Repertory Grid which maps out in a systematic way the perceptions of individuals concerning a range of pre-selected topics. This can be followed up with a discussion with the individuals concerned. (For a useful exposition, see Smith and Ashton)[24].

Knowledge, skills, attitudes or competence?

Should management development programmes aim to change knowledge, skills, or attitudes? As has already been indicated, management work is usually highly complex, and all three can be relevant. Training needs analysis will highlight where the emphasis should lie. As discussed in Chapter 4, skill rests upon a foundation of basic knowledge plus considerable practice and feedback of results. Traditional management training programmes have tended to concentrate on knowledge, and have neglected skills and feedback of results. Where the diagnosis clearly points to a need for knowledge, well-presented lectures and seminars still have much to commend them, aided by modern techniques such as programmed learning (referred to in Chapter 5).

In recent years there has been increased emphasis on skill training in management development programmes. The focus has usually been on some form of interpersonal skill with the objective of assisting the manager to communicate more effectively, lead better, and generally impress others within and without the organisation. Programmes rarely aim to change attitudes in an overt manner, and managers are naturally suspicious of attempts to indoctrinate or brainwash them. However a knowledge of group dynamics can be used by a training manager to induce change of attitudes by means of group pressures. Some of these techniques are examined in the next chapter.

The concept of 'competence' and its application in management development has recently attracted considerable attention. This stems from dissatisfaction with what has been perceived as too little attention being paid to practical application in traditional management education, plus too little attention to rigorous and scientific analysis of the abilities required and managers. Competence is seen as more than skill, encompassing the successful completion of tasks which require knowledge, skills, application and appropriate levels of motivation.

Definitions vary, from the ability to perform the activities within an occupational area, to the levels of performance expected in employment[24], to the ability and willingness to perform a task[25]. As John Burgoyne comments, 'one of the attractions of competence is that it concerns doing and action, rather than the mere possession of knowledge. It is however a broader concept than skill, and can usefully be thought of as encompassing knowledge, skill, understanding, and will'[26]. The classification of competence developed in the USA by the American Management Association, which has influenced subsequent development on the subject, created four categories encompassing:

1 dealing with people (subordinates, peers, clients, customers, superiors)

2 managing activities (financial, systems, functional)

3 sensitivity to environment (customers, legal, social, economic, political)

4 personal effectiveness (communications, numeracy, people, results, and self awareness).

The assumption of this approach is that one can identify 'clusters of behaviour that are specific, observable and verifiable, and that can be reliably and logically classified together'[27].

The evidence so far indicates that a structured and tightly defined approach to competence may be appropriate to large bureaucratic and well established organisations but is less appropriate to organisations operating in turbulent and rapidly changing markets who have to operate using 'organic' organisation structures, and who are therefore concerned with identifying personal qualification and values likely to lead to successful performance in particular situations[28]. One recent study of British companies concluded that 'good decision making in one company means taking innovative decisions. In another, it means analysing hard data and minimising commercial risk[29].

The onus is therefore on the organisation to identify the skills attitudes and competencies which are relevant to its own situation. As outlined in the opening chapter on strategy, management development programmes must be relevant to the structure and culture of the organisation, and to its mission and environment.

Management development methods

As already indicated, a range of methods is available for formalised management development programmes, and the principal ones are outlined briefly as follows. A number of these will be familiar to readers. Methods especially relevant to organisational development are left to the next chapter. All methods should be evaluated after use within the organisation.

General management training programmes

General management training programmes covering a range of management topics and usually lecture-based have been the most widely used form of management training. Such programmes usually last for one or more weeks and can be run either within the organisation or outside in a business school or similar milieu. In spite of criticism, they continue to prove popular and obviously satisfy a range of needs, not all of which are strictly to do with developing managers. Their popularity with participants and for training managers usually depends on the presence of one or more of the following:

1   lecture material of genuine relevance to participants;
2   speakers who are entertaining, humorous, or challenging;
3   good food and pleasant surroundings;
4   attendance seen as a mark of status or a reward for good service;
5   financial grants attracted from training boards and the like;
6   senior management accept them as evidence that the training department is justifying its existence.

A further need which is frequently not recognised but which can be important is satisfied by the opportunity they provide for managers to come together and discuss their problems and exchange notes on their situation. This tends to happen informally on general management training programmes, where the discussion in the bar afterwards can be more important than the lecture in the conference room.

Short specific training courses or 'workshops'

A short training course for managers can concentrate on one particular topic or skill, and therefore has much to commend it. The objective should be clear to all and the benefits easier to calculate. Skills workshops aim to provide practice and feedback in developing a relevant skill e.g. appraisal interviewing. A series of 'workshops' can be of greater practical use to managers than an extended general programme.

Management education programmes

The emphasis in management education programmes has traditionally been upon the acquisition of relevant areas of knowledge and the development of analytical skills. Recently there has been increased attention to skills and competence. Management education programmes are offered by a variety of business schools, independent management centres and colleges, and professional institutions. The programmes range from short courses lasting just a week or two to postgraduate programmes leading to awards such as the MBA.

It makes sense for companies to sponsor the attendance of their own managers on a relevant management education programme at an appropriate stage in their career. A period away from the daily grind enables managers to recharge their batteries, update their ideas, and learn from fellow participants. Companies have been reluctant to sponsor managers on full time MBA type programmes, because of the risk that the managers may choose not to return at the end of the programme. The recent growth in part-time management education programmes, making use of part-time study, block release, and distance learning, has proved increasingly attractive. This trend has been given added impetus by the Handy report and the Management Charter Initiative in the UK[30].

Job rotation

It is the practice of a number of large organisations to facilitate the development of managers considered to have potential for general management positions by giving them experience in a number of different departments on a planned basis. In each department they are required to hold down a responsible position, which allows them to gain an overview of the organisation, and prevents them from becoming too insular or stuck in a rut.

Again this method has high face validity, but is difficult to evaluate. Managers specially selected for training for top management posts tend to make good progress because it becomes generally known that they are being groomed for stardom (sometimes referred to as the 'crown prince effect' or an example of a self-fulfilling prophecy). Drawbacks to this method include the confusion created in departments as new managers arrive who lack relevant experience, and the loss experienced by their former departments.

Special projects and action learning

Instead of being transferred to other departments as part of a job rotation programme, managers can be required to undertake a special project which sets them a challenge, requires them to acquire new skills and knowledge, and generally 'stretches' them. Such a move can also serve as a test of the manager's initiative and adaptability, and can indicate potential for promotion.

One version of this approach has been popularised by Revans. Sometimes termed 'action learning', it involves the exchange of managers between companies. Managers are transferred on a temporary basis into a fresh situation in another organisation and are then required to tackle a novel set of problems. It is claimed that the manager, thus freed from worries about impressing peers and superiors in the old organisation, will be stimulated to develop new skills and knowledge of practical relevance. At times during this secondment the manager meets with a group of managers undertaking similar projects elsewhere for discussion and exchange of ideas. Revans has defined action learning as '. . . a means of development, intellectual, emotional or physical, that required its subject, through responsible involvement in some real complex and stressful problem, to achieve intended change sufficient to improve his observable behaviour henceforth in the problem field[31]. Considerable success has been claimed for this method, but it does require co-operation between organisations and the necessary resources. Evaluation presents problems, and participants are unlikely to deny that they have benefitted from this process.

Coaching

Coaching consists of on-the-job development by a superior. Senior managers frequently claim that they made the greatest strides in their own development when working for an outstandingly good boss earlier in their careers. Coaching implies more however than just working for a good boss. It represents an active process, in which the boss provides feedback on performance to the subordinate and gives advice and encouragement that fosters development. A good appraisal interview usually involves some coaching.

Realistically speaking the supply of good managers willing and able to give up time to coaching their subordinates is limited. Many appraisal forms omit reference to development of subordinates. In some circles the philosophy of Machiavelli is encouraged, which means that managers are careful not to develop subordinates to the point where they might represent a threat or challenge to their own boss.

It follows therefore that successful coaching is only likely to take place in an organisation where there exists an open and supportive culture as well as capable managers. Management development executives have a special responsibility for encouraging management coaching and for running courses on how to coach. But the prime responsibility lies with line management. This point is underlined by the Stewarts, who comment that 'Our preference remains for coaching to remain in the hands of ordinary managers: rough and unprofessional though it may seem, it has enormous credibility when the managers believe in it and are supported by the training department[32]. In some organisations junior managers and graduate trainees are provided with 'mentors'. These are experienced managers from other departments who keep an eye on their progress, and provide friendly advice from time to time.

Self development

A number of the approaches to management development outlined above include an element of self-development, recognising that managers are likely to develop best when actively involved in the process.

There has also been a strong trend towards self-development, a process described by Burgoyne as '. . . self development as personal development, with the manager taking primary responsibility for his own learning, and for choosing the means to achieve this'[33]. The extent to which the manager is involved in his or her own development can vary from minimal consultation to the point where he or she takes complete control without let or hindrance from the organisation.

Table 6.6 Guide to management self-development

Self-Development Methods Qualities of an effective manager	Experimental Groups	Learning Communities	Autonomy Labs.	Action Learning	Joint Development Activities	Structured or Experimental Exercises	Coaching/Counselling	Resource Centres	'Academic' Education	Outward Bound	Meditation	Programmed Learning	Self-Improvement Tradition	At-the-job Activities
Basic facts														
Professional knowledge														
Sensitivity to events														
Analytical, problem-solving and decision-making skills														
Social skills														
Emotional resilience														
Proactivity														
Creativity														
Mental agility														
Balanced learning habits														
Self-knowledge														

Source: Bourgoyne *et al.*

Burgoyne *et al.* offer nine different versions of self-development, varying from the use of 'real time' management situations to structured exercises designed by business school academics rather along the lines of 'do-it-yourself' physical fitness programmes. By way of illustration, Table 6.6 is taken from a guide to self-development by Burgoyne, Boydell and Pedlar[34].

The trend to self-development has had a healthy influence on traditional management development programmes, but can be taken past the point where benefits to the organisation are any longer discernible. 'Our experience tells us', cautions Alan Mumford[35], that the problems to be overcome include specifying clear objectives for the process, distinguishing those working environments in which it is likely to succeed or fail, and defining the competencies required of management development advisors who wish to sponsor the process'. The more idealistic exponents of self-development neglect the harsh economic and social realities of the real world in which managers and organisations have to survive.

Career planning

Management development is concerned both with helping managers to perform better in their current positions, and to prepare them for promotion when the time comes. Ambitious managers are keen to climb the career 'ladder' to senior positions. No large organisation can neglect career planning, particularly succession planning. In theory, succession planning is quite simple. As described by Gratton, 'It involves having an accurate knowledge of the management talent you have in the organisation. It requires knowing what qualities you need in the future and is about identifying the gaps you have and developing the talent to fill them. It is very difficult however to put these concepts into practice when many organisations do not have a clear idea of where they will be more than five years in advance'[36].

Career planning fits nicely with traditional practices and large bureaucratic organisations operating in relatively stable environments. Succession planning becomes relatively simple in such a context, and succession charts present no great problems. But the trend is towards more flexible organisation structures with fewer levels of management attempting to cope with an increasingly turbulent environment. Few of today's managers can look forward to an uninterrupted career in the same organisation for their entire working life. As described in the chapter on strategy, many organisations in the future will employ just a core of full time employees, contracting out much of their work.

The implication for management development is that managers must be prepared for an increasingly uncertain future, by developing qualities of enterprise self reliability and flexibility. Organisations require a cadre of such men and women who can act as a pool from which managers can be drawn to fill vacancies as they arise.

Evaluating management development

Methods for evaluating training programmes were considered in the previous chapter. These methods are also relevant to those aspects of management development programmes which resemble traditional training courses, i.e. where it is possible to define the objectives of the programme in behavioural terms, and where an easily identifiable skill or area of knowledge is concerned.

However it follows from the nature of managerial work and managerial effectiveness, as briefly presented at the beginning of this chapter, that management development is concerned with a far wider range of objectives. Managers should not be treated as passive objects, to be subjected to simple conditioning programmes. Managers exercise discretion, make decisions, and exercise leadership in situations where clear-cut or mechanistic solutions are not possible or appropriate. It follows then that the evaluation of management development must actively involve the managers themselves as well as developing criteria related to the effectiveness of their behaviour.

Measuring changes in the job performance of managers following training is difficult, except in the areas of discrete skills mentioned above. It is possible, for example, to measure whether a manager's behaviour in conducting an appraisal interview has changed following a course in appraisal interviewing. It is rather more difficult to measure whether he or she has therefore become a better manager; personal weaknesses, or faults in his or her organisation's use of appraisal schemes, may negate this change in behaviour.

One school of thought advocates that only training which can be shown to be beneficial in strict economic terms[37] should be offered. This approach is also likely to appeal to more traditional directors of finance. While the costing of programmes is clearly important, if strictly applied this rule would jeopardise most attempts at management development, including on-the-job coaching. It might also jeopardise the position of directors of finance!

Methods useful in the evaluation of management development programmes include the following:

1 *Immediate pre-course and post-course questionnaires and rating scales* Managers are asked to state their objectives prior to a course, and then to state their satisfaction with the course upon completion. Sensibly carried out this method treats the manager as a responsible adult capable of evaluating personal progress. However, there is a tendency for participants to rationalise their experiences, particularly if they have chosen the course themselves. Trainers should be aware of Festinger's 'Theory of

Cognitive Dissonance' in this respect, which indicates that we value more highly those events in which we actively participate in order to minimise 'dissonance' with our existing value systems. See 'Behavioural Sciences for Managers', *op. cit.*, for a discussion of 'cognitive dissonance'.

2   Measures of attitude change   Managers can be asked to complete attitude questionnaires both before and after training. Repertory Grid, already referred to, is one example.

3   *Measures of changes in behaviour*   Managers and their superiors can be asked to describe any changes in behaviour that result from training. Appraisal forms and work diaries can provide further evidence of behaviour changes.

4   *Measures of changes in performance*   Success in reaching targets following training can be evaluated, e.g. a reduction in accident rates, or higher sales figures. Again appraisal results can be used as evidence of change in performance.

Although it presents problems, evaluation of management development is important because managers are important. 'Management trainers', comment the Stewarts, 'can be divided into those who know evaluation is impossible, which is why they have never tried it, and those who treat evaluation as an integral part of training design'. The real answer to anyone who objects that evaluating the training takes time away from the serious business of training is that any serious attempt to evaluate training is bound to lead to massive improvements in training itself[38].

References

1   McGregor, D., An uneasy look at performance appraisal', *Harvard Business Review*, **35**, no. 3, pp. 89–94, May/June 1957.
2   Long, P., 'Performance Reviews', *IPM Digest* no. 249, April 1986.
3   Drucker, D., *The Practice of Management*, Ch. 11, Mercury Books, 1961.
4   Humber, J. W., 'Improving management performance', British Institute of Management, 1965.
5   Williams, M., *Performance appraisal in management*, Heinemann 1972.
6   Kane, J. S. and Freeman, K. A., 'MBO and Performance Appraisal: A mixture that is not a solution', *Personnel*, pp. 26–32, February 1987.
7   Ungerson, B., 'Assessment centres – a review of research findings', *Personnel Review*, **3**, no. 3, 1974.
8   Peach, L., 'Highflyers at IBM', *Personnel Management*, September 1979.
9   Stevens, C., 'Assessment Centres: the British experience', *Personnel Management*, July 1985.
10   Fletcher, C. and Williams, R., *Performance Appraisal and Career Development*, pp. 110–111, Hutchinson 1985.
11   Campbell, J. P. *et al.*, 'The development and evaluation of behaviourally based rating scales', *Journal of Applied Psychology*, 57, pp. 15–22, 1973.

12 Williams, M., *op. cit.*, p. 55.
13 Lawler, E. E., *Pay and organisational effectiveness*, McGraw Hill 1971.
14 Meyer, H. H., Kay, E. and French, J. R. P., 'Split roles in performance appraisal', *Harvard Business Review*, **43**, no. 1, 1965.
15 Beveridge, W. E., *The Interview in Staff appraisal*, Allen and Unwin, 1975.
16 Fletcher, C. and Williams, R., 'The influence of performance feedback in appraisal interviews', *Journal of Occupational Psychology*, 49, pp. 75–83, 1976.
17 Randall, G. A., 'Performance appraisal: purposes, practices, and conflicts', *Occupational Psychology*, 47, pp. 221–224, 1977.
18 Fletcher, C. and Williams, R., *op. cit.*, p. 103.
19 Mangham, I. L. and Silver, M. S., *Management Training – context and practice*, Economic and Social Research Council Ref., F0240 000Z, 1986.
20 Lord Young Speech to BIM Conference, quoted in *Transition*, Autumn 1986, pub, MSC.
21 Stewart, R., *Contrasts in Management*, McGraw Hill, 1976.
22 Mintzberg, H., *The nature of managerial work*, Harper and Row, 1973.
23 Cowling, A. G. *et al.*, *'Behavioural Sciences for Managers'*, Edward Arnold, 1988.
24 Smith, and Ashton, D., 'Using repertory grid techniques to evaluate management training', *Personnel Review*, **4**, Autumn 1975.
25 Reay, P., 'Management competences project', *Personnel Management*, p. 36, June 1989.
26 Burgoyne, J., 'Creating the managerial portfolio: building on competency approaches to management development', Management Education and Development, **20**, part 1, pp. 56–61, 1989.
27 Thornton, G. C. and Byham, W. C., *Assessment Centres and managerial performance*, Academic Press, New York, 1982.
28 Jacobs, R., 'Getting the measure of management competence', *Personnel Management*, June 1989.
29 Hirst, W., quoted in Syrett, M. 'Managers have skills, but just what are they?', *Sunday Times*, 6 March 1988.
30 Handy, C., *The making of British managers*, National Economic Development Organisation, 1987.
31 Revans, R., 'The nature of action learning', *Management Education and Development*, 10, 1979.
32 Stewart, S. and Stewart, A., *Managing the managers' growth*, Gower Press, 1978.
33 Burgoyne, J., 'A new approach to evaluating management development programmes: some exploratory research', *Personnel Review*, **2**, no. 4, Autumn 1973.
34 Burgoyne, J., Boydall, T. and Pedlar, M., *Self Development*, Association of Teachers of Management.
35 Mumford, A., 'Self development – flavour of the month', *Journal of European Industrial Training*, **3**, no. 3, 1979.
36 Gratton, L., quoted in Syrett M. 'Star spotting, and how it works', *Times*, 15 February 1989.
37 Odiorne, G. S., *Training by Objectives*, MacMillan, 1970.
38 Stewart, S. and Stewart, A., *op. cit.*

7

Organisation development and change

The most pressing problems facing today's leaders are those associated with change. Government, industry, unions and professional bodies are all having to adapt to their changing environments. Despite their verbal protestations some organisations underestimate the need for change in order to maintain their competitiveness. Those that do initiate major change discover the problems which arise when trying to persuade different interest groups to agree on a particular direction and strategy for change, and when dealing with the emotional uncertainties accompanying change. Whatever the source of the problem, the end result is a display of behaviour often labelled 'resistance to change'.

Organisation development (OD) is a term which has come to be associated with a particular area of knowledge concerned with planned change. Although there is a vast literature on the subject, there is surprisingly little consensus in respect of its definition and boundaries. This is all to the good, because it is a sign of a growing and dynamic field of knowledge, and one which has been adapting to new research findings and theories. What help can OD give to those managers trying to improve the effectiveness of their organisations in a changing environment? Or to put it another way, the competitiveness of their organisations?

This chapter attempts to answer such questions by:

1 identifying the main influences which have shaped the emergence and development of OD;

2 presenting a framework which clarifies the nature of the conceptual and methodological resources which OD makes available to the manager;

3 outlining some ways in which these OD resources can be most effectively utilised by management.

110

Main influences on OD

OD theorists and practitioners are continually trying to find valid answers to two basic questions: What changes do organisations need to make to their culture, and to the way in which they organise and manage themselves, in order to remain competitive? How should organisations go about introducing these changes so as to achieve their objectives efficiently and effectively? These *content* and *process* issues have been particularly influenced by the concepts and approaches outlined below.

Open socio-technical system model

A system is an orderly grouping of different components for the purpose of achieving some given objective. The essential difference in thinking of an organisation as an open rather than a closed system is that due emphasis is given to its dependence upon the environment for its continued existence. Closed system thinking tends to encourage the adoption of a problem solving approach which focusses attention on internal causes of stress, rather than those causes stemming from an organisation's relationship with its external environment.

The open system model of an organisation is essentially very simple. The organisation is seen as:

1 importing energy from its environment (in the form of labour, materials, finance and equipment);

2 transforming this energy into some product or service which is characteristic of the system (e.g. paper products, financial services);

3 exporting the product or service into the environment;

4 re-energising the system with further resources from the environment.

The open system model highlights the need for an organisation to adapt to changes in its environment. This model has therefore led OD theorists to research and propose those characteristics which are likely to increase the capacity of an organisation to adapt to environmental change. The term organisational effectiveness as opposed to organisational efficiency is often used to denote the goal of enabling organisations to grow and survive over time, rather than achieving short-term efficiency or profitability. OD is very much concerned with organisational effectiveness, and therefore with those organisational properties which are conducive to learning or adaptability, flexibility, and innovativeness.

The socio-technical component of the open system model has its origins in the pioneering work of the Tavistock Institute for Human

Relations in London. Their research in British coal mines and in Indian textile mills demonstrated the interdependence of the social and technical sub-systems within an organisation[1]. Mechanisation inevitably had repercussions on roles in the social system, and restructuring had implications for the efficiency of the technical system. The main lesson to be learned was that in introducing changes to the place of work the needs of both the technical and the social system have to be taken into account. Ignoring or misunderstanding social needs will eventually be reflected in such criteria as productivity, quality of output, accidents, absenteeism and turnover.

Subsequent research has increased our insight into the relationships between technology, organisations and their environments. In a study of the electronics industry in Scotland Burns and Stalker[2] found that the less successful organisations tended to be 'mechanistic'; i.e. a greater reliance placed on formal rules and procedures, narrow spans of control, and decision making at the highest levels. The successful organisations tended to be more 'organic', i.e. less emphasis placed on formal procedures, wider spans of supervisory control more common, more decisions taken at the lower levels. The explanation for these findings was that organically structured organisations were able to adapt to change more quickly, and were therefore a better match for an environment which was itself rapidly changing.

In a study of one hundred firms in South East Essex, Woodward[3] found that as the technology involved progressed from small batch or unit production, through large batch or mass production, to process production, certain structural characteristics also changed (e.g. the span of control of the chief executive). She found that different technologies imposed different kinds of demands on organisations, and that these had to be met by an appropriate structure. Those organisations whose structural characteristics remained close to the pattern for their particular technology tended to be more effective.

A refinement to the organic/mechanistic model has come from the work of Lawrence and Lorsch[4] who have further elucidated the complexity of the relationship between an organisation and its environment. Through their differentiation/integration model they have drawn attention to the fact that different parts of an organisation may interact with quite different environments. Thus an organic structure and climate may be appropriate for the R & D department, but a mechanistic structure more appropriate for the production department.

Humanistic psychology and human relations

OD has been particularly influenced by certain values which are associated with humanistic psychologists such as Abraham Maslow and Carl Rogers. These values stress the importance of developing human potential, giving individuals opportunities to influence their work environment, providing them with interest and challenge in their work, and recognising their unique and complex needs. These values were very visible in the pioneering OD activities of such Americans as Chris Argyris and Douglas McGregor. They received new impetus through the almost missionary zeal of Thorsrud, Cherns and others in Europe[5]. The latter found expression in the industrial democracy (ID) and quality of working life (QWL) movements. While these developments incorporated similar values as those promoted by the OD practitioners, they were much more explicit in the values which they were trying to change. Those most closely involved in ID and QWL were disillusioned with the slow rate of progress in trying to get individual organisations to change their culture to incorporate the new values; their primary targets for change were therefore governments and societies. In the UK a visible sign of their success is the promotional and advisory activities of the Work Research Unit, which is now part of ACAS.

The human relations movement was influenced by the value systems we have just referred to as well as those studies which highlighted the importance of social relationships, group membership and leadership style in determining the performance and well-being of people at work. Seminal studies included: the Hawthorne studies[6]; Lewin's studies[7] of the benefits of group decision making; Coch and French's study[8] of the superiority of a participative approach to change. Of particular importance to OD were the group approaches to individual learning and change as developed by the National Training Laboratories in the late forties, and referred to as T-groups or sensitivity training. Most of the early giants of OD such as Bennis, McGregor, Argyris and Schein, were all heavily involved in T-groups[9]. A key feature of T-group culture is the climate of openness and trust which is established. The benefits of this climate for learning, communication, problem solving and making full use of human resources, have meant that T-group based OD programmes were popular during the early development of the movement.

Force field model

One of the most enduring conceptual models in OD was originated by an American social psychologist, Kurt Lewin[10]. In order to cope with various forces which can facilitate or inhibit change, Lewin formulated his 3-step model:

1   Organisations have an inherent capacity to maintain the status quo by a balance of driving and restraining forces. In order to introduce change one must disturb this equilibrium by introducing new forces, removing old ones, or both. This *unfreezing* process can be achieved by making people feel dissatisfied with the present state of

affairs, and motivating them to seek improvements. A strategy of simply increasing the driving forces for change, without decreasing the restraining forces, is likely to lead to excessive levels of resistance to change.

2   Once the unfreezing process is well under way then the *changing* process can be initiated, and participants can be encouraged to seek new solutions to old problems.

3   The final phase is to *refreeze* or stabilise the forces operating in the new situation. This involves ensuring that the changes are legitimised and integrated into the organisation so that their maintenance is not dependent upon temporary forces, such as the presence of an external consultant.

The value of this unfreezing/changing/refreezing model is that it encourages those responsible for managing change to identify those forces which are supporting the desired change, and those opposing it. A systematic analysis of these opposing forces is more likely to result in a successful strategy for change. The three sequential steps also ensure that each phase of the change process is attended to, thus reducing the incidence of resistance to change symptoms.

Action research

The action research approach to change was another valuable contribution made by Lewin[11]. He was one of the first to argue that research in the behavioural sciences would have limited impact if the researcher was involved in the research process (i.e. developing hypotheses and gathering information), but not in the action process (i.e. planning, implementing and evaluating subsequent actions), hence the attraction of his concept of action research, where the researcher collaborates with the client in both research and action components of the problem solving process. Pioneering studies of the action research mode include: Lewin's work on changing food eating habits, Coch and French's study on overcoming resistance to change, and Jaques' studies[12] in the Glacier Metal works in the UK. Many OD practitioners adopt this process model when intervening in organisations.

Change agents

In the early conceptualisations of OD, change agents were the internal or external consultants who intervened in the processes of organisations in order to bring about certain changes as effectively as possible. They were usually well versed in psychology or the behavioural sciences. Their style of intervention was very much that of a joint problem solving approach. The implications of this style, and the reasons for it, can be best understood by comparing and contrasting three types of role relationships which a consultant can adopt toward a client system: the *expert*, the *teacher* and the *counsellor*.

The expert The client system experiences a problem; it makes an approach to a consultant with the expectation that the latter will diagnose and prescribe a solution to the problem. The consultant is thus put in the position of expert and plays a fairly directive role. Often the client prejudges the problem by approaching a consultant who is an expert in a given type of solution, e.g. management by objectives, assessment centres, autonomous work groups. This sort of relationship has many attractions: the solutions applied have usually already been researched and developed by other organisations, thus reducing cost and risk of failure; the employment of an expert generates confidence in what is being done, and provides a feeling of security; if the consultant's solution is not attractive or is threatening, it can often be rejected or shelved with the minimum of disturbance to the client system.

Possible drawbacks include:

1 Superficial diagnosis and treatment: sometimes the function of the expert is merely to provide additional authority to introduce changes which top management see as desirable.

2 The non-participative style of many experts may arouse unnecessary resistance to change, particularly where this involves breaking social norms.

3 The expert's terms of reference may severely limit the area of the client system within which he can operate. Thus the changes proposed or introduced may be incompatible or threatening to other sub-systems.

4 Solutions applied may be the result of a consultant's sales ability or of current fashion, rather than the outcome of a proper diagnosis of the problem.

The teacher In this role the consultant is primarily concerned in bringing about change through the transmission of knowledge and skill. This means that the immediate target for change is the individual and his problem solving behaviour, rather than the structural and technological variables affecting behaviour. Learning usually takes place at internal or external formal courses where simulated rather than real life problems are tackled; although in recent years formal learning experiences are increasingly being designed to be built around actual problems. The advantages of this approach include the following:

1 A high degree of control can be maintained over what is learned.

2   Large numbers of individuals can be exposed to new thinking at relatively low cost.

3   It is not too difficult to design formal learning situations to which participants will react favourably.

There are potential weaknesses, e.g. transfer of knowledge and skills to on-the-job behaviour is often negligible particularly where attitudes or managerial style are concerned, individuals can find themselves on courses, especially external courses, which neither match their needs nor those of their organisation.

The counsellor   Sometimes a consultant takes on a role very similar to that of a counsellor in a therapeutic situation, i.e. a joint problem solving approach. In the individual counselling situation, the counsellor does not try and impose a particular solution on the client, but encourages the client to arrive at a joint solution for which the client shares responsibility. While the counsellor is non-directive with respect to the solution, he or she does guide the problem solving process through its various stages: the client will be encouraged to undertake a thorough diagnosis of the problem before thinking about solutions, and to choose a solution only after exploring a range of alternatives. Where an OD consultant adopts this role in relation to a client, the mechanics of the process are somewhat different since the client is part of a larger system; this means that the problem solving stages leading to change must involve those individuals, groups, or their representatives, who have a vested interest in the problem and the power to implement or to frustrate a proposed solution. It is this counselling model which comes closest to describing the typical role played by a consultant in an OD intervention. The origins of this counselling approach can be seen in the thinking of Carl Rogers, in action research and in T-groups.

OD interventions and technology

Gaining insight into the main influences on OD is the first step toward learning to use this resource for competitive gain. The next step is to become more aware of the available technology, and the situations or context in which they are likely to be valuable. Table 7.1 is a framework for exploring these issues.

Intervention goals

Many of the early accounts of OD included the goals of improving organisational effectiveness or health. These terms were often used to differentiate between economic criteria applied to organisations (e.g. input-output efficiency measures), and the socio-psychological criteria which emphasised the softer variables of job satisfaction, innovativeness, flexibility, organisational loyalty and commitment, and so on.

Implicit in the latter criteria was the notion that certain types of behaviour were more conducive to an organisation successfully adapting to changes and new competition in its environment. Developing these desirable characteristics became a goal of many OD programmes.

An example of an influential model of these characteristics was Likert's System 4 or participative management[13]. Key features of this ideal management system were: high performance goals; an overlapping network of cohesive teams (the linking pin structure); a climate of openness; and a supportive managerial style (individuals felt that their needs for self-esteem etc. were being met). An extensive research programme provided the evidence which encouraged managers to develop their organisations along these lines through an appropriately designed OD programme.

One of the terms used in the OD literature is that of organisational self-renewal. This is the idea that it is not sufficient for organisations to change only in response to planned OD efforts, but that a climate for change needs to become an inherent characteristic of the organisation. This is a powerful idea given the rate and continuous nature of environmental change. In more recent years a similar idea is being promoted but under a different label, i.e. the learning organisation[14]. An organisation which is continually able to transform itself as the need arises has an obvious competitive edge over others. We are still at an early stage of research and model building in this area, and consequently there are few reliable guidelines or programmes for managers to follow in improving their organisation's capacity with respect to this 'desirable' quality.

In the last decade one topic which has aroused considerable interest in the management literature is that of *organisational culture*. The topic has been stimulated by such best sellers as Peters and Waterman's *In Search of Excellence*[15], which highlighted the key role of culture in achieving organisational success. By culture we are referring to the shared beliefs and values which underlie many aspects of behaviour displayed within an organisation. The importance of culture within the context of implementing strategic plans is clear when we consider the importance which many organisations are now attaching to quality and customer care. These attributes of products and services will only be consistently achieved if they are compatible with the culture of the organisation, hence the recent spate of organisational change programmes to bring culture into line with corporate strategy[16]. Many of these programmes may not be labelled OD because of the less dominant role enjoyed by the internal or external consultants, but they should be seen as just another variation of the evolving OD knowledge base if they are planned and used techniques associated with OD.

Table 7.1   Intervention goals and OD technology

Intervention goals	OD Models and technology
Improving organisational effectiveness and health	
Improving organisational learning capacity	Changing job attributes e.g. Job redesign
Improving the match between corporate strategy and organisational culture	Changing team attributes e.g. Team development Role analysis Intergroup development
Basic approaches	Changing organisational attributes e.g. Managerial Grid Sociotechnical system analysis Human resource development
Process-oriented	
Technostructural	
Integrated	

Basic approaches

Table 7.1 lists three basic approaches. Process-oriented interventions are those which are primarily directed at changing attitudes, values, norms, goals and relationships influencing behaviour. Technostructural interventions on the other hand are primarily directed at changing technological and structural variables influencing behaviour. Integrated interventions are those which combine both approaches. In the early days of OD the first approach dominated practice, but evaluation studies revealed its limitations and the strengths of the technostructural approaches. Now it is generally acknowledged that for effective change to take place an integrated approach is preferable.

Changing job attributes

Many behavioural scientists have criticised the person/job relationship which exists for the majority of people at the lower levels of organisations. These criticisms are usually based on theories of motivation, on the values underlying the quality of working life philosophy, and on certain aspects of sociotechnical systems thinking. The result is that various theorists and practitioners have arrived at certain principles of 'good' job design which it is argued will not only lead to greater individual job satisfaction, but to benefits to the employing organisation (e.g. better quality performance, lower turnover and absenteeism) and even to society itself in the form of improved mental health of its working citizens[17].

Some OD interventions are aimed at developing the person/job relationship in the direction of normative job design principles. Thus consultants guided by Herzberg's motivation-hygiene theory will seek to enrich jobs by building into them more opportunities for experiencing achievement, recognition, interesting work, responsibility, and advancement. Consultants attracted by features of sociotechnical systems thinking may want to redesign production systems along the lines of autonomous work groups, i.e. operators divided into cohesive teams which match the technology they are using, given meaningful units of work to perform (e.g. servicing all the needs of a client or assembling complete television receivers), and allowed significant autonomy in organising and monitoring their work (e.g. determine their own work pace, distribute tasks among themselves, carry out their own quality control).

There are now many examples of interventions of this nature. Buckingham[18] describes a programme where job enrichment principles were successfully applied in restructuring the role of foreman in nine factories in a tobacco manufacturing firm. The Work Research Unit in the UK Department of Employment has reported on many case studies relating to job redesign, and to the formation of autonomous work groups, in a wide variety of work settings. Most of the successful interventions have seen the early involvement of workers and their union representatives in the change processes.

Changing team attributes

Improving team effectiveness is an important objective of organisations, since much of the work is accomplished through teams and it is recognised that work-team culture has a significant effect on individual behaviour. McGregor[19] was typical of an early group of psychologists who tried to identify the characteristics which differentiated the more effective managerial team from the less effective team. Table 7.2 incorporates these criteria into a form which he used in an intervention activity at Union Carbide Corporation. Individuals are asked to analyse their team by rating it on a scale from 1 to 7 with respect to each of the variables. The whole team is then asked to discuss in depth the situation with respect to each variable, and to formulate ideas as to why these perceptions exist. The objective is to try and get the group to agree on those characteristics which require improvement, to formulate action plans, to implement the plans, and to evaluate the value of the team development exercise.

The above is just one example of a technique used to build or develop effective teamwork. There are a host of others. Some are primarily designed to improve teamwork in an established group, some more useful for building-up the effectiveness of a newly formed team. An example of the latter is the role analysis technique. This

Table 7.2   Team development scale

1. Degree of mutual trust:		
High suspicion_____		_High trust
(1)	(4)	(7)
2. Communications:		
Guarded, cautious_____		_Open, authentic
(1)	(4)	(7)
3. Degree of mutual support:		
Every man for himself_____		_Genuine concern for each other
(1)	(4)	(7)
4. Team objectives:		
Not understood_____		_Clearly understood
(1)	(4)	(7)
5. Handling conflicts within team:		Acceptance and
Through denial, avoidance,		'working through'
suppression, or compromise_____		_of conflicts
(1)	(4)	(7)
6. Utilisation of member resources:		
Competencies		Competencies
used by team_____		_not used
(1)	(4)	(7)
7. Control methods:		
Control is imposed_____		_Control from within
(1)	(4)	(7)
8. Organisational environment:		
Restrictive, pressure		Free, supportive,
for conformity_____		_respect for differences
(1)	(4)	(7)

Source: Bennis[19]

intervention is aimed at clarifying the role expectations and obligations of team members, and is particularly useful where role ambiguity or confusion exists. The assumption behind the intervention is that consensual determination of the content of roles for individual members of a team will lead to more satisfying and productive behaviour.

Often the creative and productive energy of an organisation is sapped by intergroup conflict. The factors which contribute to intergroup conflict (e.g. competition), and the consequences of conflict, are well understood in the literature and have been succinctly summarised by Schein[20]. The consequences include: each group develops negative stereotypes of the other; interaction and communication between them decreases, and when it takes place information is distorted; each thinks that it is better than the other with respect to its products, methods of work, and so on. These consequences are less likely to occur where the groups can identify a common enemy, where the nature of their tasks forces them to interact and communicate with each other frequently, or where a higher goal exists which transcends conflicting interests but is only attainable through cooperation. The problem is how does one go about creating the conditions when intergroup conflict is the norm rather than the exception?

The development of techniques to improve sub-systems larger than single teams was a major advance within OD. The most influential model of intergroup development is that of Blake, Shepherd and Mouton[21]. The following steps are typical of the process:

1   The two groups (or their leaders) meet to discuss ways of improving intergroup relations.

2   If commitment is obtained the intervention process proceeds by asking each group to prepare two lists, working independently of each other. One list describes their perceptions of the other group; the second how they think the other group will describe them.

3   The groups come together to share the information on the four lists. Discussion is limited to questions of clarification.

4   The groups separate again, to complete two tasks: to discuss what they have learned about themselves and the other group; to list the priority issues which need to be resolved between the two groups.

5   The groups come together to share the information on the lists, create a joint list of issues to be resolved in order of priority, generate action plans, assign responsibilities.

6   Sometimes a follow-up meeting is organised to evaluate progress on action plans and implementation.

This type of intervention has been carried out in order to improve collaboration not only between functional groups within an organisation (e.g. marketing and production), but also between representatives of head office and a field sub-system, between union and management representatives, and between representatives of merging organisations[22].

Changing organisational attributes

Although the popularity of the managerial grid OD programme[23] is in decline, it is worth describing since it incorporates the classic features of OD. It is designed to change an organisation's culture so that it moves from its present state to an ideal state as indicated by an influential body of knowledge. It is a good example of what may be called a 'packaged' OD programme, since it is run mainly by internal change agents and is structured around printed learning materials. Table 7.3 summarises the six phases of the grid; each phase consists of several days intensive study directed by line managers, themselves under the guidance of a skilled OD coordinator.

On paper, grid OD is an excellent example of applying behavioural science knowledge to change. Attractive features of this approach are: the organisation-wide perspective; it attempts to change in a logical sequence the basic sub-systems of an organisation; it gives managers a large part of the responsibility for directing formal learning experiences; plans for change are the result of joint problem solving; the unfreezing/changing/refreezing model underlies the structure of the learning activities; it is based on a coherent management philosophy. It is therefore not surprising that many organisations have made use of the grid. However, few have gone through all six phases, since this would involve several years of commitment for large organisations. It is perhaps significant that the most frequently quoted evaluation of the grid was published when it was first being widely marketed[24], and that apart from British-American Tobacco[25] there are few examples of UK organisations having made systematic and extensive use of grid OD.

Survey feedback is an OD technique which has been in use for many years and is flexible enough to remain popular. It is an intervention technique which managers can readily comprehend since it has grown out of a fairly traditional management tool – the attitude survey. The latter is a systematic attempt to assess attitudes of organisational members to their jobs, and to existing and proposed company policies and practices. This information is used to aid management problem solving. There are several literature reviews which amply demonstrate

Table 7.3   The six phases of the managerial grid

Phase 1   Introduces individual managers to a 9 × 9 grid (showing concern for production on the horizontal axis and concern for people on the vertical axis) which is used to present assumptions underlying five main managerial styles. Managers learn to recognise the gap between their own style and the ideal style, and through standard exercises are encouraged to acquire new behaviours to reduce the gap.

Phase 2   A team or 'family group' examines itself in terms of grid theories, barriers adversely affecting its performance are identified and plans made to overcome them.

Phase 3   Key managers heading interdependent teams are brought together so that grid learning can be applied to resolve problems preventing co-operation between divisions, departments, etc.

Phase 4   Top management contrast current objectives and culture of their organisation with a model of what it would be like if it was truly excellent. Objectives are identified to bring the organisation nearer to this ideal model.

Phase 5   Stated objectives in phase 4 are implemented.

Phase 6   Overall accomplishments of grid OD are reviewed and the need for further change identified.

the potential value of attitude surveys as diagnostic instruments for throwing light on problems of morale, turnover, absenteeism and performance. On the other hand, their contributions to organisational change have often been fairly limited. It has been common practice for the full report on the survey to be treated as confidential and restricted to top management in its uncensored form. The pressure to unfreeze and change is slight, and the report can always be shelved if it threatens the status quo or criticises policies or practices which are regarded with favour by senior management.

The model which OD consultants most frequently refer to when talking about survey feedback has been described by Mann[26]. The data is collected on an organisation wide basis, fed back to top management, and then down the hierarchy through the medium of functional teams. At each feedback meeting the superior takes the chair, and together with subordinates they interpret the data, make plans for desirable changes and for introducing the data at the next level. Because of the overlapping nature of functional teams within an organisation (through the dual membership of the superior), the outcome of discussions is fed both up and down the hierarchy. Thus a head of department who is in a subordinate position at a plant meeting will report to subordinates at a departmental meeting the outcome of discussions at the plant level, and report to his or her superior at a plant meeting the outcome of discussions at the departmental level. The data fed back to a given functional team will be relevant to the problem solving activities of that group. Thus the top management team would see the data relating to all departments and sections of the organisation, but the marketing department may only see data relating to that department and, for comparison, the average organisational responses to those questions which were also asked of other departments (comparative data can encourage the unfreezing of attitudes by creating dissatisfaction with one's own showing).

The consultant usually attends the meetings and serves as a resource person and 'counsellor'. Sometimes the consultant may have an important role to play in preparing a superior for a meeting, particularly if the data is critical of the management team and the superior not accustomed to joint problem solving sessions with subordinates. The consultant may only see his or her role as encouraging the team to analyse the problem solving processes used during the feedback sessions. This 'process consultation' is intended to help the team learn more effective problem solving behaviour from its own experiences – a sort of team development exercise.

There are studies to suggest that in the right cultural setting survey feedback can be a successful intervention technique[27]. However, it has its limitations. The objective of survey feedback is to induce the organisation to change itself; this removes from the consultant's shoulders the responsibility of deciding what structural and functional changes should be made. The disadvantage of this is that an organisation may reinforce its present mode of operation even if this had certain basic defects. Thus a non-union organisation is likely to remain a non-union organisation even after a survey feedback exercise. The changes made are likely to be in the form of mild reform, and there are unlikely to be fundamental shifts in information flow, power handling, or basic structure. The goal of the consultant is not to suggest actions, but to enable individuals and groups to identify important problems and their solutions. This takes place in the feedback sessions. These are often voluntary; unfortunately it is the supervisors with the most 'problems' who are least likely to hold them.

These two examples of applying OD techniques to changing organisational attributes are primarily process led interventions. In a sociotechnical systems analysis, structural change becomes a prime target. With these and other theoretical frameworks in mind, a consultant can enter into a collaborative relationship with a client system based on the action research model. Clark describes a project of this nature[28]. Over a period of three years the project was concerned with the organisational aspects of designing an advanced and technologically integrated factory that was intended to replace three semi-autonomous factories. For the most part the client consisted of a specially constituted design team drawn from R & D, production, industrial relations, finance and engineering services. The consultants did not see their task as trying to push any particular solution, but tried through jointly conducted projects in the existing factories to re-educate the client; that is, to help them to re-appraise some of the design-related beliefs they held in the light of alternative designs and their accompanying consequences.

There is an emerging management model which is less clearly structured and theoretically bound than others, but is exerting considerable influence on management action and on academic research[29]. This may be referred to as the human resource development model. It is characterised by renewed importance being attached to line managers becoming skilled in human resource management, by an attempt to develop human resource policies which are compatible with and reinforce corporate strategies, and by aiming to achieve high levels of employee involvement, commitment and self-development. There are many ways in which an organisation can attempt to bring about these attributes. To do it effectively in most organisations will involve changing their culture, since the changes will mean a fundamental shift in shared beliefs about the ways in which human resources are managed.

Still on the theme of culture it is worth pointing out that many organisations are now trying to change their cultures, so as to bring about a better match between culture and corporate strategy[30]. Although few organisations are attaching the label of OD to these activities, many are nevertheless using OD techniques in managing key elements in the process of change. The approach used is also more likely to be integrated, i.e. it will cover both process issues (e.g. changing attitudes through training), and technostructural issues (e.g., changing reward systems, job redesign).

Effective use of OD resources

Now that we have discussed some of the intervention goals associated with OD, and some of the approaches and techniques being applied to achieve these goals, it remains to provide a few guidelines in the effective use of OD resources. The manager who is seriously interested in learning more about OD resources than is appropriate to describe here, will find it rewarding to study French and Bell[31] or one of the other detailed texts on OD. By OD resources I am including the conceptual models which have been developed to guide managers as to the direction in which change should be made (content issues), the tools and techniques which have been developed to bring about change successfully within organisations (process issues), and the skills of OD consultants (professional change agents).

The model of factors influencing planned change in Figure 7.1 is a convenient structure for this discussion:

1 *Strategic goals*
One of the weaknesses of many early OD efforts was that they tended to become an end in themselves rather than being closely linked to the organisation's strategic plans. To indulge in OD in order to 'make the organisation more effective', or to follow the lead of competitors, is a luxury to be dropped as soon as finance is tight, the senior manager sponsoring the programme leaves, or the novelty value of the programme wanes. For a successful change programme to be initiated more enduring forces need to be operating such as: agreed change objectives to support the business strategy; informed decision making by the chief executive officer and his or her team when committing themselves to particular change objectives, and the means of achieving these objectives; an adequately resourced and skilled coordinator(s) to oversee the implementation of plans. Planned change must be an integral part of the strategic plans of an organisation. An OD intervention should not be seen as a means of changing the internal environment of an organisation to conform to an ideal state, but as a means of establishing a better fit between corporate strategy and the internal environment.

2 *Attributes conducive to goal attainment*
As we have seen in our discussion of the main influences in the

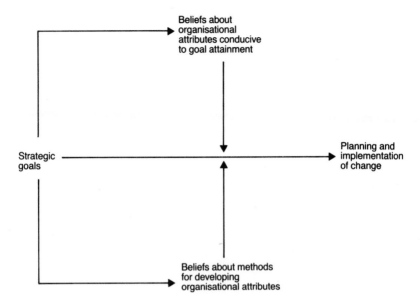

Figure 7.1   Factors influencing planned change

development of OD, research in the behavioural sciences has led theorists and practitioners to believe that certain attributes of jobs, teams and organisations will lead to certain consequences. Accumulated research findings have meant that some of these beliefs have had to be radically modified, others have only needed fine tuning. We now know more about the conditions (e.g. dominant technology used by the organisation, national culture) under which certain types of solutions (e.g. participative management) are likely to achieve expected outcomes. Managers initiating planned change need to be well informed, or to have access to appropriate experts, before selecting given behavioural science solutions to achieve their strategic goals.

3   *Methods conducive to change*
Our knowledge in this area is substantial. We have some proven models to help us in managing the process of change (e.g. force field model). We have a range of reliable and valid techniques for arriving at action plans, and for ensuring commitment to implementation (e.g. action research, survey feedback). We know about the importance of giving the ownership of change to those who have to implement it and make it work, and that this relationship is more likely to hold in certain situations than others (e.g. in Western democratic cultures). We know about the techniques which will facilitate individual and group learning

(e.g. modelling). We know the key role of power in bringing about change.

One of the factors accounting for the limited success of many of the early OD efforts was the weak power base of the external consultant; a feature which was exacerbated by the value system of many OD consultants. Considerations of ownership and power have led to many current OD interventions to become more management-centred and less consultant-centred. This is particularly noticeable in current attempts to change organisational culture[32]. Consultant-driven change is more likely to occur where a packaged programme such as the managerial grid is used, or where a prestigious consultant is employed to steer through the programme. The switch to more management-driven OD recognises the source of power within the client system, the need for more flexible and less value-laden change programmes, and the fact that a key task of general managers in any organisation is managing change. For change programmes to support corporate strategy management-driven OD is essential. There are clear implications here for the training of general managers to acquire some of the knowledge and skills normally associated with the OD consultant. Managers must also learn to use the latter in the most appropriate way – sometimes as counsellors, sometimes as experts and sometimes as teachers. OD consultants in turn need to re-examine their traditional role in the light of evaluation research.

References

1 Trist, E. L. *et al.*, *Organisational Choice*, Tavistock, 1963.
2 Burns, T. and Stalker, G., *The Management of Innovation*, Tavistock, 1961.
3 Woodward, J., *Industrial Organisation*, Oxford University Press, 1965.
4 Lawrence, P. R. and Lorsch, L. W., *Developing Organisations; Diagnosis and Action*, Addison-Wesley, 1969.
5 Davis, L. E. and Cherns, A. B., *The Quality of Working Life*, Free Press, 1975.
6 Roethlisberger, E. J. and Dickson, W. G., *Management and the Worker*, Harvard University Press, 1939.
7 Lewin, K., 'Group decision making and social change' in Swanson *et al.*, *Readings in Social Psychology*, Holt, 1952.
8 Coch, L. and French, J. R. P., 'Overcoming resistance to change', *Human Relations*, 1, pp. 512–532, 1948.
9 Bennis, W. G., *Organisation Development: its nature, origins and prospects*, Addison-Wesley, 1969.
10 Lewin, K., 'Frontiers in Group Dynamics: Concept, Method and Reality in Social Science; Social Equilibria and Social Change', *Human Relations*, 1(1), pp. 5–42, 1947.
11 Lewin, K., *Field Theory in Social Science*, Harper and Row, 1951.

128   *Organisation development and change*

12   Jaques, E., *The Changing Culture of a Factory*, Tavistock, 1951.
13   Likert, R., *New Patterns of Management*, McGraw-Hill, 1961.
14   Pedler, M., Boydell, T. and Burgoyne, J., 'Towards the learning company', *Management Education and Development*, **20**(1), pp. 1–8, 1989.
15   Peters, T. J. and Waterman, R. H., *In Search of Excellence*, Harper and Row, 1982.
16   Williams, A. P. O., Dobson, P. and Walters, M., *Changing Culture: New Organisational Approaches*, Institute of Personnel Management, 1989.
17   Warr, P., *Work, Employment and Mental Health*, Oxford University Press, 1987.
18   Buckingham, G. D., Jeffrey, R. G. and Thorne, B. A., *Job Enrichment and Organisational Change: a Study in Participation at Gallaher Ltd*, Gower, 1975.
19   Bennis, W. G. op. cit.
20   Schein, E. H., *Organisational Psychology*, Prentice-Hall, 3rd edn., 1980.
21   Blake, R. R., Shepherd, H. A. and Mouton, J. S., Managing Intergroup Conflict in Industry, Gulf, 1965.
22   Blumberg, A. and Wiener, W., 'One from one: facilitating organisational merger', *Journal of Applied Behavioural Science*, **7**(1), pp. 87–102, 1971.
23   Blake, R. R. and Mouton, J. S., *The Managerial Grid*, Gulf, 1964.
24   Blake, R. R. *et al.*, 'Breakthrough in organisation development', *Harvard Business Review*, **42**(6), pp. 133–155, 1964.
     Personnel and Organisational Effectiveness, McGraw-Hill, 1972.
26   Mann, F. C., 'Studying and creating change' in Bennis *et al.*, *The Planning of Change*, Holt, 1961.
27   Bowers, D. G., 'OD techniques and their results in 23 organisations: the Michigan ICL study', *Journal of Applied Behavioural Science*, **9**, pp. 21–43, 1973.
28   Clark, P. A., *Organisational Design: Theory and Practice*, Tavistock, 1972.
29   Storey, J., 'The people-management dimension in current programmes of organisational change', *Employee Relations*, **10**(6), pp. 17–25, 1988.
30   Williams, A. P. O., Dobson, P. and Walters, M., *op. cit.*
31   French, W. L. and Bell, C. H., *Organisation Development*, Prentice-Hall, 3rd edn., 1984.
32   Williams, A. P. O., Dobson, P. and Walters, M. op. cit.

8

Pay policy and the management of rewards

The effective management of rewards lies at the heart of successful human resources management. The rewards available to managers include both extrinsic rewards of which pay is the most important, and intrinsic rewards such as recognition and status. This chapter concentrates on pay while drawing attention to the importance of satisfying the other needs which employees bring to the work situation. Pay represents both a cost and an investment to the organisation. It is the largest cost item for many employers. Consequently studious attention to budgeting and control is paramount. Pay is also an investment because it represents money spent in pursuit of productivity. Ensuring that the money devoted to pay is invested wisely is the prime objective of a company's pay policy.

Economic conditions have in recent years particularly forced most organisations to become leaner, fitter and more customer-oriented. This has been reflected in their pay structures. In the past pay policy was often exemplified by bureaucracy, inflexibility and adherence to the status quo. Today, pay policy in the more successful organisations is fully integrated with corporate strategy and with an emphasis on rewarding individual and group contributions to corporate goals.

The objective of reward management is to motivate and retain a productive workforce. Pay policy aims to facilitate the attraction and retention of employees and to encourage effort, cooperation as well as a willingness to learn new skills and to adapt to change. Pay policy has to be administered in a manner perceived by employees to be equitable and fair. Traditional pay schemes have frequently engendered distrust, encouraged demarcation disputes and provided trade unions with a list of grievances; while those employees contributing an above average performance may have earned no more than below average performers. These were the times when pay tended to reflect status, age, length of service and the power of trade union bargaining groups. This is now changing as organisations respond to the challenge of competition and attempt to stimulate greater participation and productivity in their human resources.

In this chapter we examine methods of updating policies on pay and developing rewards appropriate to organisational goals and strategy. While the administration of pay has become increasingly specialised in larger organisations more recently, pay policy is too important to be left with the specialists. Corporate strategy as outlined in the opening chapter, must provide the overall direction, with line management involved in all stages of its operation and the personnel function providing advice and support.

Market forces

Any review of pay policy must start with economic considerations: there are limits as to what organisations can afford to pay; the objective must be to make pay increases self-financing through higher productivity. Those leaner and fitter organisations can permit higher levels of pay which in turn can foster improvements in productivity. The basic price of labour in a free economy is determined largely by the forces of supply and demand in the labour market and no organisation can afford to let itself be too far out of line. Pay policy has to be incorporated into budgets which in their turn require accurate forecasts of trends in external pay levels. The 'reward package' offered by most employers consists of much more than a basic wage. Most employees are looking additionally for 'deferred' pay in the form of pensions, job security, opportunities for self-expression and job satisfaction, such human factors being frequently neglected by labour market economists. The principal source of intelligence concerning the labour market, available to companies is provided by pay surveys which take various forms.

Pay surveys

Systematic investigation is essential if the correct conclusions are to be drawn since haphazard and 'off the cuff' investigations are liable to mislead. Job titles can also mislead so adequate job descriptions are vital. The five factors of skill, responsibility, mental effort, physical effort and working conditions provide a popular and well tried set of headings for this purpose[1].

Systematic investigations into pay levels frequently concentrate on so-called 'bench mark' jobs. These are jobs considered to have special significance for the pay structure on account of custom and practice, their use in pay bargaining, and the number of workers covered. A number of sources of information on pay levels are usually available to management. As many as are convenient and practicable should be used and results compared. Typical sources include:

1   the firm's employment office;

2 job advertisements in papers and journals; (Treat with caution as they can mislead, and may not be based on adequate job descriptions);

3 employment agencies. Private agencies are usually helpful, but have a vested interest in inflating rates. Public agencies, such as Department of Employment 'Job Centres' also provide limited labour market information.

4 published surveys. Though their publishers charge a high fee to cover costs, reputable publications such as 'Incomes Data Services' provide excellent information.

5 official publications. Publications such as DE Gazette provide useful general information but are of limited use in the local labour market situation.

6 participation in an inter-firm pay survey. This can be an excellent source of information. Regular inter-firm pay surveys are carried out by a large number of organisations. It is vital that such surveys are carried out on a systematic basis.

It is not enough to limit labour market surveys to basic rates of pay. The financial rewards offered by many organisations embrace a complete package of basic pay plus a variety of allowances, opportunities to earn overtime, and fringe benefits. Data generated on earnings should be in a format suitable for simple statistical analysis. A wide spread of earnings is frequently found within and across a sample of organisations. This information should be further simplified by calculating the respective ranges, medians and quartile statistics. Management is then in a position to decide whether to maintain or establish a position as a relatively high, average, or low paying firm. The economic state of the organisation, the need to attract large numbers or a high class of recruit, the level of labour wastage, the need to placate trade unions and the general employment philosophy of the organisation are all relevant considerations.

Having taken external economic forces into account, we turn now to internal considerations.

Motivation and pay

Every manager knows from experience how complex individual motivations can be. People are motivated by money and by a lot more besides. Furthermore, money can be used in a number of different ways to motivate people. Pay policy has to reflect the complexity of human nature if it is to succeed in its objectives. Both the amount of money and the manner in which it is offered have to be kept under continuous review in order to achieve optimal results.

The work of behavioural scientists provides a useful contribution to the management of human resources and money and pay have featured in their research. The best known work perhaps is that of Herzberg in the US[2]. While his research methodology is open to some criticism, many managers find that his results correspond with their own practical experience. Herzberg's 'two-factor' theory likened the role of pay to 'hygiene' in the maintenance of public health. He suggested that in the same manner in which hygiene was essential to health, adequate pay is essential to motivation. However, just as good health requires much more than hygiene, so high levels of motivation require much more than a weekly wage since they also require a sense of achievement, recognition and responsibility. Managers require little reminding that it is difficult (but not impossible!) to motivate staff who feel inadequately paid. Pay moreover, is not just a hygiene factor; pay can actively motivate employees to greater effort and productivity. The old 'economic' model of man is no longer good enough. Pay must not be used simply as a carrot. This is particularly true of skilled employee grades who look for a reward 'package' to match their expectations. A more sophisticated approach is required. The so-called 'expectancy theory' recognises that individuals come to work with different needs to satisfy and will be motivated to greater effort if and only if employers provide the rewards they seek. The key to motivation lies in their expectations: this is shown in simplified form in Figure 8.1:

The key lies in gaining employees' confidence. Extra effort will only result if they believe strongly that appropriate rewards will be forthcoming. Lest this should appear obvious it is worth reflecting on the prevalence of pay schemes which make little or no attempt to match rewards to performance, or if they do, are viewed with distrust or dissatisfaction by employees. Using research from the US making use of expectancy theory Porter and Lawler[3] advise management to ensure that:

1   the rewards given are those most desired in return for performing the job well,

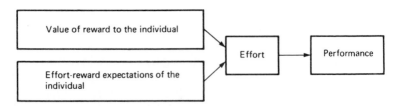

Figure 8.1 Efforts, rewards, and expectations (adapted from Porter and Lawler[3]). Role of attitudes other than satisfaction in performance

2 superior performances are given more extrinsic rewards (e.g. salary and bonuses) and are provided with more opportunities to gain intrinsic rewards (e.g. challenging and varied work) than are given to inferior performances

3 Most individuals in the organisation see and believe that first class performance leads to both extrinsic and intrinsic rewards*:

Internal equity and job evaluation

The concept of a fair day's pay for a fair day's work is deeply engrained into our thinking. A fair day's pay tends to be defined by workers consciously or subconsciously, by reference to what fellow workers in similar jobs are earning, particularly their colleagues at their place of work. While an internal structure of differentials is generally accepted as necessary by most workers, their feelings concerning equity and fairness demand that the size of differentials be regulated in accordance with some open and rational system. A professional approach to wage and salary administration by management likewise demands a rational and acceptable structure of differentials. These demands have given rise to the technique and widespread popularity of job evaluation.

Job evaluation is not a new technique. Most commonly found methods have been in use for the last fifty years. But in recent years there have been a number of attempts to adapt traditional methods to fit in with social and technological change, notably in the use of participation, consensus, and computers.

Exponents of job evaluation have sometimes claimed that it represents a truly scientific method of payment. This is an exaggeration. In the last resort it can only rely upon subjective judgement. But there are many benefits that can accrue from a well installed job evaluation scheme, including:

1 *Cost Control* Where specific rates and differentials are established and maintained, labour costs can be analysed, budgeted, and controlled.

2 *Fairness* Employees can see that an impartial system is being used to establish differentials, and pay rates are not just subject to favouritism or whim.

3 *Simplification* Instead of a large number of different job rates, some perhaps only differing by a penny or two, jobs can be slotted into a simple graded structure.

---

*A fuller outline of relevant theories of motivation is provided in Chapter 4 of 'Behavioural Sciences for Managers' published by Edward Arnold in this series.

Job evaluation is essentially concerned with actual job content and not with either the individual job holder or outside market forces. In real life it is not always easy to ignore the job holder, who may in fact have had a large say in developing the scope of the job he or she occupies, nor the presence of supply and demand for particular job skills. However management should aim for a practically useful scheme that is acceptable to both management and workers, rather than one that is technically pure.

The essence of job evaluation is job analysis. The successful operation of a scheme requires that thorough job studies are carried out by trained analysts. Also basic is the concept of 'bench mark' jobs. As already mentioned these are jobs which are accepted by all parties concerned as being fairly paid at the current time in relation to each other, and also have sufficient in common with the other jobs to be used for comparison. At the start of a job evaluation scheme considerable time needs to be spent on establishing satisfactory bench mark jobs. A method of checking on their usefulness is given under the points method outlined as follows.

Traditional approaches

Different job evaluation techniques have their own peculiar advantages and disadvantages. Four techniques of job evaluation have been in use for many years. These are 'ranking', 'grading', 'factor comparison' and 'points method'. The first two are based on 'whole job' comparison and are therefore, referred to as 'non analytic' to distinguish them from the latter two that analyse job content under a number of 'factor' headings.

1   Ranking

The object of ranking is simply to establish a rank order or hierarchy of jobs. Pay rates will then reflect this hierarchy. Evaluation is carried out by comparing the contents of jobs with the contents on the bench mark jobs, and putting the job into its appropriate place in the hierarchy. Evaluators must use their judgement as to whether one job is to be rated higher or lower than another job. In a typical machine shop we might finish up with the following rank order.

(1)   Tool room fitter
(2)   Maintenance fitter
(3)   Machine setter
(4)   Semi skilled machinist
(5)   Unskilled labourer

Rates of pay will then reflect this simple hierarchy, although the actual differentials must be settled by judgement or negotiation. The principal advantage of this method is its simplicity. It is easily under-stood, and is not complicated to carry out. But because it is so simple it is not appropriate when a large number of jobs of varied content need to be included. For example, we would have difficulty in fitting jobs such as 'secretary' or 'sales representative' into our rank order above. But where a small homogeneous 'family' of jobs is concerned, ranking can be useful.

2 Grading

This technique is also referred to as 'classification'. As its name implies, it is based on the establishment or maintenance of a graded, hierarchical, structure. Frequently a simple grading structure with a strictly limited number of grades is the objective. To illustrate: we might have five basic job grades representing highly skilled (appren-ticeship plus toolroom training), skilled (apprenticeship), partly skilled (two years' training), semi skilled (four weeks' minimum training) and unskilled work in an engineering workshop. These might be labelled as grades A to E respectively, and the same five jobs would then be slotted into the appropriate lettered grade.

Simplicity is its principal virtue. It is extensively used in manufactur-ing industry and in office jobs. But again it can only be effectively used within a homogeneous family of jobs.

3 Factor comparison

This method is less often used in practice. Jobs are compared on the basis of their relative importance under a set of different job 'factors', such as 'training', 'responsibility', 'skill' and 'physical effort'. A rank order is established under each of these headings, and the factors are then weighted in accordance with the ideas of the evaluators. For example, under the factor heading of 'physical effort' our five machine shop jobs may show up in this rank order.

(1) Semi skilled machinist
(2) Machine setter
(3) Maintenance fitter
(4) Unskilled labourer
(5) Toolroom setter

Therefore, the machinist should be paid more under this factor than the toolmaker. The rank order might of course be different under other factor headings. Translating factor comparison into actual pay is something of a headache, and so the usual way out of the dilemma is to use a quantitative approach based on points, which leads us to the points method.

4   *Points method*

Points method achieves a system of differentials by ranking jobs in accordance with the number of points they have been awarded during a job evaluation exercise.

Firstly, a set of factors must be drawn up that will permit satisfactory analysis and comparison of the jobs in question. Typical factors might again be 'responsibility', 'training', 'skill', 'experience', and 'decisions'. A weighting exercise has then to be carried out to decide what possible maximum total of points shall be permitted under each factor heading.

We can illustrate the application of a points scheme by referring to our simple list of five jobs in a typical machine shop. Let us assume that we are using just the four factors of 'training', 'responsibility', 'skill' and 'physical effort', and that as a result of the weighting exercise each factor initally carries a maximum of 25 points out of a grand total of 100 points. The results of evaluation might then look like this:

	Factor				
Job Title	1. Train- ing	2. Respon- sibility	3. Skill	4. Physical effort	Total
Toolroom setter	20	15	20	5	60
Maintenance fitter	15	12	16	7	50
Machine setter	10	10	10	10	40
Machinist	6	4	5	15	30
Labourer	2	3	2	8	15

If pay is directly related to points, it would mean in this case that toolroom setters earn four times as much per hour as labourers. As differentials of this order are not acceptable in our society, this difficulty can be overcome by giving an initial allocation of points to all jobs. Here we might allocate 50 points to all jobs at the start of the exercise giving a final differential between toolroom setters and labourers of 110:65 i.e. if the toolroom setter earns £220 per 40 hour week the labourer earns £130. This example highlights the fact that any job evaluation scheme must be tailored to individual company pay policy and practical objectives.

The relationship between points and pence to be aimed for is normally a linear one with pay rising in proportion to the allocation of points. Such a points scheme can be portrayed on a graph. Graphs show up anomalies which it is the prime purpose of job evaluation schemes to correct. Figure 8.2 shows the results of an evaluation exercise which has allocated points totals to a number of jobs. Some of these jobs are in a correct relationship with each other and therefore fall on or near the straight line that relates points and money. A few jobs are some way from the line indicating that job holders are either being paid too much in relation to the agreed bench mark jobs (where they appear above the line) or are being paid too little (where they appear below the line). As will be seen in Figure 8.2 jobs A and B are being paid too much in relation to the points total credited to them, whereas jobs C and D are being paid too little. The remaining jobs are receiving the correct rate per hour.

Strictly speaking, the pay for jobs A and B should be reduced, and that for C and D increased to bring them into line. In practice, individual rates of pay are usually only increased or maintained, never decreased. An undertaking to this effect is usually given in advance of the exercise to ensure both employees' and unions' full co-operation. Thus the rates for jobs A and B may be reduced to the appropriate level, but individuals currently occupying those jobs will be allowed to keep the higher rate, the difference between the newly adjusted rate and their own higher rate being expressed as a personal 'plus' rate in the pay record books. These individuals may not share in annual cost of living or general increases until such time as the adjusted rate for the job has caught up with their hourly rate of pay, subject of course to negotiation and consultation.

Frequently a job evaluation scheme is linked to a grading structure. A particular grade then includes all jobs that achieve a total of points falling within the minimum and maximum for that grade. For example, using the scheme set out in Figure 8.2 above, we could create five

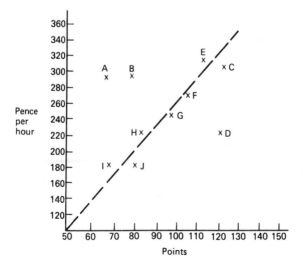

Figure 8.2   Job evaluation graph: points and pence

grades lettered from A to E, and give each grade a twenty points span. Grade A would then include all jobs amassing between 50 and 70 points, grade B all jobs amassing between 71 and 90 points, and so on. In practice the actual demarcation points are likely to be subject to negotiation and consultation. (Grading schemes are dealt with further in the section on Salary structures.)

Modern variations and trends

Recent attempts to update traditional methods of job evaluation incorporate certain trends. The first of these is emphasis upon participation and consensus. In part this arises from general social pressures towards greater consultation, and in part the realisation that workers have something useful to contribute. Today joint management-union committees are frequently set up to monitor the progress of a job evaluation scheme.

Secondly there is more emphasis on the importance of decision-making as a factor in evaluating a job. This arises from the realisation that in large part both workers and managers are paid to make correct decisions in their work, be they concerned with the operation of machines or major policy decisions.

Thirdly, the trend is towards modern technology, such as computers, in large organisations where many jobs need to be compared, and where bench mark jobs for a start may well exceed fifty in number. This is especially the case when paired comparisons are made between jobs under factor headings, necessitating a large number of calculations and the need for a memory data-bank.

A final trend has been for individuals or consultancy firms to attempt to give a 'brand image' to their own particular version of job evaluation. In general these versions emphasise one or more of the considerations outlined above. And so we find methods with labels like 'Decision Band Theory' (by Professor Tom Paterson, emphasising the different levels of decision-making); 'Time Span Theory' (by Professor Elliott Jaques, emphasising the time span between the making of a decision and the point when the success or otherwise of that decision can be properly reviewed); the 'Guide Chart Profile Method' (by Hay MSL Management Consultants, emphasing know-how, account-ability, and problem-solving); the 'Direct Consensus Method' (by AIC Inbucon emphasising consensus and paired comparisons) and the 'Profile Method' (by Urwick Orr, and Partners, Consultants, emphasising 'job profiles' constructed from the factors of 'responsibility', 'knowledge', 'mental demands', 'social demands', 'physical demands and work environment', and joint management union participation). (See Livy[5] for a fuller treatment of these techniques.)

Introducing and maintaining job evaluation

The practical problems of introducing and maintaining a job evaluation scheme can exceed the technical problem of understanding and choosing the best method. Starting from scratch is an expensive business, because of the man hours required in analysing jobs and servicing consultative committees. Frequently union consent needs to be gained and this can lead to tough bargaining. The official trade union line is not usually hostile to job evaluation, but trade unions not surprisingly demand adequate union representation on committees supervising the project. Naturally union representatives may try to wrest maximum financial advantage for their members. Frequently job evaluation schemes are introduced as part of a package deal with the unions when bargains are struck on related matters such as manning levels and pay increases (discussed further in Chapter 9).

Once a scheme has been installed there is a dangerous temptation to assume it will continue to operate successfully for many years without much effort. But all job evaluation schemes decay over a period of time, as the organisation itself changes to meet new situations. Resources have to be made available to carry out regradings as job content changes. It is probably necessary every five years or so to undertake a major revision.

Reservations concerning job evaluation

Employers have in recent years expressed a number of concerns about job evaluation relating to sex discrimination, possible loss of flexibility, lack of sensitivity to market forces and neglect of individual contribution: While the legal position concerning sex discrimination and equal opportunity in the UK is examined more fully in Chapter 11, it is appropriate to note here that under the equal value amendment to the Equal Pay Act 1970 any woman can claim equal pay with any man (or vice versa) if she believes her work is equally demanding, under such factors as 'effort' 'skill' and 'decision making'. The one circumstance in which an employer can seek to have an equal value claim set aside at an early stage is where the work of both claimant and comparator has been rated differently under the same job evaluation scheme, provided that the scheme is analytical and free from sex bias. To achieve this it has to avoid discriminatory factor weighting[6].

It take time to evaluate jobs and reach agreement on relative worth, a fact which may lead to some loss of flexibility. The advantages have to be weighed against the disadvantages. Job evaluation has also been criticised for reinforcing the job demarcation practice of trade unions[7]. This is more of a criticism of old fashioned management practices and a weak response to trade union pressures to preserve the status quo. As long as jobs are graded at different levels and paid accordingly there has to be some fair way of determining their relative worth. Job evaluation does not claim to take account of market forces, because it focusses on internal relativities. Market forces are catered for by superimposing special allowances to reflect the current state of the market. Nor does job evaluation claim to recognise individual effort, hence the need for performance-related bonuses and payment by results schemes as described below.

Payment by results

For the greater part of this century, 'payment by results' has been the term given to pay schemes which link earnings to output and attempt to motivate workers, usually manual workers, to higher levels of productivity. The term reflects the tradition of distinguishing between pay schemes for manual (or blue collar) workers and office (or white collar) workers, hence the terms 'wages' and 'salaries'. Traditionally payment by results has been seen as part of wage administration and the domain of work study engineers. Happily these status distinctions are being broken down, with the adoption of single status agreements.

Payment by results systems remain widely used in industry – an estimated 40% of manual workers receiving some form of payment by results[8]. But modern methods offer a considerable improvement on old fashioned piecework techniques.

Traditionally, payments by results (PBR) was payment by unit of output. Widespread introductions of time and method study led to systems based on time allowances, arrived at by using a range of techniques, from the simple stop watch to complex synthetic data and Predetermined Motion Time Systems (PMTS). As part of this process 'effort rating' undertaken by time study engineers may help to achieve *fair time allowances* i.e. a systematic estimate of the effort being put into jobs by workers to determine the time a worker of 'effective worker standard' (EWS) should take for job completion, making due allowances of fatigue, rest pauses, and unavoidable interruptions. This can then be converted into standard minute values (SMVs) enabling workers to be measured and paid according to a standard performance scale, such as the popular 60/80 scale, or the 0–100 (British Standards Institute) scale.

These scales are based on the notion that workers on payment by results are likely to work faster than workers on a time-rate, and should be rewarded accordingly. Thus with the 60/80 scale the time-worker is estimated to put in a '60' performance, the PBR worker an '80' performance (i.e. $\frac{1}{3}$ higher). Target remuneration for a PBR worker should therefore be set correspondingly higher. PBR workers have the opportunity to earn considerably more than time workers, how much more depending on the system in use. The ILO defines four

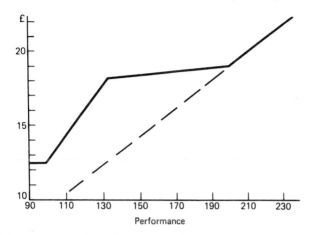

Figure 8.3 Example of 'variable' payment by results system using BS1 scale

types of gearing of performance to pay, namely *proportional, regressive, progressive*, and *variable*. Under a 'proportional' system payment increases in the same proportion as output. A 'regressive' scheme means that payment increases proportionately less than output. Such well known schemes as Bedaux, Halsey and Rowan fall in this category. Because payment per unit decreases as output rises, labour costs decrease as output increases, although the worker has to work harder to increase his income. Under a progressive scheme the reverse happens i.e. payment increases proportionately more than output. Employees are thus encouraged to achieve higher levels of output, but management encounters problems of cost control. With variable systems, payment increases in proportion which differ at different levels of output, as illustrated by Figure 8.3.

Such schemes may encourage higher output up to a certain level of performance, but can be complicated to instal and difficult for employees to understand.

Many firms operate PBR schemes which are based on 'time rate plus' i.e. workers are guaranteed a certain basic rate, and payment by results are then added to this. Frequently 'fall-back' rates also operate or other methods of guaranteeing earnings in the event of stoppages. 'Lieu bonuses' are often paid to certain categories of timeworkers, usually skilled workers such as maintenance craftsmen, to preserve differentials between them and production workers. Group bonus and PBR schemes operate along similar lines, but with the output targets set for groups of workers e.g. on a production line. Bonus payments are then shared by members of the group. Such schemes may encourage group co-operation but discourage individual effort.

Misuse of PBR: pros and cons

PBR systems have frequently been criticised, especially where they have been used indiscriminately or been installed by unqualified rate fixers. On many occasions they have been blamed for industrial disputes, wide fluctuations in earnings, poor workmanship, and restriction of output. Other criticisms (see for example Lupton 1961[11]) also cite high administrative costs, difficulty in achieving consistency in effort rating, the fact that technology often dictates the pace of work rather than effort, and difficulties workers frequently have in understanding the operation of these schemes. Lupton (op. cit.) quotes one female worker as saying 'We have been to ask them to explain but the gentleman in the office says it is in decimals which we couldn't understand, and that we must go back to work and not make a fuss'!

Defenders of PBR however claim that it leads to increased output, higher earnings, and lower costs of production – when properly applied. The National Board for Prices and Incomes concluded that '. . . properly controlled, conventional PBR is generally more effective in encouraging workers to produce more than simply paying them so much an hour for the time they spend at work'[9]. There exist many examples of schemes that have been installed with full trade union agreement.

Describing PBR schemes in black or white terms is a mistake, rather one should ask whether a particular system is appropriate to a particular situation, and if not, in what ways it might usefully be modified. This point is taken further in ensuing sections of this chapter[10].

Modified forms of PBR

In order to overcome some of the problems associated with traditional PBR systems a number of modified schemes have been designed. *Measured Day Work* schemes for example determine the level of performance to be expected of an effective worker using work measurement techniques, and then fix an appropriate level of payment. Workers are expected to maintain this level of performance and to co-operate with management in return for guaranteed earnings and job security. *Premium payment Plan* (PPP) is a graduated form of measured day work allowing workers some choice of performance level and the associated rate of pay. Under this system a worker can improve his pay in two ways – by achieving a higher level of performance over a specified period in his present job or by moving to a job in a higher classification.

Value-added pay schemes

These schemes have been adopted by a number of employers who feel strongly that employees should see a connection between the contri-

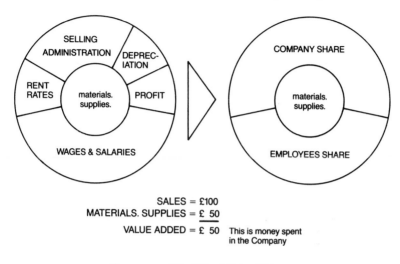

SALES = £100
MATERIALS. SUPPLIES = £ 50
VALUE ADDED = £ 50   This is money spent
in the Company

Wages average 45% of Value Added = £22.50
Productivity Standard £2.22

Figure 8.4   The Value Added 'Doughnut'

bution their efforts make to the prosperity of the enterprise, and the rewards they receive as a share of the value added to the product or service. Value-added schemes are also referred to as 'gainsharing'. Thus it is felt that employees can be encouraged to identify with the fruits of their labours and to participate in improving working methods. Such schemes require a high degree of commitment by management, a willingness to disclose information, good labour relations and careful measurement. Wages are an agreed proportion of the monetary sum derived by subtracting the cost of materials and other supplies, from sales revenue. A simplified version is illustrated in Figure 8.4.

The two best known versions of value-added schemes are the Scanlon Plan and the Rucker Plan. The first, developed in the 1930's in USA by Joe Scanlon (an ex steel worker and union official who wished to see a sensible conclusion to the conflict between management and employees over pay levels) focussed on the whole organisation, and involved unions and employees as well as management in productivity improvements. The Plan provides for 75% of gains being distributed to employees with 25% going to the firm. A similar idea was inherent in the Rucker Plan except that it modified the distribution to reflect the relative contributions of labour and capital in the particular organisation.

A number of successful value-added schemes are currently in operation in the US[11]. Typically, the successful scheme shows productivity improvements of between 5% and 15% in the first year of operation together with an improvement in product quality. But there have been failures too, notably associated with bonus levels which fell short of employees' expectation as well as inconsistencies in the treatment of different groups. A modified version of a value-added scheme has been in operation at Volvo's plant at Kalmar, Sweden, where gains from productivity are shared between the company and employees all of whom receive regular briefings from team representatives. In addition plant-wide assemblies take place twice each year[12].

Pay-for-skill

When skills are in short supply it can make sense to reward the acquisition of special skills. Modern production systems frequently require multi-skilled operators who can operate in teams. Pay-for-skill schemes award pay increases to employees as they progress from single to multi-skill status, acquiring 'skill blocks' en route. Supporters of such schemes claim that contrary to expectation, unit costs decrease in spite of higher individual wages. This occurs because both productivity and quality improve and supervisory posts can be eliminated[13].

Salary structures

Most of us are familiar with salary structures composed of a range of pay grades and incremental scales within each of those grades. If they are to work effectively these structures must be based on the tech-

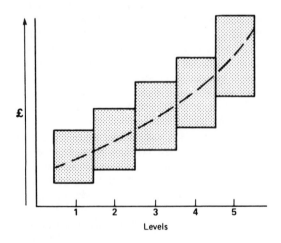

Figure 8.5 Example of graded salary structure with varying overlap

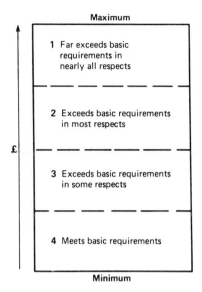

Figure 8.6 Salary range broken into quartiles to provide a section for each of the categories of performance

niques described earlier in this chapter. The final outcome can be represented by the type of structure depicted in Figure 8.5.

Three fundamental decisions in developing such a structure concern the number of pay grades, the range within each grade, and the amount of overlap between each grade. Incorporating a large number of grades, as found in many public sector organisations, makes promotion a relatively easy matter whilst devaluing the significance of promotion. Conversely the structure with relatively few grades enhances the significance of promotion but decreases flexibility. Grades with a large measure of overlap devalue the financial significance of promotion but may lead to less pressure for promotion. Grades that embrace a wide range of pay permit a large number of incremental increases (usually justified on the grounds that experience and service deserve some reward) but can mean that two persons with different lengths of service doing the same job receive widely different rates of pay.

It is possible to control progression through a pay grade in order to ensure higher rewards and faster progress for staff earning good appraisal reports. This is illustrated in Figure 8.6.

A system of differential rewards can be taken one stage further by use of so called 'salary progression curves'. These curves depict the movement of employees' salaries over a period of time, and can be

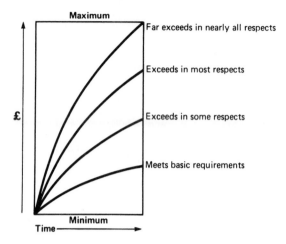

Figure 8.7   Salary progression curves

viewed both as a historical process and a prediction for the future, as shown in Figure 8.7.

Merit awards

Merit rating was examined briefly in Chapter 6 when we considered appraisal. Merit awards for salaried staff have multiplied in recent years in an attempt to reward higher levels of performance. Fewer pay schemes now award annual automatic cost of living increases to all employees; instead all pay increases are referred to as 'merit awards' and some employees receive no increase. Usually this is linked to some form of appraisal. The evidence in favour of such merit awards is not clear cut: while in theory they should stimulate greater effort, in practice they can run into a number of practical problems. Staff may not be convinced that the merit awards are fairly based and the value of the awards may be insufficient to motivate staff. There is evidence that an increase of at least 10–15% is necessary to stimulate greater effort[14]. In the UK such awards have averaged only 7%[15]. 'Pay for performance' schemes are now making their mark and have replaced many former merit schemes.

Pay for performance

Where some form of measurement is possible performance of salaried grades of staff can be rewarded in several distinct ways. Before any such scheme is launched some basic considerations are necessary. Armstrong and Murlis[16] have highlighted the following:

1 the choice of performance measures – financial or non-financial or a combination between the two;

2 how far the scheme should be tied down to a formula, or should it permit discretion when making awards;

3 the need for a link between the pay scheme and the performance appraisal system;

4 the level of payments to be made according to performance which will take account of the target level, the starting point and any limits or 'caps' to be placed on incentive earnings;

5 action to be taken over any 'windfall' profits;

6 how often payments should be made.

In UK the most frequently used financial measures of performance of the work of senior managers, is pre-tax profits followed by return on capital employed[17]. As well as individual financial incentive plans, group bonus schemes may be operated, bonuses being either discretionary or awarded from a special pool and distributed pro rata as a percentage of salary.

Non-financial measures of performance include the following:[18]

1 Narrative descriptions of performance

2 Evaluation scales using ratings which may vary from poor to excellent

3 Time limits and target dates for completion of projects

4 Ratios, such as number of errors per employee

5 Objective and quantifiable measures of output

Interesting examples of performance-related pay schemes in UK are provided by Mars Confectionery, Jaguar Cars and Rank Xerox. These cover all employee grades. Mars operate a 'status free' culture where all employees, termed 'associates' participate in a bonus scheme. All jobs are evaluated in the same system. The acquisition of skills and experience is rewarded by increments. The company bonus plan pays out bonuses in the range 10–25%, depending on financial results[19].

At Jaguar Cars policy is to keep bonus earnings as a significant proportion of total earnings for all employees. To this is added a profit sharing scheme in which, at the discretion of the board, a percentage of profits is distributed annually in the form of shares, equally to all employees with more than one year's service. These have to be kept in trust for two years after which they can be sold or transferred into the employee's name. There is also a save-as-you-earn share purchase option scheme[20]. At Rank Xerox bonus payments to managers are linked to the return on assets, growth in revenue, and profits before tax. In recent years bonuses have typically run at 25% on top of basic salary.

An essential preliminary to all successful pay for performance schemes is a soundly based business plan and sensibly structured organisation. As one senior director commented: 'Incentives will not move the business'[21]. A radical shift in rewards from an emphasis on hierarchy and status to performance and contribution is not without its difficulties and challenges. Old habits often die hard. A recent review of the American scene comments: 'A source of trouble to most corporations is the fact that various forms of contribution-based pay also tend to shake up the hierarchy, challenge traditional authority relationships and weaken the meaning of organisational status'[22].

Employee benefits

The management of employee benefits is an important part of pay policy and reward management. The cost of benefits can amount to more than a quarter of direct pay costs, and benefits play an important role in attracting and retaining staff. Many employee benefits which are now part of the employment package started out as welfare services.

As well as pensions and holidays, typical large company benefits include company cars, subsidised catering, life assurance, private health insurance, day nurseries and social facilities. To this list some would add forms of deferred pay such as share options and profit sharing[23].

A philosophy of pay for performance favours 'clean cash' in preference to expenditure on benefits so as to reinforce the link between rewards and results. However benefits are popular with many employers. The company car is now established as an important 'perk' in UK. Some companies favour a 'cafeteria' approach for executives allowing a degree of choice between various benefits and cash, as long as the cost to the firm remains the same. This element of choice is held to increase the attractiveness of the rewards.

Employee benefits should be reviewed on a regular basis to ensure that they are still achieving the desired results and that the organisation is getting good value for its money.

References

1 Lupton, T. and Bowey A. M., – *Wages and Salaries*, Ch. 2, Penguin, 1974.
2 Herzberg, F., 'One more time: how do you motivate employees?' *Harvard Business Review*, 46, 1968.

3 Porter, L. W. and Lawler, E. E., 'What job attitudes tell about motivation', *Harvard Business Review*, Jan/Feb 1968.
4 Cowling, A. G. *et al.*, *Behavioural Sciences for Managers*, Edward Arnold, 1988.
5 Livy, B., *Job Evaluation – a critical review*, George Allen and Unwin, 1975.
6 Fouracre, S., 'New Factors in Job Evaluation'. *Personnel Management*, May 1986.
7 Wickens, P., 'Job Evaluation mitigates against change'. *Personnel Management*, April 1988.
8 IDS Study no. 170, 'Payment by Results', *Incomes Data Services Ltd.*, May 1978.
9 NBPI Report no. 65, *Payment by results systems*, HMSO, 1968.
10 Bowey, A. *et al.*, 'Effects of incentive payment systems. United Kingdom 1977–80, London', Department of Employment, Research Paper 36, 1982.
11 Kanter, R. M. *et al.*, 'From status to contribution: Some organisational implications of the changing basis for pay', *Personnel*, pp. 27–33, Jan. 1987.
12 Hanck, W. C. and Ross T. L., 'Sweden's Experiments in Productivity gainsharing: A second Look', *Personnel*, Jan. 1987, pp. 61–69.
13 Kanter, R. M. *et al.*, *opus cit.* pp. 34–35.
14 Kanter, R. M. *et al.*, *opus cit.* pp. 14–16.
15 Murlis, H. and Wright A. 'Rewarding the performance of the eager beaver', *Personnel Management*, June 1985.
16 Armstrong, M. and Murlis H., *Reward Management*, Kogan Page, 1988, pp. 210–211.
17 Monks Guide to Performance Related Bonuses, 1988.
18 Fowler, A., 'New Directions in performance pay', *Personnel Management*, Nov., 1988.
19 Bowden, J., 'Rewarding Executive Performance in a Status Free Culture', Conference Paper, IPM National Conference 1987.
20 Edwards, K., 'Rewarding Executive Performance – The Jaguar Experience', Conference Paper, IPM National Conference 1987.
21 Edwards, K., *opus cit.*
22 Kanter, R. M., *opus cit.*, p. 36.
23 Webb, S., *Employee Benefits Annual Survey*, 1983. BIM Information and Advisory Services.

9

Welfare at work

'It is unfortunate that so much of the business world confuses caring, involvement, and compassion with outdated concepts of paternalism and treating your employees as if they were incapable of looking after themselves. True caring is a matter of respect for the individual and the individual's different aspirations, accepting them as his or her right, and trying to acknowledge and assist them'.*

John Harvey-Jones

Welfare is a different topic from most of the others to be found in this book. Welfare is not directly about the provision of clean washrooms, or children's creches, or about safety or equality legislation although all those things are important. Nor does welfare enjoy the academic status of having various models with which to help the manager manage. It is a topic which is essentially 'soft'. It can be observed, experienced and enjoyed; but its effectiveness may be more difficult to measure. In the world of human resources management there are remuneration systems, succession plans, appraisal techniques and communication strategies, but where are the welfare systems, plans, techniques or strategies? Welfare is not like that.

Defining welfare

Welfare is a corporate attitude or commitment reflected in the expressed care for employees at all levels, underpinning their work and the environment in which it is performed. In management terms it is concern for the community that works together. Welfare is almost a variation on Descartes' dictum: cogito ergo sum (I think, therefore I am) 'We work together, thus we care for each other'. Obviously there must be financial constraints but a concern for welfare is a commitment to employees for their own sake as employees, not because in the long term it improves the bottom line.

However what is interesting to note is that those firms who are

* John Harvey-Jones ('Making it Happen', by Fontana, 1989, on page 149).

committed to the welfare of their employees such as Marks and Spencer, The Body Shop, Shell, Lever Brothers are also successful in financial terms. Welfare is not always an either/or: either welfare or profit. Welfare is very much a both/and: profit and welfare achieved together by the right corporate attitude and actions.

The provision of a programme for women returners due to the 'demographic time bomb' of fewer school leavers is not welfare; it is manpower resourcing. Senior line managers chairing a health and safety committee is not welfare; it is fulfilling legal responsibilities. Welfare is about asking simple questions such as 'How can we make our employees' work as safe, enjoyable and as challenging as possible because they are our employees?' 'How can we help each other give of our best and grow in individual respect?'

Anita Roddick, The Body Shop entrepreneur encapsulated this concept when talking about her company: 'I employed workers but people came instead'. Part of Roddick's success is no small way due to the attitude she and her management have towards their employees.

Nor should welfare be viewed as the largesse of management to be given to or witheld from the workforce. It is mutual and reciprocal. In management generally and even in the extensive literature welfare has never topped the subject popularity stakes. The reasons why this may be so are both obvious and legion.

Firstly, there are what may be termed 'operational' reasons. In the main line managers do not see welfare as their responsibility. Occasionally in job descriptions one might see, (often the last item), a statement about health and safety of subordinates, but direct accountability for welfare is perceived as enjoying a home elsewhere. Perhaps it is because a concern for welfare makes no immediate contribution to perceived managerial priorities. Indeed it could be argued that a practical concern for welfare mitigates against efficiency and productivity *in the short term*. Is it not strange that even after 50 years many managers still have a Taylorite view of human resources? No doubt 'speedy' Taylor would support two possible reasons which hinder keen management interest:

1 welfare is difficult to measure, and

2 there is very little reward for getting it right.

Welfare is unfortunate, for unlike good quality in a product or service or good design, it is not immediately saleable to customer or client. At most it may be viewed as an overhead cost which cannot be passed on. In fact welfare is rather like a jelly fish: difficult to describe, no clear boundaries, impossible to grasp and may cause exceptional pain to those who ignore it.

However, it is too easy to suggest that managers are totally responsible for this lack of concern. Employees too have played their part.

All too frequently protective clothing or safety measures are seen as 'namby pamby' and for some strange reason it is 'macho' to go without ear defenders, helmet or goggles or whatever else should be worn for protection. Employees also take unnecessary risks with their own lives and sometimes those of their workmates. Perhaps it is because the effects of non-compliance, like wearing ear defenders, are not perceived immediately. Perhaps gradual deafness is acceptable to some. The need to shout at those who have suffered the effects of years of noise at work in traditional heavy industries makes this point most forcefully. Even with employee representatives safety was not always a main issue. Safety was negotiable, certainly in the early days; the concept of compensation and danger money being better established than good practice and safeworking. If it was dangerous, one was paid more, rather than making safe that which was dangerous.

There may have been cultural reasons as well. Certainly with industry we still prefer the cult of the winner. Welfare has always had close links with the weak and the disadvantaged and to express care and concern is not always seen as fashionable by policy makers.

Welfare could be regarded as an old fashioned, even quaint, concept. Today there are very few welfare departments. Somehow the title has more to do with old style paternalism than with human resource management – a Quaker enthusiasm no longer appropriate in today's world.

Finally welfare is not easily implemented because it requires the co-operation of all the major parties involved with the enterprise: management, employees, trade unions, shareholders and government. Forced compliance from any one of these major players will almost certainly guarantee non-compliance. An example of this is the equal opportunity legislation: it is now over twenty years since it was enacted, but women still lag behind in pay compared with their male counterparts. If compliance with the law is not easy, compliance with the spirit and values that gave legislation birth is far more difficult.

A framework for welfare provision

After such an introduction, does welfare still have a place in the management of human resources? The answer has to be 'yes'. Increasingly in these days society is witnessing a change in values. This means: 'that the use of individuals to satisfy the economic goals of an organisation is no longer a viable social value. People will not let themselves be used'[1].

Management prerogative brings with it management responsibilities towards the employees in an organisation. Employees, in their turn, have responsibilities towards management. At work employees can reasonably expect to enjoy basic rights and it is within this framework that welfare will always have a place in the management of human resources. These rights fall into three categories:

1 *The right to enjoy health and safety*   to be free from the risk of injury to body or mind and to be granted basic facilities.

2 *The right to enjoy information and communication*   to be able to express a point of view directly or through a third party concerned with work without fear of recrimination; to communicate freely with other employees on matters of interest; to be given information concerning major factors affecting individual work and continuing livelihood.

3 *The right to be managed fairly*   not to be treated arbitrarily and to be able to participate in consultations about proposed changes with a right to appeal against perceived unfairness.

It is within this context of rights that welfare issues can be addressed. The impetus for action comes less from statutory obligations or from what can be afforded and more from a standpoint of mutual concerned care. Welfare is the support that can reasonably be expected by employees from their employers. As long ago as 1776 Adam Smith wrote:

> 'The man whose life is spent in performing a few simple operations, of which the effects too are, perhaps, always the same, or very nearly the same, has no occasion to exert his invention in finding out expedients for removing difficulties which never occur. He naturally loses, therefore, the habit of such exertion, and generally becomes as stupid and ignorant as it is possible for a human creature to become'.
>
> (The Wealth Of Nations)

A trend which will continue to ensure that welfare is continually given attention by management is the increasing educational participation of the workforce. More people are being educated for longer; more are enjoying further education at all levels. This process brings about four consequences: a rise in skill and ability levels; increased aspiration for jobs which call for personal skill and ability; a demand for a better quality of life at work; an increased ability to request and negotiate for basic welfare rights[2]. It has been argued that we have today an overeducated workforce whose abilities exceed their job requirements. They are no longer prepared to accept the standards of the past and, if their legitimate aspirations are not recognised, they will use their skills and abilities to initiate the appropriate changes.

The right to enjoy health and safety at work

Freedom from the risk of injury at work is the driving force behind the safety legislation beginning in the UK in 1802 with the Health and

Morals of Apprentices Act and culminating in the Health and Safety at Work etc. Act 1974 and the work of the Health and Safety Commission. In spite of this legislation something in the order of 900,000 people are injured at work in the UK every year. Such a figure cannot be acceptable to a modern society. The requirements of the legislation are well documented elsewhere and so in this section more space will be given over to the welfare implications covering the qualitative aspects of employee work. It is axiomatic that physical safety is part of welfare but there is also mental safety to be considered.

The predominant paradigm in manufacturing is the 'main effects' model which predicts that assembly work will bring about higher absence, lower job satisfaction and deterioration in mental health when compared with other methods of manufacture, which include self-pacing or less repetitive work[3].

A concern for welfare suggests a need for management action to reduce the harmful effects of boring monotonous work. Job rotation, operator quality control and even, in some plants, permission to talk would be beneficial. Social facilitation and job interest for operators can and should be built into production by industrial engineering. Questions such as 'How can we make work more enjoyable, more interesting for our operators?' are worthy of consideration at the same time as questions of efficiency and production maximisation are being discussed. These questions are not mutually exclusive.

The other model for the effects of assembly work is the 'interactive model' which suggests that the effects of the assembly method of working depends on factors or contingencies in the individual environment. Broadbent's work goes a long way to suggest that where there is strong social support, mental health can be maintained in such an environment[4]. In this study female workers stated that fellow employees, co-confidants and friends had a part to play in that they provided strong social support.

The influential study by Walker and Guest suggests an inverse relationship occurring between the number of required operations and job interests and absenteeism[5]. The larger the job, the more interest in it resulting in less absenteeism. It is strange that some managements will take to excess the steps to effect a percentage uplift in output but neglect to take positive action to reduce the absenteeism of the operator working the system. It is unfortunate that in many organisations absenteeism is picked up through the disciplinary procedure rather than a welfare audit, which might enable management more easily to root out the real causes of absence from work.

Sadly employees are still often treated as extensions to machines rather than vice-versa. Kornhauser found that employees whose skills are underutilised were more likely to suffer a deterioration in their mental health[6]. Also daydreaming was positively associated with mental health. Harrison, (*op. cit.*) suggests that there should be a match between the requirements of the job and the abilities of the individual.

Could it be that we are now ready for the Copernican revolution at work; the employer revolving around the employee, jobs structured for human needs? For the last two decades the wealth of evidence challenges the technocratic or Taylorist view point where the sole motivation to work was financial. Marx as long ago as 1844 in the Paris Manuscripts warned of the dangers of alienation of the workforce. Blauner has suggested that a reduction in freedom has a direct connection with alienation[7]. Where talents are wasted, so too are financial resources[8,9] (Herzberg and Likert).

Two leading manufacturing companies BICC and Rolls Royce have pioneered what has been called human-centred engineering. For example conventional automation had led the computer controlled lathes to be programmed away from the shop floor. Essentially this reduced the skilled employee to a machine minder. In human centred engineering while the lathe is still computer controlled the programming is done by the operator. The BICC technologies manufacturing system provides for and encourages individuals to develop and extend their skills and knowledge. Craft skills are being valued and developed around the technology.

At Rolls Royce, human centred engineering facilitates flexibility in the work force. The aim of the programme is to increase the involvement of the skilled employee continually reducing the traditional barrier between design and manufacture.

With the same commitment to the job contract and employee involvement, labour turnover, absenteeism and stress levels, when addressed appropriately, bring about increasing productivity[10,11]. A concern for the type of work and environment of employees, will be accompanied by increased output.

Sometimes this concern for employees is motivated from the Taylorist approach. More appropriately, as BICC and Rolls Royce have demonstrated there has been a shift in values. As previously suggested, Davis puts it most eloquently: '. . . that the use of individuals to satisfy the economic goals of an organisation is no longer a viable social value. People will not let themselves be used' (*op. cit.*).

Traditionally it has always been the employee who adapts to the work; this no longer makes economic or moral sense. The options now open to management and employees are legion and include:

Job enlargement extending work cycles in content with increased task at same level.

Job enrichment where job content and responsibility can be assumed from the next person up in the hierarchy, thus making the job more interesting.

Job rotation   individuals within a team can swap jobs with each other and this will begin to mitigate the inevitable boredom of short cycle repetitive tasks.

Job information   Employees given information on their work and on the units they produce. This provides a conceptual framework. Matters like quality and sizes of production runs are then possible to put into context by employees, understanding instructions and their implications rather than just being expected to comply with instructions.

Job consultation   where employees can talk about their work and discuss problems and opportunities in an environment where decisions on improvements can be taken. Discussion for its own sake is of no value. Where an individual input can be made management will be, as Tom Peters puts it, 'drowned with ideas'[12].

Team working   where work is structured so that team commitment and social relationships may be maximised.

These and similar measures will improve not only the quality of working life but also the productivity and efficiency of the organisation.

Stress related problems

Within the area of health and safety, space must be given to stress, a major concern of those responsible for people at work. By stress we mean 'any force that places on the individual a psychological or physical factor beyond that individual's range of stability, producing a strain within the individual'[13].

Stress comes from the Latin word *stringere* (to pull tight). When the word was first used it had the meaning of having difficulty or suffering hardship or affliction, only later did stress imply strain or pressure.

In 1946 Selye provided a helpful model outlining the process of stress-related illnesses. Essentially there were three stages:

Alarm   The stressor acts upon the organism and the defence mechanisms are brought in to play.

Resistance   The organism adapts to the new stressful situation. If the organism cannot adapt or the defence mechanism is not successful then the third stage occurs.

Exhaustion   Resistance collapses and the organism can no longer perform satisfactorily.

The literature suggests four major areas which may bring about the alarm stage in an employee at whatever level from chief executive to hourly paid cleaner. They are as follows:

1 *The job itself* A sudden increase or decrease in work load or pace; changes in hours; excessive working conditions; frequent changes in procedures or policies; changes in technology 1.6; time pressures

2 *Role and job responsibility* Lack of job guidelines; under-expectations from superiors or colleagues; too much or too little responsibility; inadequate feedback on work performance; role conflict, different expectations from different groups or individuals.

3 *Relationships at work* Poor relationships with boss/colleagues/subordinates; difficulties in delegating work; lack of participation or real communication; working at the boundaries/interfaces between departments, or the outside world.

4 *Career development* Over or under promotion; lack of job security; lack of scope for self development within the job.

Stress can be recognised by line managers looking for major changes in these major areas:

Mood:
Increases in anger or irritability; self condemnation; depression or continual sadness.

Work Patterns:
taking longer to do things; an increase in error rate; an increase in absenteeism; increase in smoking or drinking; difficulty in making decisions; difficulty remembering things.

Cooper recommends various strategies open to organisations to reduce stress at work[14]. He divides them into two categories:

Operational Strategies which modify existing human resource systems

Influential using a human resource specialist to mitigate stress

In the operational category Cooper suggests making appraisal less judgemental and more developmental, the introduction of stress counselling and stress awareness training, increasing professional training and providing clarity of promotion criteria. In the influential category Cooper includes opportunities to talk through problems reducing job relocation requirements and improving selection, taking the prospective candidate's ability to cope with anxiety into account at interview.

Any welfare programme should incorporate measures to produce a working environment which is stimulating enough to encourage development and interest of the employee. Conversely, no employee should be placed under such pressure that he or she is debilitated. The strategy is to create an ideal environment avoiding both 'rusting' and 'burnout' for the individual.

In 1986 Dr Joe Kearns medical director of BUPA Occupational Health Service stated at a conference on stress that 60% of absence at work was caused by stress-related illnesses. It is estimated that 100 million working days a year are lost because people cannot face going to work. This is more than three times the number of work days lost through strikes in 1979, the year of the 'winter of discontent'.

Many major organisations have found it worthwhile to invest in stress counselling. The Post Office has counsellors as does the TSB. Other organisations have encompassed stress counselling within a wider problem solving service such as that provided by Control Data's Employee Advisory Resource or The Wellcome Foundation's career-counselling and self development programme.

Employee assistance programmes

A growing trend in America also being adopted in the UK is the development in Employee Assistance Programmes (EAPs) to save the careers of employees who for a variety of reasons are under-performing.

Line managers are trained to deal with absenteeism, lateness, poor performance, poor interpersonal behaviour but not trained to deal with the underlying problems that bring about aberrant behaviour in their subordinates. To deal with this problem about 10,000 American organisations now use EAPs which are essentially company referral schemes to ensure that employees receive the type of counselling they require.

EAPs are normally for valued employees who for some reason have dipped in their performance. A not untypical situation is where a previously dependable employee may have begun to miss deadlines, upset fellow employees and taken time off work. EAP operates as a support before the employee gets picked up through the disciplinary procedures. Thus EAPs are the occupational equipment of preventative medicine. The American experience suggests that EAPs save $3.50 for every dollar spent. It is too early for the UK experience to suggest such significant savings. However, American Express Travel Division have found it sufficiently successful to extend their EAP pilot study. In Data General it is a permanent feature of the human resource department.

Occupational health care

Many British manufacturers have traditionally had an occupational health service to provide advice on health and welfare of employees to line management. The John Lewis Partnership for example has had an occupational health unit in London since 1920 when its Sloane Square store appointed a Matron. Today the Partnership's occupational health service has the following objectives:

To promote and maintain the health and safety of people at work.

To provide immediate treatment for sick and injured people at work, including customers.

To advise management on the provision of a safe and healthy working environment.

To provide expert medical advice when requested.

To educate Partners in the attainment and preservation of good health.

To advise on rehabilitation and placement in suitable jobs of Partners who have had serious illnesses or injuries or if necessary to advise retirement on medical grounds.

Many firms find it commercially advantageous to provide occupational health care for their employees. Lord Sieff of Marks and Spencer is quoted as saying 'People at work are human beings, not industrial beings'. Marks and Spencer have had a medical service for well over half a century with full time doctors ever since the war. The company spends 1% of pre-tax profits on health care. Each of the stores has its own visiting doctor who carries out health checks and counselling. It is also interesting to note the spouses of employees can also make use of this service.

Acquiring counselling skills

All managers and supervisors may expect to be faced at some time with an employee for whom they have responsibility, coming to them, perhaps in an anxious or unhappy state for advice about some problem which besets them and which may be affecting their work performance. Or, a situation may arise where the manager becomes aware of some underlying difficulty even though the employee concerned has said nothing. Whatever the case, on occasions such as these the manager's interpersonal skills will prove vital. The counselling role has not sprung up overnight; it formed part of the Hawthorne experiments in the 1930's, but until recently it has been a more restricted activity in the UK. The pace of change has brought the need for it more into the limelight, some of the areas of expansion include career, health and marriage counselling, and to assist those now involved in this field, the British Association for Counselling has been set up as a resource centre, whilst the British Psychological Society has done much to promote counselling as an area worthy of research and professional interest.

The skills of counselling include:

1 Actively observing and listening

2 Developing rapport and empathy (seeing things from the other's perspective)

3 Preventing one's personal views and feelings from interfering

4 Being patient

5 Analysing the other's decision-making processes and progress

6 Helping the other to identify and implement solutions and strategies.

The manager or supervisor likely to be faced with the counselling role, even if only occasionally, may find it helpful to focus on the following areas:

- discovering the facts and the employee's attitudes and needs.

- creating rapport by relieving the employee's tension, anxiety or anger.

- helping the employee identify and accept a problem.

- helping the employee to identify and implement a solution to the problem.

- help restore the employee's sense of dignity and responsibility.

Managers and supervisors involved in counselling employees will be better able through experience to recognise problems when these present themselves and know when to accept those that are 'true' and those that are a cover for a deeper problem. In such cases the employee's emotions may act as a major barrier to communication.

In smaller organisations with resources too limited to permit the development of counselling services along the lines of the 'employee assistance programmes' discussed above, the manager may have to walk a fine line with tact and sensitivity in deciding how far he or she can go towards helping an employee through a crisis or involving other specialists to assist.

(For a fuller account of counselling and associated skills, see the companion volume Behavioural Sciences for Managers, A. G. Cowling *et al.* Edward Arnold 1988.)

Issues concerning sex and violence

Sexual and physical harassment is an age-old problem now being given increased attention. The basic right to be treated with respect has implications not just for management style but also for gender issues. Now the topic is being properly examined, the facts are alarming. In 1989 the Suzy Lamplugh Trust commissioned, through LSE and sponsored by Reed Employment, a review of this area which was publicised under the title of 'True risks of going to work'. Of the 1,000 people surveyed, (800 female, 200 male), 486 reported work-related aggression, 1 in 5 professional women had suffered sexual harassment. 4% of females had been physically attacked as had 1 in 7 males. Of the total respondents 8% ran the risk of being assaulted either on their way to work or from work during the course of a year.

A concern for welfare means management action in terms of a 'code of practice' to ensure that physical and sexual abuse, both actual and possible, can be reported and dealt with. Improvements to security arrangements should be made not just to protect stocks or assets but for the safety of individual employees at risk and potentially violent employees are to be screened out at selection.

Essex County Council set up groups with union representatives to examine the problem of increasing and widespread violence particularly in the social services department. As a result of confidential questionnaires they decided to treat the problem on a department by department basis rather than by a county wide approach.

A further difficult issue which the employer must face up to in the years ahead is AIDS. The World Health Organisation has confirmed that Britain is fourth in the world table for aids sufferers. At the beginning of 1988 between 20,000 and 50,000 people in England and Wales were HIV-positive. By the end of 1992 between 7,500 and 17,000 will die. This is an issue which will demand increasing attention.

Welfare policies on this topic are now well established in the US. Bank of America runs special programmes for its employees with the disease and has advanced training concerning the medical and communication implications given to appropriate personnel. In Wells Fargo Bank AIDS is covered within its EAP but the bank recognises that each situation has its own special problems which must be addressed. Levi Strauss employees have the benefit of informational videos, brochures and managers' training materials. Question and answer sessions take place about the virus. The American experience suggests that employees welcome information on AIDS and they also see corporate action on this topic as the firm making an effort on their behalf.

The right to enjoy information and communication

A concern for welfare is a concern to ensure that employees have sufficient information to understand the context of, and be able to perform their work. Some managements still put far more effort, professionalism and cash into communicating with their customers and shareholders than into communication with their employees, research on the topic is surprisingly barren, other organisations have devoted considerable resources to improving the flow of information in a more readily digestible manner. A survey by MORI noted that the most widely used way of communicating with employees is through the notice board[15]. MORI points out that this is unpopular, as is hearing news through the grapevine! Company newspapers and videos are increasingly being used to communicate information, but all these methods only really allow information to flow one way. The difficulty here is that the employee cannot participate. Not surprisingly, the most popular way reported by employees to receive information is directly, in face-to-face conversation with their boss. This can either be informal as in day-to-day contact at work, (Tom Peters, *op. cit.* dubbed this MBWA – Managing By Wandering About) or it can be formal through briefing sessions or appraisal.

Employees also have special needs in the type of information they require from management. In the MORI report 61% said that they wanted to be told on a regular basis about their job performance. Employees were less interested in finance, but had a strong concern for future plans and reasons behind major decisions that would directly affect their lives at work.

The MORI survey, 'Working in Britain today' found that staff wanted to know where their company is heading, and want a genuine dialogue with management. They complain that management is more interested in talking than listening.

More than half the unskilled manual workers surveyed admitted that they could work harder without too much effort. The survey found that only 55% of manual grade supervisors feel that they can express their ideas. Only three out of five say they are usually told the reasons for what they are asked to do. But those who are, are more satisfied with their jobs. Many managements still have a long way to go to get communication right in their organisations.

Improving the flow of communication

Here are some basic guidelines for improving information exchange.

1   Keep lines of communication as short as possible, especially between the person who has the problem and the person who has the authority to do something about it.

2   Ensure that all concerned have a clear idea of what is trying to be accomplished. Give clear direction so everyone can appreciate the direction of the organisation.

3   Everyone needs to know what they are individually responsible

for and how this fits in with the rest of the team/department organisation.

4 Give as much feedback as possible. Encourage comments and ideas particularly from those who are directly affected by management decisions.

5 Ensure that things happen after they have been agreed. Reward good communications and feedback with perceived action. Make information flow be seen to be worthwhile and beneficial.

Specific mechanisms exist to improve information flow. None of the programmes stated below is superior to another, but each will contribute to a better communications environment!

Management By Wandering About (MBWA)

Managers and supervisors should take time to walk the job and talk to those for whom they are responsible. It is as simple as it is straightforward. Difficulties can be answered, explanations given as well as opportunities for recognition and support. At Hewlett-Packard this is termed 'Management by Wandering About'. Robert Carlson, when he was Chief Executive at United Airlines adopted MBWA as part of his policy of 'visible management'. He succeeded in turning a largely bankrupt airline into a successful one[16].

Team briefing

This is a method of communication, promoted actively by the Industrial Society in UK, for employees in their teams or natural groups to receive significant organisational information and to be able to comment about it. It facilitates the information flow both up and down the organisation. It ensures that senior management review regularly what is significant to members of the organisation and what employees need to know to perform their jobs effectively. It also ensures that valuable employee views and comments flow back to senior management. In this way management action and direction can be modified in the light of employee comment.

Works committees and employee meetings

These provide a forum for issues and other employee concerns to be made known to management. In these meetings employees, through their elected representatives, are encouraged to express their needs, problems and difficulties, including management practices that interfere with job performance. Essentially it is a process of consultation offering senior management an insight into the concerns and feelings of those who work for them.

Open door policy

This is a statement to the effect that an employee can see any manager on any matter of concern once the employee has discussed the matter with his/her immediate supervisor. Open door policy is the 'flip side' of MBWA where the initiative for the 'Wandering about' lies with the employee to go and see the manager about a particular concern. The whole object is to remove the blocks to upward communication. What is important here is not so much the policy, but making it work. Employees are easily put off if a manager does not make him or herself accessible to subordinates.

Speak Up programmes

This is similar to 'open door' but more formalised in that managers must see in private, usually once a month, each of their subordinates to review work or progress. Many managers find it hard to talk to their employees in a formal way about their jobs. Even in the less frequent appraisal (usually on an annual basis), face-to-face discussion is still actively avoided by some.

One-way communication systems

Not so effective but still necessary in the devising of a total information programme are the more familiar ways of passing information – usually downwards. They include information booklets, employee bulletins, corporate videos, shareholder and employee reports and company journals and, the ever popular, notice board.

In welfare terms these methods of communication are not so effective because it is difficult for discussions, comment and feedback to senior management to occur through their use.

The right to be managed fairly

Over the last two decades there has been a significant move away from autocratic management as the preferred style to a more participative approach. This trend can be attributed to, in part, employees demanding a greater say in the way that they are managed, and to the work of humanistic management theorists like McGregor (1960), Argyris (1964) and other researchers who advocate participation as a means of self-expression and fulfilment. In addition to this, the growth of democratic forms of work organisation actively encourage joint decision-making and problem-solving.

In such a participative environment, employees enjoy equal place with those who manage them in the achievement of work and organisational goals.

Changing management style

Within this climate there needs to be a concern on management's part for 'how' people are managed and organised. This can be approached either in terms of a participative managerial style often called 'Theory Y' or in terms of more formal mechanisms such as work councils or negotiated procedural agreements[17]. The underlying principle is that individuals should, by right, be able to exercise some influence over the decisions that directly influence them at work. For participation to become a reality, it can only occur when the majority of the employees are both willing and able to participate. Experience shows that it is easier to achieve by worker representatives at the top of organisations than to get worker participation on the shop floor involved in programmes to increase productivity. Employees are often unwilling to be actively involved in the process of management at the production level.

The whole key to this area of participative rights is the value systems of those who work together. Legislation can insist that participative and democratic mechanisms are initiated, but it needs the support of those who manage and those who are managed. A concern for welfare is to ensure and facilitate understanding on both sides.

Signs of poor welfare

It may be helpful to consider some of the signs of a lack of welfare in an organisation, giving indications perhaps that a welfare review might be a positive step. Below are listed some of the 'signals' which would suggest such action would be useful.

Low productivity   where production or output continually remains below that which is technically feasible, where output suddenly drops from the usual level.

Low quality   where quality of product or services decreases below the norm. Where there is a continual focus of complaints in one particular area or process.

Machine down-time   where the downtime or maintenance of equipment is far greater than expected. Where down-time cannot always be explained by technical deficiencies.

Higher illness rate   when visits to the Medical Department suddenly increase.

Increased accident rate   when accidents suddenly increase in frequency or severity.

Complaints about the food   Sometimes expressing grievances against management practice is difficult for employees. The catering facility is a useful surrogate and a legitimate substitute.

Machine/product abuse employee discontentment expressed by deliberately abusing machinery and equipment and spoiling the product.

Increased absenteeism where absenteeism is higher than the average for the organisation or for the industry. Comparison of the organisation's absenteeism with the national figures is a useful exercise. Absenteeism resulting from psychosomatic causes with symptoms such as headache, migraine, backstrain and tummy upset.

High staff turnover where employees decide that the job is not worth it and pursue their careers elsewhere. The nature of the job, the environment, the management or the rewards or a combination of all four aspects may push employees out of an organisation. A concern for welfare will ensure that the major issues affecting employee dissatisfaction can be identified and appropriately managed.

Increased industrial relations activity here individuals are acting collectively against the difficulty. Employees usually accept the status quo. It is when standards are infringed that they may take the matter into their own hands.

Redundancy and outplacement

Welfare not only extends to the organisation's current employees but also to those who usually, through no fault of their own, find themselves made redundant or 'let go' from their jobs. Organisations are in constant change due to mergers, acquisitions, new markets and technologies and this inevitably means that staff are released. This phenomenon has given rise to a new firm of consultancy which, began in North America, and now has firmly taken root in UK. The generic term for this welfare provision is outplacement or career transition.

Outplacement came to prominence when large corporations who were losing senior executives took the welfare responsibility of helping the executive into his or her next position. This goes beyond the golden hand shake and involves a process of counselling, including client assistance in job search or earlier change.

The processes involved within outplacement are now well established. First, the individual is counselled through the immediate anxieties brought about through job loss. It is important for the individual to be able to look forward to the next stage in their career rather than look back to the jobs they have lost.

The next phase is a review of personal strengths, weaknesses, opportunities and threats which assists the individual to gain direction and insight into various career options. Once direction has been confirmed the individual is given coaching in cv preparation. To assist with self marketing the executive is told about the approach, the four main entry points to the job market namely agencies, adverts, networking and 'cold approaches'. This activity will lead to interviews and so the next stage is self presentation, grooming and interview training. The outplacement procedure is completed with job offer selection advice and salary package negotiation training. It is not uncommon for the released executive to gain a significant increase in his or her remuneration package.

Where a company has to release large numbers, a 'job shop' facility is often set up to supplement and support outplacement training. This acts rather like a job centre but is somewhat more pro-active in that counsellers in the job shop contact all the local employers to establish job opportunities. Released employees are then matched to the vacancies offered and also given specific training. The job shop also arranges the interview with the prospective employer. Job shops have been employed with great success in a variety of industries and locations including Caterpiller in Glasgow where there was high unemployment, to Duracell in Crawley which has the lowest unemployment rate in the UK. They have also been used to great effect in the City post 'Black Monday'.

The added advantage to the employer of providing such outplacement provision is that it shows that it cares – not only to those it releases but also to those that stay. It is very important to convince employees who remain that the organisation will look after its employees. This is another example of how welfare provisions can promote good employee relations.

In the same way that many organisations have a policy on training and development so it is not uncommon for them to have an outplacement policy as well. In some firms, contracts of employment, particularly at senior levels, have a clause guaranteeing outplacement should the manager unfortunately find him or herself released from employment. A firm such as Rowntree found this provision useful when suddenly they became owned by the larger Swiss conglomerate, Nestlé.

Welfare and profitability

A concern for welfare is a concern for employees driven by and through values. In my introduction it was hinted that perhaps it was those values more akin to the Human Relations School than the simplistic and unitary model of 'Economic Man' born out of Scientific Management. In the latter, welfare is a matter of cost-benefit analysis, technical efficiency and productivity. It is Scientific Management by another name. It could be argued strongly that it is all the same to the recipient. Good working environment is a good working environment with the employee benefiting from it, irrespective of the Scientific Management motives that underpin the welfare provision. But this just means that human resources are not managed but used. Welfare, to be genuine, should include social goals and values including the design of working environments and technology to suit people rather than the other way round; it is about opportunities for autonomy and individual growth; social concerns and fairness: a view of work and employees with a strong humanistic, liberal and altruisic orientation.

However, it should be stressed that a concern for welfare is not at the expense of profitability. Dr Derek Taylor the Chief Medical Officer in Marks & Spencer has stated that 'A decent environment, profit sharing, subsidised meals, and other benefits, lead to a productive work force. The president of Marks & Spencers was once asked how could the firm afford an occupational health service. His answer was, 'how can we afford not to?'

It is the responsibility of all those who manage and also can influence human resources to recognise the needs of those who they employ.

References

1   Davis, L. E., 'Reading the Unready: Post Industrial Jobs', *California Management Review*, 13, 27–36, 1971b.
2   Burris, V., 'The Social and Political Consequences of Over Education', *American Sociological Review*, 48, 454–467, 1983.
3   Harrison, R. Van, 'Person and Environment Fit and Job Stress', Cooper C. L. and Payne, K. (eds), *Stress At Work*, Wiley, 1978.
4   Broadbent, D. E., 'The Clinical Impact of Job Design, *British Journal of Clinical Psychology*, 24, 33–44, 1986.
5   Walker, C. D. and Guest, R. H., *The Man on the Assembly Line*, Harvard University Press, 1952.
6   Kornhauser, *The Mental Health of The Industrial Worker*, Wiley, 1965.
7   Blauner, *Alienation and Freedom*, University of Chicago Press, 1964.
8   Herzberg, *Work and the Nature of Man*, World Publishing, 1966.
9   Likert, R., *The Human Organisation: Its Management And Value*, McGraw-Hill 1967.
10 Hackman, G. R., Pearce, J. L. and Wolfe, J. E., Effects of Job Changes and Job Characteristics on Work Attitudes and Behaviours: Organisation Behaviour and Human Performance, 21, 289–304, 1978.
11 Dijkhvinen, N. Van., 'Towards Organisational Coping With Stress', *Coping With Stress at Work*, Cooper, C. L., Marshall, J. (eds) Gower, 1981.
12 Peters, T., *Thriving on Chaos*, Macmillan, 1987.
13 Cooper, C. L., Cooper, R. D., Eaker L. H., *Living with Stress*, Penguin, 1988.
14 Cooper, C. L., *The Stress Check*, Spectrum, 1988.
15 Mori, *Working in Britain today*, November, 1985.
16 Pascale, R. and Athos, A. G., *The Art of Japanese Management*, pp. 156 –170, Penguin Books, 1982.
17 McGregor, D., *The Human side of Enterprise*, McGraw Hill, 1960.

10

Employee relations

In many organisations trade unions exert an important influence over many of the issues discussed in this book and the management of human resources in general. This chapter is intended to provide readers with an introduction to management-worker relations in the UK and some of the key developments taking place concerning them.

Major changes have occurred during the 1980's which have had an impact on employee relations. Unemployment and structural changes in the economy have adversely affected trade union membership and bargaining power, strike activity has declined significantly, legislation has been introduced which has increased the legal liabilities of unions and their members, and innovative collective agreements have been concluded which incorporate 'no strike' provisions and provide for closer links between pay and performance, extensive labour flexibility, and harmonised terms and conditions of employment for both manual and non-manual workers. Yet it is important not to overstate the scale and significance of these changes. Employee relations in general have not undergone a dramatic transformation during the last decade. In many organisations, what has taken place has been marked more by incremental evolution rather than by radical change.

The chapter attempts to capture this combination of continuity and radical change. However, inevitably given its nature, attention is focussed primarily on the present rather than the future, and the normal rather than the exceptional. Material in the chapter is presented under four broad, but inter-related headings: organisational approaches to employee relations; the structure of collective bargaining; the conduct of bargaining; and the assessment of employee relations. A brief final section considers the future importance of collective bargaining in the UK by reference to likely trends in union membership and other influences.

Organisational approaches to employee relations

As with many tasks of management, there is no one correct way of managing employee relations. Organisations need to develop the

169

policies and strategies that best suit their individual circumstances. A wide variety of factors may have to be taken into account. For example: the type of product and labour markets in which an organisation operates, the type of technology it uses; its internal structure and culture, and the degree and nature of trade union organisation within it.

Employee relations policies not surprisingly vary considerably between organisations. Two leading academics, John Purcell and Keith Sisson, have attempted to classify them into four 'ideal typical' styles of management: *traditionalist, sophisticated paternalist, sophisticated modern and standard modern*[1].

Traditionalists, according to Purcell and Sisson, adopt a policy of 'forceful opposition' to trade unions and an often overtly exploitative approach towards their employees. *Sophisticated paternalist*, a category held to include companies like IBM, Hewlett-Packard, Marks and Spencer and Kodak, also tend to be non-union, but differ from the *traditionalists* in that they spend considerable time and money developing personnel policies which ensure that unions are seen as unnecessary and inappropriate by their employees. *Sophisticated moderns*, such as Ford, ICI and most of the large oil companies, by contrast, adopt a rather more positive approach to trade unions, legitimising their role in certain areas on the grounds that they can help maintain stability, promote consent, assist management-worker communications and help the process of change. Finally, the standard modern category, which is considered to be the largest and to include companies like GEC, Tube Investments, and Guest, Keen and Nettlefolds, is characterised by an approach to industrial employee relations which is essentially pragmatic or opportunistic. While they recognise unions and employ specialists to handle employee relations, they tend to view the employee relations function as primarily a 'fire-fighting' activity.

In arguing that the *standard modern* category is the most common, Purcell and Sisson highlight the fact that most UK employers do not tend to approach employee relations in a particularly strategic manner. A further illustration of this point comes from a recent study of practice in 175 large multi-establishment enterprises which found that while over 80% of firms claimed to have an overall industrial relations philosophy, only half said this was written in a formal document and even fewer that a copy of this was given to employees. The authors went on to conclude that 'the general weight of evidence would seem to confirm that most UK owned enterprises remain pragmatic or opportunistic in their approach' to the management of employees[2].

Moreover the presence of a particular philosophy or policy at company level does not necessarily mean that it is actually implemented. Managers within companies differ in terms of both the work they do, and their attitudes, philosophies and personal experiences. These differences must influence how they personally approach the management of their employees. Managers facing tight production deadlines and a militant work group may, for example, be more inclined to circumvent established procedures and agreements in order to maintain output at an acceptable level and quality than those not subject to such pressures. Differences of this type are likely to be particularly important where a company does not espouse a clear employee relations style or philosophy. They are also likely to be relatively important where the employing organisation makes little effort to communicate and clarify to managers what they need to know about its employee relations policies and procedures, or to monitor whether they are being carried out.

This last point serves to highlight the importance of providing managers and supervisors with sufficient training so that they are knowledgeable about the procedures they are expected to operate, understand the philosophy underlying them, and possess the skills necessary to carry out the duties relating to them[3]. The same point may be made in relation to shop stewards. Such union officials in any event have a right under the Employment Protection (Consolidation) Act 1978 to receive paid time off to receive training approved by their unions or the TUC (see Chapter 11). As a result a management which fails to provide appropriate training for its managers may find that they are less knowledgeable about employee relations than the shop stewards with whom they have to deal. Union officials incidentally are also entitled to time off under the same legislation to carry out duties connected with industrial relations. A Code of Practice produced by the Advisory, Conciliation and Arbitration Service provides guidance on this latter right[4].

The structure of collective bargaining

Collective bargaining arrangements vary in terms of who they cover, the subject matter they encompass, the form they take and the level at which they operate.

Collective bargaining coverage

Collective bargaining determines the terms and conditions of employment of 60% to 70% of the UK workforce. Since the likelihood of unions being recognised in a particular establishment increases with workforce size, the proportion of workplaces covered by collective bargaining is rather lower. The 1984 Workplace Industrial Relations Survey found that in workplaces with 25 or more employees collective bargaining formed the basis of the most recent pay increase for manual workers in 62% of workplaces and for non-manuals in 54%[5].

Union recognition not only varies with workforce size. It also varies between sectors of the economy. It is most common in the public sector, where the 1984 Survey found that unions were recognised in over 90% of workplaces. It is less common in private manufacturing industry, where unions are recognised in 56% of workplaces and even rarer in private services, where just 44% recognise unions.

The decision as to whether to recognise trade unions has considerable implications for an organisation, and needs to be considered carefully. Recognition has a number of potential advantages and disadvantages for management. On the negative side, unions will inevitably restrict the freedom of management to organise work and reward employees in the way they wish, with potentially adverse consequences for organisational efficiency and costs. Employers may also fear that their recognition will lead to the creation of an 'us and them' divide within the company and necessitate considerable amounts of management time being tied up in negotiations over possibly trivial matters. On the positive side, managements, particularly in larger workplaces and companies, may see unions as providing a valuable means of two-way communication with the workforce. Collective bargaining may also be considered a useful means of gaining workforce commitment, particularly to change, and a relatively efficient way of altering the employment contracts of large numbers of employees simultaneously.

The subject matter of bargaining

The subjects covered by management–union negotiations can be considered under two broad headings: *procedural* rules which lay down the regulatory framework within which management–union relations are to be conducted; and *substantive* provisions which lay down the terms and conditions under which workers are employed. For obvious reasons managers need to keep up-to-date with changes in both these areas.

Procedural rules

Procedural rules can cover a wide variety of issues including the types of workers covered by collective bargaining, the composition of the machinery through which management–union discussions and negotiations are to take place, the appointment and constituencies of shop stewards, and the rights, facilities and training to be provided to them, the subject matter to be discussed and negotiated, and the procedures which are to be followed when attempting to resolve or handle particular issues. Subjects commonly covered by such procedures include, discipline and dismissal, grievances, disputes, new technology, redundancy, equal opportunities, and health and safety.

Where more than one union is recognised for bargaining purposes, a not uncommon situation in Britain, separate procedural arrangements will frequently be agreed with the different unions. This is particularly likely to be the case where both manual and non-manual unions are recognised. However, it may also be the case where more than one manual union is present. In manufacturing, unions representing production workers will frequently bargain separately from those representing craft workers.

Multi-unionism, and the multiplicity of bargaining units frequently associated with it, has been a long criticised feature of British industrial relations. It is seen to have a number of potential drawbacks for employers[6]. Inter-union disputes over who has the right to recruit particular types of workers, demarcation disputes over whose members can do particular work, inefficiences arising from job demarcations, and the greater complexity of collective bargaining are among the potential problems frequently highlighted. In existing multi-union workplaces employers are increasingly attempting to minimise such problems by enlarging the boundaries of bargaining units and hence reducing their number, by persuading different unions to negotiate together. For example, negotiations covering process operators, craft workers, supervisors and staff at Pilkington Insulation's Ravenhead works have since 1985 been conducted in a single forum rather than a series of separate negotiations[7]. Similar developments have recently taken place at the health products company Johnson & Johnson.

Where organisations are setting up operations on 'greenfield sites' for the first time they are frequently seeking to avoid the problems associated with multi-unionism by recognising just one union, that is if they are willing to concede recognition at all. Organisations which have adopted this approach include a number of Japanese companies, such as Nissan, Sanyo Industries, Toshiba, Hitachi and Komatsu. Employee relations arrangements developed in these companies have attracted considerable attention, some commentators seeing them as heralding a 'new style' of industrial relations[8]. Key features of these arrangements include, harmonised terms and conditions of employment for all staff (including a common grading structure), the application of incremental pay structures and appraisal systems to manual as well as non-manual workers (see Chapter 6), wide-ranging labour flexibility, and the establishment of negotiating and consultative machinery consisting of workforce rather than union representatives.

Substantive provisions

The *substantive* content of collective agreements can encompass a vast array of issues: Hours of work, holidays, staffing levels, payment systems, pensions, gradings, redeployment, physical working conditions, job content and pay are just some of the topics that may be covered[9]. Provisions negotiated relating to these issues may last varying lengths of time, ranging from a few weeks to several years. Negotiations over pay typically take place annually. However, a number of companies have negotiated longer-term pay deals in recent years as a way of creating a more predictable and stable employee relations environment. These agreements, which generally still provide for annual pay increases, usually last either two or three years. Agreements lasting four and six years respectively have however been concluded at Metal Box's Swindon plant and Borg-Warner's Kenfig factory, in Wales. Organisations have negotiated significant changes in the *substantive* content of collective agreements over the last decade[10]. For example, grading structures have been simplified to remove restrictive distinctions between different categories of jobs, sometimes as part of harmonisation programmes. Closer links have been established between pay and performance through merit pay and profit sharing. Working practices have been reformed to acquire greater labour flexibility by, for example, breaking down demarcations between different types of craft worker and making production workers responsible for inspecting the quality of their work and carrying out routine maintenance. Working hours have also been reformed and greater use made of part-time, temporary and sub-contract staff, to achieve a better match between labour supply and demand. New patterns of working hours to emerge include changes to shift patterns, the use of 'min-max' contracts under which employers are able to vary the number of hours an employee works during a particular week up to a specified maximum, and annual hours schemes which enable the number of hours worked in a defined period – for example where the work has seasonal fluctuations – to be varied in relation to a given number of working hours per year.

In many cases these changes have been introduced through the medium of comprehensive and wide-ranging flexibility agreements. A good example of such an agreement is that signed at Metal Box's plastics container factory at Swindon which also illustrates how developments on existing 'brownfield sites' are tending to follow similar lines to those in operation on many 'greenfield' ones[11]. This 1988 Metal Box agreement, provided for:

- a shift from a regular three-shift pattern spread over five days to a four-shift pattern over six days;
- the introduction of unified terms and conditions for all employees below management level;
- the implementation of a new four-grade, incremental pay structure covering both manual and non-manual grades, progression

within each grade being based in part on the acquisition of new skills;

- complete labour flexibility, subject only to restrictions stemming from the individual capacities of workers;

- the introduction of team working on the shop floor under which work groups consisting of electricians, printers and engineers are expected to work without demarcation limits and to be responsible for product flow and quality; and

- the establishment of a joint negotiating committee consisting of representatives of all four unions on site.

There has been much debate during the 1980's as to whether employers have reduced the range of issues over which they are prepared to negotiate with unions. The available survey evidence on this is rather contradictory[12]. Some studies suggest that employers have indeed been tending to narrow the issues over which they are prepared to bargain. Others suggest that the opposite has in fact been the case!

All the available studies indicate however that in most workplaces little change has taken place. Given this evidence, the safest conclusion would seem to be that the subject matter of collective bargaining has neither increased or reduced dramatically during the 1980's.

This conclusion points to the danger of assuming automatically that macro-level changes in unemployment and union membership enhance the bargaining position of individual employers and lead them to adopt a more aggressive approach towards unions[13]. Individual employers faced with difficult trading and financial conditions may well take the view that the last thing they need is to run the risk of a potentially costly industrial dispute in an attempt to increase the scope of managerial prerogatives, while those facing a favourable market situation may prefer to try and secure the changes they want by offering generous pay increases in return. More positively, in an increasingly competitive economic environment employers may be concerned to increase employee commitment and involvement, both through collective bargaining and other means.

Certainly employers during the 1980's have been active in taking initiatives designed to improve management–worker communication, and to involve individual employees more closely in decision-making, at least at the level of their job. A variety of different means have been used to achieve these objectives including videos, in-house newspapers, employee reports providing information on the employer's financial results, team briefing, profit sharing and share option schemes, quality circles and autonomous work groups[14].

The form of agreements

Collective agreements in Britain are, with a few exceptions, not legally binding on the signatories, although some of their terms may be incorporated into employees' individual contracts of employment. They also tend to be relatively insubstantial and imprecise when compared with those in more legally-based industrial relations systems such as are found in North America.

In the 1950's an eminent labour lawyer, the late Otto Kahn-Freund, drew a distinction between what he called the static and dynamic models of industrial relations[15]. The former, he argued, characterised the systems found in North America and much of Western Europe, and was marked by the conclusion of comprehensive collective agreements which detailed at great length the mutual rights and obligations of the collective parties. During the currency of these agreements the parties were precluded from lodging claims to improve their terms with the result that disputes could legitimately only arise over points of interpretation. In other words a clear distinction was drawn between *conflicts of right* and *conflicts of interest*. In contrast, the common law model, which was held to operate in Britain, involved a greater reliance on informal agreements and understandings and an almost continual process of adaptation, with no clear distinction being drawn between disputes relating to either rights or interests.

Kahn-Freund's analysis remains to a large degree valid today and serves to highlight the relatively greater degree of informality that has traditionally been embodied in the British system of industrial relations. The extent of this informality was in fact a major theme of the Royal Commission report on trade unions and employers' associations[16]. Known as the Donovan report, after the commission's chairman, this criticised the degree of reliance then placed on informal understandings and agreements on the grounds that they were a major source of disorder in periods of high employment and rapid change. The commission went on to recommend that companies should develop comprehensive and authoritative collective bargaining machinery at the company and/or workplace level.

The period since Donovan has undoubtedly seen a considerable increase in formality. The vast majority of medium and large workplaces, for example, now have formal procedures covering union recognition, grievances and discipline[17]. Nevertheless a considerable degree of informality remains. Indeed some commentators argue that employers, against the background of a very different economic climate, are currently seeking to move away from the increasing formalisation of the 1960's and 1970's in order to give themselves greater flexibility and freedom of action[18].

The continued importance of informal agreements and understandings suggests that they continue to have certain attractions and benefits for both employers and unions. Their potential advantages were usefully summarised by McCarthy in a research paper prepared for the Donovan Commission[19].

With regard to procedural arrangements, McCarthy found that informality was largely attributable to management reluctance to convert 'de facto' practices into 'de jure' rights. Three main reasons were put forward to explain why management might prefer to continue to rely on informal arrangements and understandings: they make it easier to withdraw concessions granted to union representatives; informal concessions are less easily used by shop stewards to get even more advantageous concessions; and informality enables management to grant concessions which they would not be prepared to admit publicly because of the extent to which they infringe managerial prerogatives. In contrast, McCarthy argued that both managers and shop stewards saw advantages in informality, in the area of substantive terms and conditions. Shop stewards found that management were frequently prepared to discuss a wider range of issues on an informal basis, while managers felt that informal negotiations were less likely to give rise to precedents in the future and could avoid the embarrassment of having to discuss certain controversial issues on a more formal basis.

A degree of informality is perhaps an inevitable feature of management–union relations[20]. However, care needs to be taken to ensure that informal understandings and agreements do not undermine established policies and procedures and create the kinds of inefficiences and disorder criticised by the Donovan Commission. Supervisors and first line managers play a potentially important role in determing the scale and significance of such understandings and agreements. Yet many organisations pay relatively little attention to defining the employee relations roles of supervisory and junior management personnel and providing them with the training necessary to carry those roles out.

The status and role of supervisors, both in regard to employee relations and more generally, has recently received considerable attention in a number of organisations. In some cases this has led employers to enhance significantly their employee relations responsibilities as part of a strategy of making line management more responsible for personnel issues. At Nissan, for example, supervisors take part in job interviews, mark the aptitude tests given to job applicants and, working with team leaders, make the final decision as to who is appointed[21]. They also play an important role in identifying staff training needs. To ensure that supervisors have the skills necessary to carry out their production and person-management responsibilities the company takes considerable care over their selection, using a combination of aptitude tests, role playing and formal interviews (see Chapter 3), and provides them with extensive training.

Levels of bargaining

Collective bargaining can take place at industry level through the medium of employers' associations as well as in individual organisations. Within individual organisations it can take place at a number of different levels, the most important being at company, division and establishment levels. The accompanying table, taken from the Workplace Industrial Relations survey 1980–84, shows the relative importance of the different levels of bargaining.

Industry-wide bargaining is of declining importance, and has been throughout the post-war period. However, it continues to operate in a number of sectors, including engineering, electrical contracting, construction, local government and transport, and is estimated to be the principal means of fixing pay for one in five private sector employees[22]. Where industry level bargaining continues to take place it generally sets only minimum rates of pay which are often considerably exceeded as a result of negotiations conducted within individual organisations. Industry-wide terms concerning matters like overtime premium, sick pay, hours of work and holidays are, however, usually followed.

Management needs to take into account a wide variety of factors and considerations when deciding the level at which to bargain within their organisations. Centralised and decentralised bargaining arrangements both have potential advantages and disadvantages[23]. Centralised arrangements can make labour costs more predictable, enable a common approach to be adopted towards union recognition, and ensure that negotiations are carried out by skilled and experienced negotiators. They also ensure consistency between workplaces

Table 10.1   Basis for most recent pay increase (% of workplaces)

	Manual workers		Non-manual workers	
	1980	1984	1980	1984
Result of collective bargaining	55	62	47	54
Most important level:				
National/regional	32	40	29	36
Company/divisional	12	13	11	13
Plant/establishment	9	7	4	4
Not the result of collective bargaining	44	38	53	46

Source: Millward, N. & Stevens, M., British Workplace Industrial Relations 1980–84: the DE/ESRC/PSI/ACAS Surveys, Gower, 1986, p. 255.

thereby avoiding jealousies and rivalries between plants and the comparability-based pay claims that these may generate. On the other hand, central negotiations can be very time-consuming and lead to delays in resolving disputes. They also tend to mean that pay rates have to be set at the level sufficient to recruit and retain labour in the most expensive of the labour markets in which the employer is operating. In addition it is rather difficult to take account of differences in the performance of different workplaces and the types of work they carry out, and to engage in detailed discussions about ways of improving efficiency. A further potential problem is that where negotiations break down, any resultant dispute is likely to affect the whole of the company rather than just one part of its operations.

A number of factors need to be taken into account when considering the relative strengths and weaknesses of these arguments[24]. These include: internal management structure, existing patterns of union representation and collective bargaining, types of payment system in use, geographical location of plants, nature of labour and product markets, and types of work carried out.

Current trends show companies tending to move away from highly centralised bargaining arrangements and seeking to negotiate at divisional or workplace level. Lucas, Philips, Royal Insurance, Courtaulds, GEC and Pilkington are just a few of the companies that have gone down this road. The trend appears to be very much associated with a change in corporate strategy and business policy towards local profit centres, and the granting of greater autonomy for business unit managers[25]. It is also seen to reflect the greater emphasis being placed on the cost-effective use of human resources[26].

The decentralisation of bargaining does not, however, necessarily mean that local managers are given a completely free hand with regard to how they conduct industrial relations. In fact rather the opposite appears to be true. The study of multi-establishment companies mentioned earlier, for example, found that two-thirds of those with establishment-level bargaining had a policy on pay settlements or issued pay guidelines and a similar proportion indicated that there were consultations with management at higher levels before the start of negotiations. Only 17% of the establishments surveyed in the study indicated that there was no such higher-level policy, guidelines or consultation[27].

The conduct of collective bargaining

The conduct of collective bargaining is considered under four headings: the context of management–union negotiations; the nature of such negotiations; the bargaining encounter; and the procedures used to resolve disputes.

The context of negotiations

Collective bargaining is part of an ongoing relationship between management and unions. This needs to be borne in mind during negotiations, and care taken to ensure that relatively minor short-term gains are not obtained at the cost of harm to the long-term relationship. Nevertheless, disagreements will inevitably occur which will prove difficult, if not impossible to resolve in a way that is reasonably acceptable to both management and union.

Negotiations involve a combination of coercive and persuasive strategies. The latter encompass both threats and arguments. The former the application of direct sanctions intended to inflict harm on the opposing side and prompt it to shift its negotiating position.

Threats and arguments can take a number of different forms and those used will inevitably be influenced by the issues under discussion and the particular circumstances surrounding those discussions. With pay negotiations union claims will often be supported by reference to one or more of the following: movements in the cost of living, improvements in productivity, trends in company profitability, the level of settlements negotiated elsewhere in the industry or the economy, and the earnings of other groups of workers, either inside or outside the company. Notions of equity, fairness and justice will frequently underpin, either implicitly or explicity, the arguments put forward in respect of pay and other issues. For example, in discussions over a disciplinary matter union representatives may well argue that the proposed penalty is out of all proportion to the offence committed, or that management is guilty of inconsistency in that a lesser penalty had been imposed when a similar situation occurred in the past. It is important not to underestimate the importance of such notions when handling industrial relations issues[28].

Threats involve one party threatening to impose sanctions on the other unless a more favourable settlement is offered. Sometimes these threats may be meant. On other occasions they may involve an element of bluff. A crucial task for the other party is to try and assess which of these situations apply. Sanctions can be imposed by both sides. Management may, for example, threaten to lock the workforce out, cease negotiations and impose a pay settlement unilaterally, dismiss any workers taking industrial action, or close the workplace down. Union initiated sanctions can include, strikes, go-slows, work-to-rules, overtime bans and the withdrawal of co-operation.

Calculations about the ability of members to take effective action will influence the willingness of unions to impose sanctions over a particular issue. These in turn will reflect assessments of the degree of support among members and the capacity of those members to disrupt their employer's operations. The nature of the employer's products, the position the workers occupy in the work process, and in particular the immediacy and extent to which they can affect the supply of goods and services, and the ability of the employer to find alternative means of meeting customer demand, such as through the use of alternative labour or production from another plant, are some of the more important factors which will influence the disruptive potential of particular employee groups[29].

The nature of negotiations

The process of negotiation has been defined by Gottschalk as 'an occasion where one or more representatives of two or more parties interact in an explicit attempt to reach a jointly acceptable position on one or more divisive issues'[30]. Various models have been put forward to analyse management–union negotiations. One of the most influential is that developed by Walton and McKersie[31] who argue in their model that negotiations consist of four sub-processes: *distributive bargaining*, *integrative bargaining*, *attitudinal structuring* and *intra-organisational bargaining*.

Distributive bargaining exists where the function of the negotiations is to resolve conflicts between the parties, the resolution of which requires by definition one party to win, the other to lose. Walton and McKersie argue that this form of bargaining is the dominant activity in management-union negotiations.

Integrative bargaining, in contrast, refers to negotiations over issues which are not marked by fundamental conflicts of interest and hence are capable of solutions which benefit both sides to some degree, or at least do not result in the gains of one side representing equal losses for the other. The productivity bargaining carried out in the 1960's and 1970's under which employees agreed to accept more efficient working practices in return for improved terms and conditions provides a good example of this type of bargaining[32]. The same is true of many of the flexibility agreements signed in more recent years.

While most bargaining situations will involve elements of both distributive and integrative bargaining, they will generally approximate to one or other of these two 'ideal types'. According to Walton and McKersie, '*integrative bargaining* is tentative and exploratory and involves open-communication processes, whereas *distributive bargaining* involves adamant, directed, and controlled information processes'[33]. *Integrative bargaining* is consequently facilitated by a supportive and trusting climate which encourages the negotiators to behave spontaneously without fear of sanctions.

Attitudinal structuring, is more concerned with the process by which one party to the negotiation attempts to influence the attitudes of the other in a way favourable to itself. Attitudes can be influenced both during negotiations and before they start. For example, management and unions may try to influence the expectations of the other side with regard to forthcoming negotiations during discussions in forums like joint consultative committees[34]. Management may also try to influence attitudes in the build up to negotiations through the provision of information on financial performance, future trading prospects and likely future developments in the enterprise. In connection with this, it should be noted that under the Employment Protection Act 1975 officials of independent, recognised unions have a right, on request, to be provided with information without which they would be 'to a material extent impeded' in carrying out collective bargaining. Employers have a similar obligation to provide information which it would be in accordance with good industrial relations practice to disclose for the purpose of such bargaining (see Chapter 11). An ACAS Code of Practice provides guidance on the types of information that employers should disclose in order to meet their statutory requirements[35].

Intra-organisational bargaining, the final subprocess distinguished by Walton and McKersie, reflects the fact that those directly involved in negotiations are acting as representatives of their respective parties. Consequently an important aspect of negotiations is the process of discussion and debate that goes on within each of the parties involved in order to reach consensus on matters like the offer which should be made to the other side, the tactics that should be employed during negotiations and the acceptability of a proposed settlement. As one writer has observed, 'when two organisations are party to negotiations, it takes, in effect, three agreements to achieve a negotiated settlement between the parties: an agreement within each party and between them'[36]. In the public sector this process of intra-organisational bargaining can be particularly complex since the government will frequently try, either formally or informally, to influence the policies and strategies adopted by management.

Negotiatiors need to bear in mind these intra-organisational considerations. A sensitivity and awareness of the internal political pressures which the negotiators 'on the other side' are under can be helpful in the search for the compromises and packages necessary to resolve disputes. Management negotiators, for example, need to appreciate that even if their union counterparts find an offer acceptable, they may have to reject it because of the views of their members.

Negotiations may involve union full-time officials, shop stewards or a combination of the two[37]. Shop stewards are elected by union members in a particular location, department or section to represent their interests. Traditionally they were associated with manufacturing industry and manual workers, their widespread appointment developing first in the skilled engineering trades during the 19th century. Today it is estimated that there are more shop stewards in the public sector than in the private, and that there are nearly as many representing non-manual employee grades as manual[38].

Shop stewards are to be found in the majority of workplaces where unions are recognised[39]. Where two or more stewards are present, they will often appoint senior stewards, and/or convenors. Committees representing stewards from one or more unions may also exist. When negotiating, stewards consequently have to take account, not only of the policies of the national union, and the expectations and aspirations of their members, but also the views of their fellow stewards.

The nature of the relationship existing between shop stewards and the members they represent will reflect the composition of the workforce and of their own personality and opinions. In a study of shop steward organisation in a car factory Batstone *et al.* distinguished four different types of steward based on the extent to which they espoused trade union principles and the nature of the relationship they had with their members[40]. The most important distinction was that drawn between what they termed *leader* and *populist* stewards. *Leader* stewards adopted an initiator role in decision making, actively shaping the issues raised on behalf of members, and sought to achieve objectives supportive of wider trade union principles. *Populists*, in contrast, saw themselves more akin to a delegate whose role was to carry out merely the wishes of the membership what ever these might be. Interestingly, Batstone found *populists* to be more common among white collar groups and *leaders* among manual workers.

The bargaining encounter

Negotiations can range from relatively informal discussions between a supervisor and a shop steward to a large set piece affair involving a number of representatives from each side. In this second situation, it is important to clarify the roles to be played by each member of the negotiating team before the start of negotiations. Roles commonly distinguished are those of chief negotiator, the person who does most of the talking, the secretary, who is expected to keep notes and look for any verbal or non-verbal signals from the other side, and the analyst, whose role is to scrutinise and analyse what is being said and to summarise the issues, if and when this is appropriate. Negotiating teams may also include, one or more specialists who possess technical knowledge and experience relevant to the issues under discussion[41].

It is vital to ensure that team members do not give contradictory messages, since this is not only confusing, but may give the other side an opportunity to exploit any differences of opinion that exist. Disagreements within a negotiating team should be discussed during adjournments, an important part of negotiations. Adjournments give negotiators time to consider the arguments and offers put forward by the other side, re-appraise their bargaining tactics and to seek clearance from senior management if a change in bargaining objectives is thought desirable.

Good preparation is an essential prerequisite for effective negotiations. Each side needs to consider carefully what its negotiating objectives are to be, including fall back positions, and the arguments that are to be used to support them. Where a number of issues are to be discussed it may be useful to allocate the various objectives to one of three categories: *essential, desirable* and *optimistic*[42]. Thought also needs to be given to the objectives likely to be pursued by the other side, and the arguments that they may use to support them. Also to be considered must be the necessary bargaining tactics. For example, management may choose to make a relatively generous opening offer which leaves little subsequent room for manoeuvre, or it may adopt the opposite approach.

Once negotiations start the convention is that the party seeking the negotiation should open the encounter. Thus, in the case of a pay claim, the union will start the process by outlining its claim and the rationale underlying it. At this stage it is important for management to listen carefully to what is being said, seek any necessary clarification and make sure that what the union is asking for is fully understood. Indeed these three techniques should be used throughout negotiations. Research by Rackham and Carlisle, for example, has found that 'skilled negotiators' tend to seek more information, and more frequently to summarise and test understanding, than 'average negotiators'[43].

Agreement by definition only becomes possible if one or both sides are willing to make concessions and move from their opening positions. But both sides may be wary of offering concessions for fear that they will not be reciprocated. The use of what has been called signalling can be used to try and 'break out' of circular and non-conclusive argument in a way that minimises this danger. Signals are qualifications placed on a statement of position which indicates a willingness to consider alternative proposals. An example is where a negotiator adds the phrase 'in its present form' to a statement that 'we will never agree to what you are proposing'[44]. More generally, when negotiating, it is important to think creatively about how the various issues on the bargaining table can be combined or packaged in a way that is satisfactory to both sides.

As far as possible, exchanges that could be perceived as personalised attacks by the other side's negotiators should be avoided since this is unlikely to be helpful to the discussions and could have adverse implications for future negotiations. Similarly, where a party makes a concession it may be sensible to help them do this without losing face.

Once agreement has been reached it is important to clarify exactly what has been agreed. One way of doing this is to prepare a detailed summary which both sides then agree. A further important point is that union negotiators will frequently have to refer agreements to their members for approval before they can agree them formally. Management should seek an undertaking that they will recommend acceptance by their members.

Disputes procedures

When negotiations become deadlocked the parties will usually register a failure to agree and refer the issue to the next stage of the disputes procedure. It is normally understood, if not explicitly stated, that both sides will refrain from taking any industrial action until all stages of the procedure have been exhausted. Nevertheless, unconstitutional action, that is action in breach of procedure, can occur.

Disputes procedures are intended to aid the resolution of disputes by enabling them to be processed through a series of hierachical stages, each of which involve the introduction of more senior personnel from both sides who are less directly involved with the issues under discussion. Survey evidence shows that the majority of workplaces with 25 or more employees have formal, written procedures and that they are almost universal in establishments with workforces of over 500[45]. The absence of a formal procedure does not, however, mean that an organisation does not have any standard means of processing disputes[46].

When devising procedures it is important to incorporate only those levels of management able to play an effective role in resolving disputes and so avoid their becoming unduly cumbersome and time consuming. An important issue to be decided is whether individual grievances and collective disputes are to be covered by the same procedure. Where a combined approach is adopted, it is common with collective disputes for the procedure to provide for certain of the early stages to be omitted.

Procedures vary considerably both in relation to the number of stages they contain and the identity of those to be involved at each stage[47]. Three main levels or stages can be distinguished, although each of these may in turn include a number of different stages. These are the department, the establishment and the external. An additional corporate level stage may be distinguished in some multi-plant companies.

Not all procedures formally provide for issues to be referred outside the organisation. Where provision is made, it may take the form of reference to an industry-wide disputes procedure. Naturally, this option is only available if the employer concerned is a party to the relevant set of industry-level negotiations. Alternatively, the matter may be referred to an independent third party.

Independent third party intervention, often organised in the UK under the auspices of ACAS, can take one of three main forms: *conciliation*, *mediation* and *arbitration*. With *conciliation* the third party supports the negotiating process by assisting the parties to identify the nature of their differences and possible ways of resolving them. *Mediation*, in practice often difficult to distinguish from conciliation, permits a rather more interventionist stance in that the third party puts forward recommendations for settlement, although the parties are free to accept, reject or amend the terms proposed. Finally, *arbitration* involves an even greater degree of intervention in that the third party has to make an award which is binding on the parties.

Procedures which include provision for third party intervention differ in terms of how the process is to be triggered. In some cases this can only occur with the joint agreement of the two parties. In others, one party may have the right to refer an issue to a third party. A third possibility is for the procedure to provide for an issue to be automatically referred once a failure to agree has been registered internally. Moreover it is possible for procedures not only to specify more than one type of intervention, but to lay down different procedures regarding how they are to be initiated. For example, an agreement may provide for joint reference to conciliation, but unilateral reference to arbitration.

Procedures which provide for automatic recourse to arbitration have been central to the recent debate about 'no strike' or 'strike free' deals. This is because, when combined with the normal obligation not to take action in breach of procedure, they effectively preclude a union from calling unconstitutional industrial action. Optical Fibres, NEK Cables, Bowman Webber, Toshiba, Hitachi and Excel Wound Components are among the companies which have agreements of this type[48]. Unconstitutional action may still occur nonetheless and indeed has done so in several companies which have concluded 'no strike' agreements in recent years[49].

Arbitration can provide a valuable means of resolving disputes without costly industrial action, but it does have several potential drawbacks since, by definition, it involves management allowing a third party to decide issues which could have considerable implications for internal costs and efficiency. It may also act to undermine the collective bargaining process in two important ways: First, because it provides the parties with a way of 'getting off the hook' without having to work out their own solutions. Second, because arbitrators can, and frequently do, choose compromise solutions somewhere between the final negotiating positions of the two sides. As a result it is argued that negotiators are encouraged to hold back their final negotiating stances on the grounds that they have 'something to give' at the arbitration stage. North Americans refer to this as the 'chilling effect'.

Such potential drawbacks have prompted considerable interest in the concept of 'pendulum' or 'last offer' arbitration, a feature of most of the 'strike free' deals referred to above. Used widely in North America to resolve public sector disputes, this type of arbitration differs from that traditionally used to resolve disputes over issues like pay in that the arbitrator cannot make an award somewhere between the final negotiating positions of management and union. In other words the arbitrator has to opt for one or other side. For example, during the 1988 pay negotiations at Sanyo Industries an arbitrator was appointed to choose between a union claim for an 8.5% increase and a company offer of 6% linked to productivity improvements. The arbitrator opted for the union's position.

It is argued that pendulum arbitration serves to support rather than undermine collective bargaining since it encourages the parties to narrow their differences as far as possible in order to avoid the 'all or nothing' character of the process and minimise their chances of losing if an issue does go to arbitration. But it does have certain potential disadvantages compared with traditional arbitration[50]. These include, the difficulties surrounding what constitutes the final negotiating positions of management and union; the fact that it precludes arbitrators from considering the long-run implications of their awards for industrial relations; and the rather crude nature of the process where the dispute concerns a complex set of negotiations covering a number of different issues such as pay, holidays and hours of work.

The assessment of employee relations

Disputes procedures are intended to help management and unions to resolve disagreements without recourse to costly industrial action. However, they must guard against assessing the quality of their employee relations solely by reference to the amount of such action experienced.

Effective management-union relations take place within the context of the employment relationship more generally. Both parties to this relationship, management and workers, have objectives which they want to fulfil. Employees, for example, are likely to see their work as a means of meeting their aspirations on for example, pay levels, employment security, hours of work, and promotion. Similarly, organisations employ people to enable the enterprise to further its commercial and/or public service objectives.

As seen by the employer, the ultimate test of effectiveness should be whether their management–union relations enable the organisation to operate in a way conducive to the achievement of both its short and long-term objectives. Relevant questions to consider are therefore whether they are helping or hindering the achievement of high levels of output and productivity, satisfactory labour recruitment and retention, the maintenance of an atmosphere supportive of change, and the presence of a committed and motivated workforce. All the carefully worked out policies and practices must be seen as a means to an end, not an end in themselves.

Organised conflict can dramatically harm an employer's operations in each of the areas mentioned. It is presumably not a thing any employer positively desires. On the other hand, a low level of conflict is not necessarily a sign that relationships are satisfactory. It is quite possible for low levels of conflict to exist alongside high levels of absenteeism and labour turnover, inflexible working practices, and widespread resistance to change. As has been pointed out by Fox, 'overt and palpable expressions of conflict are no more a reliable indicator of low morale than their absence is of a clean bill of health'[51]. Such is the dilemma facing the employer.

The future of collective bargaining

The future of collective bargaining in the UK is inexorably linked to developments in union membership and recognition. The 1980s have seen unions experiencing reverses in both of these areas.

In 1979 union membership in Britain had reached an all time record level of 13.2 million, or 55% of the workforce (defined to include the unemployed but to exclude the armed forces). Since then it has fallen dramatically. Between 1979 and 1986 membership fell by nearly two million to 10.5 million, a fall which means that the union movement lost all the members it gained during the expansionist 1970's. It is currently estimated that only just over 40% of the workforce are now union members[52].

Unemployment rose steeply during the early 1980s; inevitably this had an adverse effect on union membership, unemployed workers generally having little incentive to join or remain in unions. Although unemployment is now falling, it is still high compared with the post-war period. Nevertheless, the improved employment situation has coincided with a slower decline in union membership, which in 1987 fell by the lowest amount since the start of the decade. Some individual unions have also recently reported their first increases in membership in the last decade[53].

Unemployment, is not the only factor which can adversely effect union membership. Government policies can significantly influence the climate of opinion regarding union membership and recognition, and in particular employer attitudes towards these issues. Structural changes in the economy which affect the distribution of employment between different sectors, the size of workplaces and the types of work available can also have an impact.

Successive governments since 1979 have been less sympathetic towards trade unionism and collective bargaining than their post-war predecessors. This change in attitude has been most clearly illustrated by the developments in labour law enacted since 1979. The removal of legislative support for union recognition and closed shop arrangements, the prohibition of union-only clauses in commercial contracts, and a considerable narrowing of the statutory immunities provided to protect those involved in organising and carrying out industrial action from various common law liabilities, are just a few of the legislative changes that have been made over this period[54].

At the same time employers have been considerably less willing to recognise unions and, as mentioned earlier, some argue that employers have reduced the range of issues over which they are prepared to negotiate with the unions they recognise. This shift in employer attitudes does not, so far appear to have been associated with a full frontal assault on union recognition and organisation. Shop steward organisation for the most part remains intact, if less influential, and there have been relatively few cases where employers have chosen to derecognise unions[55]. As a result, where unions were recognised at the end of the 1970s, they generally continue to remain recognised and to operate in much the same way as they did previously.

The difficulties stemming from these shifts in government and employer attitudes have been compounded by structural changes which are significantly affecting the distribution and composition of employment in a way that has adverse consequences for union recruitment. These changes include a shift in the balance of employment away from traditionally highly unionised manufacturing industry to the less well-organised private services sector; an increase in the number of white-collar and female workers; a growth in self-employment and temporary, and part-time work; and a reduction in the size of employment units. Nonetheless some unions have devised policies to combat the adverse consequences of these changes. For example, unions, such as USDAW, TGWU and GMB*, have developed campaigns aimed at increasing recruitment among female, part-time and temporary, and even self-employed workers[56]. A number of unions have also launched packages which provide members with a range of financial and legal services in an attempt to improve member recruitment and retention[57].

How far initiatives of this type will be successful remains to be seen. Some researchers suggest that they could have a significant impact on

---

* Union of Shop Distributive and Allied Workers (USDAW); Transport and General Workers Union (TGWU); and General Municipal Boilermakers and Allied Trades Union (GMB).

union membership levels[58]. Others take the view that they are likely to meet with limited success unless favourable changes occur in government policy and/or the economic variables (low unemployment, and relatively rapid rises in prices and earnings) which have been historically associated with union membership growth[59].

Whichever is the case, it would seem questionable whether union membership will in the near future, if ever, reach the level achieved in 1979. On the other hand, while the coverage of collective bargaining is unlikely to grow significantly, there are few signs that it is about to enter a period of dramatic decline. In consequence such bargaining is likely to remain the major influence on employee terms and conditions of employment in the UK for the foreseeable future.

New patterns for the future

While collective bargaining does not then seem to be in terminal decline, the evidence suggests that its content will continue to change, (as it always has done) as organisations attempt to adjust their employment practices in response to technological changes, and labour and product market developments. The introduction of flatter grading structures, the extension of incremental payment structures and appraisal systems to manual workers, the establishment of closer links between employee pay and performance, the rationalisation of bargaining arrangements, the harmonisation of manual and non-manual terms and conditions of employment, and labour force flexibility are all issues where important developments seem likely to continue to take place.

How far developments of this type will lead to improvements in organisational efficiency and finances remains to be seen. Much will depend on the ability of employers to exploit the opportunities they provide. This in turn will be influenced by their willingness to invest sufficient time and resources to take advantage of them. Appraisal systems, for example, will only work effectively if they are well-designed and training is provided to those who are to carry out the appraisals. Similarly the potential benefits of securing wide-ranging commitments to work flexibility will only be maximised if staff are given the training necessary to enable them to carry out a wider range of tasks and management structures and attitudes are adjusted to support the new working practices. Negotiating changes is one thing, implementing them effectively is another.

References

1 Purcell, J. and Sisson, K., 'Strategies and Practice in the Management of Industrial Relations', in Bain, G. S. (ed), *Industrial Relations in Britain*, Blackwell, 1983.

2 Marginson, P. and Sisson, K., 'The Management of Employees', in Marginson, P. *et al*, *Beyond the Workplace: Managing Industrial Relations in the Multi-Establishment Enterprise*, p. 120, Blackwell, 1988.

3 Jennings, S. and Undy, R., 'Auditing managers' industrial relations training needs', *Personnel Management*, February 1984.

4 Advisory, Conciliation and Arbitration Service (ACAS) Code of Practice, Time Off for Trade Union Duties and Activities, HMSO, 1977.

5 Millward, N. and Stevens, M., British Workplace Industrial Relations 1980–84: the DE/ESRC/PSI/ACAS Surveys, p. 226, Gower, 1986.

6 Royal Commission on Trade Unions and Employers' Associations 1965–68. Report. Cmnd 3623, pp. 179–186, HMSO, 1968.

7 'Integrated payment structures', *Industrial Relations Review and Report*, 367, 6 May 1986.

8 Bassett, P., *Strike Free: New Industrial Relations in Britain*, Macmillan, Revised Edition, 1987.

9 See e.g. Millward, N. and Stevens, M., *op. cit.*, Ch 9; Storey, J., *The Challenge to Management Control*, Business Books, 1981, Ch. 6; and McCarthy, W. E. J. and Parker, S. R., Shop Stewards and Workshop Relations, Royal Commission on Trade Unions and Employers' Associations, Research Paper No. 10, HMSO, 1968.

10 See e.g. Brewster, C. J., and Connock, S. L., Industrial Relations: Cost Effective Strategies, Hutchinson, 1985.

11 'Packaging flexibility at Metal Box', *Industrial Relations Review and Report*, 424, 20 September 1988.

12 Legge, K., 'Personnel Management in Recession and Recovery: A comparative analysis of what the surveys say', *Personnel Review*, 17, 1988.

13 Batstone, E., Working Order: *Workplace Industrial Relations over Two Decades*, pp. 233–236, Blackwell, 1984.

14 'Employee involvement statements – current practice', *Industrial Relations Review and Report*, 396, 14 July 1987.

15 Kahn-Freund, O., 'Intergroup Conflict and their Settlement', *British Journal of Sociology*, 5, 1954. Also see Clegg, H. A., *The Changing System of Industrial Relations in Great Britain*, pp. 115–123, Blackwell, 1979.

16 Royal Commission; *op. cit.*

17 Millward, N. and Stevens, M., *op. cit.*, p. 170.

18 Brewster, C., 'Collective Agreements' in Towers, B. (ed.), *A Handbook of Industrial Relations Practice*, Kogan Page, 1987.

19 McCarthy, W. E. J., The Role of Shop Stewards in British Industrial Relations, Royal Commission on Trade Unions and Employers' Associations, Research Paper No. 1, HMSO, 1966.

20 Terry, M., 'The inevitable growth of informality', *British Journal of Industrial Relations*, 25, 1977.

21 'Nissan – a catalyst for change', *Industrial Relations Review and Report*, 379, 4 November 1986.

22 Brown, W., The evolution of regionally-differentiated pay, Public Finance Foundation, 1989. Also see 'Developments in multi-employer bargaining: 1', *Industrial Relations Review and Report*, 440, 23 May 1989.

23   Commission on Industrial Relations, Industrial relations in multi-plant undertakings, Report No. 85, HMSO, 1974.

24   Thomson, A. W. J. and Hunter, 'The Level of Bargaining in a Multi-Plant Company', *Industrial Relations Journal*, 6, 1975.

25   Purcell, J., 'How to manage decentralised bargaining', *Personnel Management*, May 1989.

26   Brewster, C. J. and Connock, S. L., *op. cit.*

27   Edwards, P. K. and Marginson, P., 'Trade Unions, Pay Bargaining and Industrial Action' in Marginson, P. *et al.*, *op. cit.*

28   Hyman, R. and Brough, I., *Social Values and Industrial Relations*, Blackwell, 1975.

29   Batstone, E., Boraston, I. and Frenkel, S., *The Social Organisation of Strikes*, pp. 27–44, Blackwell, 1978.

30   Gottschalk, A. W., 'The Background to the Negotiating Process', in Torrington, D. (ed.), *Code of Personnel Administration*, Gower, 1973.

31   Walton, R. E. and McKersie, R. B., *A Behavioural Theory of Labor Negotiations*, McGraw-Hill, 1965.

32   See e.g. McKersie, R. B. and Hunter, L. C., *Pay, Productivity and Collective Bargaining*, Macmillan, 1973.

33   Walton, R. E. and McKersie, R. B., *op. cit.*, p. 166.

34   Marchington, M. and Armstrong, R., 'A Case for Consultation', *Employee Relations*, 3, 1980.

35   ACAS Code of Practice, Disclosure of Information to Trade Unions for Collective Bargaining Purposes, HMSO, 1977.

36   Singh, R., 'Negotiations', in Towers, B. (ed.), *A Handbook of Industrial Relations Practice*, Kogan Page, 1987.

37   Boraston, I., Clegg, H. A. and Rimmer, M., *Workplace and Union*, Heinemann, 1975.

38   Millward, N. and Stevens, M., *op. cit.*, pp. 84–89.

39   *Ibid.*, p. 80.

40   Batstone, E., Boraston, I. and Frenkel, S., *Shop Stewards in Action*, Blackwell, 1977.

41   Useful texts on the negotiating process include: Atkinson, G., *The Effective Negotiator*, Quest, 1977; Kennedy, G. Benson, J. and McMillan, J., *Managing Negotiations*, Hutchinson, 2nd edn, 1984; and Kniveton, B. and Towers, B., *Training for Negotiators*, Business Books, 1978.

42   Kennedy, *et al.*, *op. cit.*

43   Rackham, N. and Carlisle, J., 'The Effective Negotiator – Part 1, *Journal of European Industrial Training*, 6, 1978.

44   Kennedy *et al.*, *op. cit.*, Ch. 5.

45   Millward, N. and Stevens, M., *op. cit.*, pp. 169–192.

46   Thomson, A. W. J. and Murray, V. V., *Grievance Procedures*, Saxon House, 1976.

47   Singleton, N., *Industrial Relations Procedures*, HMSO, 1975.

48   'No-Strike deals: are they different?', *Industrial Relations Review and Report*, 414, 19 April 1988.

49   *Ibid.*, p. 4.

50   Wood, Sir John, 'Last Offer Arbitration', *British Journal of Industrial*

Relations, XXIII, 1985; and Kessler, S., 'Pendulum Arbitration', *Personnel Management*, December 1987.

51 Fox, A., Industrial Sociology and Industrial Relations, Royal Commission on Trade Unions and Employers' Associations, Research Paper No. 3, HMSO, 1967, p. 9.
52 Kelly, J. and Bailey, R., 'British trade union membership, density and decline: a research note', *Industrial Relations Journal*, 20, 1989.
53 'The Challenge for the unions', *Industrial Relations Review and Report*, 417, 1 June 1988.
54 Mackie, K., 'Changes in the Law since 1979: an overview', in Towers, B. (ed.), *A Handbook of Industrial Relations Practice*, Kogan Page, 1987.
55 Claydon, T., 'Union Derecognition in Britain in the 1980's', *British Journal of Industrial Relations*, XXVIII, 1989.
56 Kelly, J. and Heery, E., 'Full-time Officers and Trade Union Recruitment', *British Journal of Industrial Relations*, XXVII, 1989.
57 'Trade unions towards the year 2000', *Industrial Relations Review and Report*, 385, 3 February 1987.
58 Undy, R. *et al.*, *Change in Trade Unions*, Hutchinson, 1981.
59 Bain, G. S. and Price, R., 'Union Growth: Dimensions, Determinants and Destiny', in Bain, G. S. (ed.), *Industrial Relations in Britain*, Blackwell, 1983.

11

The legal framework of employment

Law provides an important framework to employment and no one who has responsibility for management of human resources can afford to ignore it. There is a great volume of employment law and it is both complex and subject to frequent change. All this chapter can aim to achieve is to provide a sufficient outline of how law operates to enable managers to recognise when to seek more expert advice from within their employer's organisation, or from a legal practitioner. It must be understood that the broad rules set out here are often subject to qualifications which may modify their operation in particular situations.

There are a number of valuable textbooks which give authoritative commentaries on this branch of the law and well equipped personnel departments are likely to have an office copy of one or more of these works. Journals and looseleaf publications, which are regularly updated by the publishers, are especially useful to those who have to manage within the fast changing legal environment.

The legal system

In order to understand employment law it is necessary to have a working knowledge of the legal system within which it functions in England. Unfortunately for those business men who wish to operate internationally, legal systems are relevant to, and enforceable only within, state boundaries. Even within the United Kingdom there are three distinct jurisdictions, namely, England and Wales, Scotland and Northern Ireland. However, as the three jurisdictions share one Parliament, and the Appellate Committee of the House of Lords is the highest appeal court for each jurisdiction, there are few areas, and those not related to employment, where there are any major regional differences in the laws and systems of application. Moreover, the development of the European Community is bringing a high level of harmonisation of regulatory standards throughout the member states, and the employment law of the United Kingdom has already experienced the impact of a number of Community Directives.

Sources of law

Laws stem from two important sources – litigation and Acts of Parliament. In former times litigation was the more important source of law in England. Centuries ago judges decided disputes according to local custom; in time, through reporting of these judgments, certain local customs became common to the whole country and provided the foundation of the 'common law'. The system of law reporting, which has been redefined during the past century, ensures that the more important judicial decisions are published and even a modest law library will carry many shelves of reports. Good law reporting has led to case law being held in such regard that decisions of the higher courts create binding precedents which can only be set aside with great difficulty.

A number of references are made to case law in this chapter so it may be useful to explain the referencing system which lawyers employ to denote where in a law library a case can be found. For example the reference *Gascol Conversions Ltd.* v *Mercer* [1974] ICR 420 means that this case (which incidentally bears the names of those involved in the litigation) can be found at page 420 of Industrial Cases Reports for the year 1974. Among other modern series of law reports referred to here are

IRLR   Industrial Relations Law Reports

QB ⎫
KB ⎬   Queen's/King's Bench   ⎫ The
AC   Appeal Cases   ⎬ Law
WLR   Weekly Law Reports   ⎭ Reports

Personnel departments often subscribe of IRLR: quality daily papers, such as *The Times*, usually carry brief reports of the more important of the previous day's hearings as part of their news service. As law reports are not generally accessible, members of the public who have a genuine interest in researching cases are normally admitted by universities and polytechnics to their law libraries.

The development of legal rules through case law is somewhat haphazard, since it depends on the fortuitous occurrence of situations which provoke litigation; moreover cases can create rules of law which cannot easily be adapted to accommodate the needs of a rapidly changing society. Parliament has therefore intervened and directed the development of law by making statutory rules to supersede or supplement the common law. In recent years Parliament has often been required to legislate to implement the Treaty of Rome or subsequent Directives from the EEC as to the regulatory standards to be observed in member states; for example the Sex Discrimination Act 1975 was intended to implement an EEC commitment to equal opportunities. Moreover when experience proves that UK legislation has failed to capture the intention of the EEC further amending legislation may be necessary: thus the Equal Pay Act 1970 was amended by the Equal Pay (Amendment) Regulations 1983 to introduce the concept of work of equal value into the 1970 Act.

In the UK, because legislation has developed pragmatically to deal piecemeal with defects in the law, there is no single Act of Parliament constituting a code in which all rules relating to employment are contained. The foundations of modern employment law were largely laid in the nineteenth century and a few Acts of Parliament from this early period are still in force (e.g. Conspiracy and Protection of Property Act 1875); but most of the legislation currently in force originated in the 1970s, though much of this relatively recent law has since been amended. Of major importance to the employee is the Employment Protection (Consolidation) Act 1978, as amended.

Indeed so complex has society become that Parliament no longer attempts to legislate in detail; increasingly Parliament legislates in broad concepts by 'enabling' or 'framework' acts, which delegate wide powers to Secretaries of State to make regulations to provide detailed rules of law. The Health and Safety at Work etc. Act 1974 is such an enabling Act. It has in fact been implemented by various sets of regulations such as The Health and Safety (First-Aid) Regulations 1981 whose library reference is SI 1981 No. 917.

Another regulatory device is the Code of Practice. Parliament enables, or even directs, within the parent statute, that a code of practice be made to provide guidance as to a proper mode of conduct in given circumstances within the scope of the statute's provisions. Unlike statutes and regulations, compliance with codes of practice is not mandatory, but codes are of evidential value and in reality it is very hard to justify, in a legal enquiry, why the code has not been followed, if the situation is one to which it is applicable. Thus the Employment Protection Act 1975, s.6(2)(a) enabled a code of practice to be made concerning the disclosure of information by employers to certain trade union representatives for the purpose of collective bargaining and most employers will be unlikely to deviate far from the recommendations of the code which has been published further to this provision.

Words used in Acts of Parliament often require interpretation: indeed there is an Interpretation Act 1978, which interprets words frequently used in legislation – for example, 'he' used in a statute normally includes 'she' (a lawyer's discriminatory practice adopted in this chapter!). In spite of this Act much statutory interpretation is left to courts, and case law which develops in relation to an act of Parliament can considerably influence the impact of the legislation; therefore the legal practitioner relies less on a Stationery Office copy of a statute than upon text books which incorporate subsequent judicial interpretations of that legislation.

Criminal and civil law

Rules of law fall into two main categories: criminal and civil.

Criminal law aims to regulate society, and provides for sanctions, such as fines and imprisonment, to be imposed on those who do not observe the standards it imposes. Often it aims to prevent the creation of hazardous situations or undesirable practices. Criminal cases are frequently brought to court by the police (generally through the Crown Prosecution Service) or by a special enforcement agency such as the Health and Safety Executive. Criminal law is enforced in England in magistrates' courts and the Crown Court. Minor criminal charges are tried summarily in magistrates' courts; a major charge is tried upon indictment, before a jury, in a session of the Crown Court, but only after a preliminary enquiry has been conducted in a magistrates' court to determine whether there is a case to answer. Appeal may lie from decisions of the Crown Court to the Criminal Division of the Court of Appeal and thence to the House of Lords.

The criminal law plays a relatively unimportant role in employment, with the notable exception that occupational health and safety laws are largely enforced in criminal courts. However, management should feel duty bound to inform the police and cooperate with criminal prosecutions should incidents involving theft or personal violence occur at the workplace. Also, industrial disputes have a regrettable tendency to encourage violence; for example picketing has often provoked police intervention with resultant criminal prosecutions. However, the rules invoked in these situations will be drawn from the general body of the law and be entirely, or very largely, unrelated to employment.

Civil law is intended to give parties the opportunity to obtain redress from the person, organisation or representative of government who has injured them.

Minor civil disputes are heard in county courts; major disputes are tried in the High Court. Appeals lie to the Court of Appeal and finally to the House of Lords.

The system of courts described above is for England: there are different systems in other parts of the United Kingdom.

The laws of the UK may now be subject to review in the Court of Justice of the European Community which is empowered to determine whether laws of member states meet the requirements of Community law. It hears references from national courts for rulings on the interpretation of provisions of Community law: it is also concerned with actions alleging failure to fulfil the obligations of the Treaty of Rome by member states or state enterprises (e.g. Area Health Authorities). The rights of the individual employee to apply to the court for interpretation of employment provisions are complex, depending partly upon the Article of the Treaty relied upon, and partly upon whether the employer involved is related to the 'State'.

Industrial tribunals

Employees have, since the late 1960s, been granted by statutes, certain rights (such as the right not to be unfairly dismissed) which are enforceable only through industrial tribunals. Such rights are additional to more traditional rights (such as those relating to wrongful dismissal) which were formerly, and remain even today, enforceable in county courts and the High Court. While these statutory rights are not enforceable in common law courts, often rules of law developed in common law courts influence the interpretation which an industrial tribunal places on a contract of employment when dealing with statutory rights. Appeals from an industrial tribunal lie on a matter of law to the Employment Appeal Tribunal (EAT) (a special court of High Court status); further appeal lies to the Court of Appeal and finally to the House of Lords. Since the higher appellate courts are common law courts they also tend, some believe wrongly, to infuse into the statutory system some of the principles of common law, and, unlike industrial tribunals they (including the EAT) provide binding precedents on statutory interpretation.

Originally it was imagined that industrial tribunals would provide a swift and cheap resolution of employees' complaints; so complainants to a tribunal are not entitled to legal aid. Experience has shown that issues can involve complex interpretations of law and when cases are appealed it may be a long time before the dispute is finally resolved. Recently questions have been raised as to whether the system should be reformed or whether arbitration would not be a preferable means of settling disputes.

Arbitration

Parties to an agreement may always include in that agreement a provision that in the event of dispute they will turn to a person, or institution, for arbitration of any dispute arising out of the performance of their agreement: even if the original agreement did not make provision for use of arbitration the parties may elect to go to arbitration when a dispute has actually arisen. Arbitration has not traditionally featured strongly in UK employment law, though it may be used to determine a dispute which has arisen out of a collective agreement. It is possible for provision to be made for disputes between an individual employee and employer to be resolved by arbitration but this has rarely been done in the UK. Such arrangements might be difficult to create except where there was a strong union presence at the workplace: where the workforce was unionised the arrangements could be incorporated in the collective agreement between the employer and the union, as indeed is common in the USA.

Where a provision for arbitration has been incorporated in a contract the courts will not hear a dispute which has not been to arbitration and will enforce the outcome of the arbitration: the decision to resolve a strike by arbitration would not normally be a part of a contract, but striking parties who did not observe the arbitrator's ruling would lose credibility. (For ACAS' role in arbitration see below).

Collective and individual employment law

The common law view is that the employment relationship is essentially an individually negotiated contract between employer and employee, creating personal, and non-assignable rights and duties for the parties to it (*Nokes* v. *Doncaster Amalgamated Collieries Ltd* [1940] AC 1014). In practice, however, the ability of the parties to negotiate contractual terms is somewhat restricted by statutory controls: for example the very rule as to the personal nature of the relationship has been largely undermined by The Transfer of Undertakings (Protection of Employment) Regulations 1981, which are intended to protect the employee from suffering termination of his contract when his employer transfers his business to another employer. The significance of personal relationships in employment is still further reduced by the fact that a fairly large sector of the labour force is employed in circumstances where a trade union negotiates employment terms for a class of employees with an employing organisation or its representative association. Individual contracts of employment may then incorporate collectively bargained terms.

Any study of the legal framework of employment law has therefore to consider both the contractual relationship between the employer and employee and the relationship between the employer, or employers collectively, and trade union(s). A third aspect of control of employment is the relationship between the trade union and its individual members but this aspect is beyond the scope of the present chapter.

Since collective employment law is largely concerned with the relationship between employers and trade unions it is important to have a clear idea of what is meant by the term trade union. For the purposes of legislation a trade union is defined as an organisation, whether permanent or temporary, which consists wholly or mainly of workers of one or more descriptions, whose principal purposes include the regulation of relations between workers of that description and employers or employers' associations. (Trade Union and Labour Relations Act 1974, s.28). It follows from this that there is no special procedure for creating a trade union. However many statutory provisions refer to *independent* and, or, *recognised* trade unions. To establish its *independence* the union must first be placed on the Certification Officer's list of trade unions and then make a further application for a certificate that it is independent. Whether it is deemed independent will depend upon whether, in the view of the Certification Officer, the trade union is one which:

a) is not under the domination or control of an employer or group of employers or one or more employers' associations, and

b) is not liable to interference by an employer or by any such group or association (arising out of the provision of financial or material support or by any other means whatsoever) tending towards such control.

A union is *recognised* when it has recognition by an employer to any extent for the purpose of collective bargaining. Since there is no statutory procedure for establishing that a union is recognised a union may have difficulty in substantiating a claim that it is indeed recognised.

The system of employment relationships, like any other form of agreement, is liable to breakdown. The collective bargaining process between employer and union is particularly sensitive and liable to breakdown, either at the stage of negotiating new terms (disputes of interest) or subsequently when one or other party allegedly fails to honour the bargain which has been negotiated (disputes of right). However disputes between individual workers and their employers may escalate into collective disputes, so it is not entirely accurate to associate industrial unrest solely with the collective bargaining process. Breakdowns in industrial relations result in disruption at the workplace with either the workforce withdrawing labour (striking) or the employer refusing to allow the workers to carry out their work (lockout). Disruptions of this nature, which may well involve large numbers of workers, can have serious consequences for the economy and may cause great inconvenience to the public at large, particularly if, as is often the case, the breakdown occurs in a service industry in the public sector.

Legislative machinery for promoting the improvement of industrial relations

The extent to which trade unions and employers should be permitted by the State to wage economic war by withdrawal of labour on the one hand, and imposition of lockouts on the other, is a debatable political issue. However few would doubt that any mechanisms which can be provided to improve industrial relations and reduce the likelihood of withdrawal of labour or other forms of industrial action must be valuable.

Labour governments of the 1970s held the view that industrial harmony could be promoted by encouraging recognition by employers of trade unions and also by protection of individuals from reprisals by their employers for taking part in trade union activities. These objectives were reflected in the provisions of the Employment Protection Act 1975 and the Employment Protection (Consolidation) Act 1978. Both these statutes have now been considerably amended, but the 1975 Act still contains certain provisions promoting collective bargaining and the 1978 Act remains the principal source of individual employment protection. In addition the 1975 Act revised and re-enacted official machinery for promoting harmony in industrial relations.

Statutory machinery and definitions

The 1975 Act set on a statutory footing the Advisory Conciliation and Arbitration Service (ACAS) and charged it with the general duty of promoting improvement of industrial relations, and in particular of encouraging extension of collective bargaining, and development and, where necessary, reform of collective bargaining machinery. In the event it was to become clear that extension of collective bargaining (especially by creation of new splinter groups) did not always improve industrial relations and this, as much as a change of government policy, has resulted in repeal of the original provisions relating to the role of ACAS in promoting trade union recognition.

The functions of ACAS are conciliation, arbitration, provision of advice and conduct of enquiries. The Service may also issue codes of practice.

Conciliation   Where a trade dispute exists or is expected ACAS may, at the request of one or more of the parties to the dispute, offer the parties to the dispute its assistance with a view to bringing about a settlement by way of conciliation or by other means. ACAS is also required to provide conciliation officers in respect of any matters which are, or could be, the subject of proceedings before an industrial tribunal and in this respect a major part of its work has been in connection with dismissal of employees. Its function is not, however, (in respect of either individual or collective employment issues), to advise the parties as to the probable outcome of litigation, but rather to enable them to reach agreement without resort to litigation.

Arbitration   Where a trade dispute exists or is expected, ACAS may, at the request of one or more of the parties, and with the consent of all the parties, refer all, or any, of the matters to which the dispute relates to arbitration. The arbitration may be conducted by persons specially appointed for the purpose by ACAS or by the Central Arbitration Committee (CAC). CAC was set up according to the provisions of Schedule 1 of the 1975 Act and is in effect a group of persons experienced in industrial relations from whom a panel can be selected to deal with arbitration of a particular dispute.

The term 'trade dispute' is defined in s.126A of the 1975 Act as a dispute between employers and workers, which is connected with one or more of the following:

a) terms and conditions of employment, or the physical conditions in which any workers are required to work;

b) engagement or non-engagement, or termination or suspension of employment or the duties of employment, of one or more workers;

c) allocation of work or the duties of employment as between workers or groups of workers;

d) matters of discipline;

e) the membership or non-membership of a trade union on the part of a worker;

f) facilities for officials of trade unions; and

g) machinery for negotiation or consultation, and other procedures, relating to any of the foregoing matters, including the recognition by employers or employers' associations of the right of a trade union to represent workers in any such negotiation or consultation or in the carrying out of such procedures. (Broadly the same definition is used in the Trade Union and Labour Relations Act 1974, s.29(1)).

Advice   ACAS is also empowered to provide, free of charge, advice to employers, employers' associations, workers and trade unions on any matters concerned with industrial relations or employment policies, including:

a) the organisation of workers or employers for the purpose of collective bargaining;

b) the recognition of trade unions by employers;

c) machinery for the negotiation of terms and conditions of employment, and for joint consultation;

d) procedures for avoiding and settling disputes and workers' grievances;

e) questions relating to communication between employers and workers;

f) facilities for officials of trade unions;

g) procedures relating to the termination of employment;

h) disciplinary matters;

i) manpower planning, labour turnover and absenteeism;

j) recruitment, retention, promotion and vocational training of workers;

k) payment systems, including job evaluation and equal pay.

ACAS may publish general advice on matters concerned with industrial relations and employment policies. In addition it may issue codes of practice containing such practical guidance as it thinks fit for the purpose of promoting the improvement of industrial relations.

ACAS is also empowered to inquire into any question relating to industrial relations generally, or industrial relations in any particular industry or undertaking. It may, with certain safeguards, publish the findings of any such enquiry together with any advice it has given.

Disclosure of information to trade unions

An independent trade union which is recognised by the employer has, inter alia, the right to disclosure, by the employer, to its representatives, for the purposes of all stages of collective bargaining, (subject to certain exceptions) of all such information relating to the employer's undertaking as is in his possession, which is both information without which the trade union representative would be to a material extent impeded in bargaining, and information which it would be in accordance with good industrial relations practice that he should disclose to them for the purposes of collective bargaining.

An independent trade union which has not received information to which it is entitled may complain to CAC. CAC may, if other means of settlement fail, make an award that, in respect of any description of employees specified in the claim, the employer must observe the terms and conditions which CAC has specified.

The EEC is committed to a wider concept of worker involvement with management in decision making, but the UK has always been wedded to a conflict model of industrial relations and, although it is now more than a decade since the Bullock Committee of Inquiry reported on how worker participation might be introduced in the UK (Cmnd 6706 HMSO 1977), no acceptable proposals have yet emerged. Meanwhile The Safety Representatives and Safety Committees Regulations 1978 are remarkable in that they provide the only instance in which persons (safety representatives) appointed by a recognised trade union have statutory rights and functions at the workplace in the UK.

Litigating trade disputes

It is by no means clear that rules of law and the law courts are the proper means for resolving disputes; nevertheless this is an area in which the law has been much involved throughout the twentieth century. Since the enactment of the Conspiracy and Protection of Property Act 1875, criminal liability has rarely attached to peaceful withdrawal of labour, but courts are still all too frequently called upon to determine whether or not specific industrial action is a civil wrong, actionable by the person on whom it is inflicting injury.

Common law gave trade unions no special rights to organise labour, and it proved very difficult for labour to be withdrawn by employees without liability being incurred by them in either contract or tort: in contract liability was attached to individuals for breach of their personal contracts of employment; in tort there might be liability for conspiracy or for interfering with, or inducing the breach of, the contracts of other persons. Moreover, since normally the trade union could not itself be sued, individual members and officers of the union were brought to court, to meet claims for damages, or, much more frequently, to be served with an injunction, (i.e. a court order), whose intent was to produce a return of the strikers to work.

In the twentieth century there have been numerous Acts of Parliament modifying the common law. The intention has been to adjust the balance of power between labour and capital and to protect the general public from the chaos which can so easily follow widespread or prolonged interruption of manufacturing, and, or, provision of services. Judges have had the invidious task of interpreting statutory provisions and applying them to particular strike situations. No universally agreed statutory formula has been discovered: almost inevitably successive governments of left or right have considered it necessary to amend the legislation to redress what they have perceived as imbalances of power inherent in the legislation passed by the previous government, and judicial interpretations of it. As no positive legal framework has been established, the statutory provisions have only given strictly defined immunities from the civil liability which trade unions or their members would otherwise incur under the ordinary civil law.

In very broad terms statutory protection is given to persons for certain actions done *in contemplation or furtherance of a trade dispute* (Trade Union and Labour Relations Act 1974 s.13) even though these actions might normally be tortious. S.15 of the above Act governs the right to picket. The words 'trade dispute' are defined in s.29 to cover primarily, though by no means exclusively, disputes about terms and conditions of employment (see comparable provision of the 1975 Act, above). A controversial issue has always been the extent to which 'secondary action' should be permissible in the course of a trade dispute, (i.e. interference with the commercial activities of an organisation by persons other than the workers who are involved in the trade dispute, or actions by the strikers against persons other than their own employer). The present rules about secondary action are set out in very convoluted terms in s.17 of the Employment Act 1980. The Employment Act 1982 ss.15 and 16 took from trade unions the immunity which they (as opposed to their members and officers) had previously enjoyed from liability to pay damages for activities for which they might be deemed responsible, outside the protection granted by s.13 of the 1974 Act (*supra*). The Trade Union Act 1984 and the Employment Act 1988 have sought to regulate the internal affairs of trade unions in matters such as the appointment of officers and calling of strikes, in the belief that greater involvement of members in the trade union decision-making process would restrain industrial action.

The contract of employment

A proper review of employment law has to start with a study of common law, for even though legislation has been of major importance in recent years, an appreciation of the common law of contract has always been important to an understanding of this legislation. Arguably in the recent past legislative provisions have, for a number of reasons, been less relevant than they were in the 1970s and the role of common law has again become more prominent.

The concept of contract has played an important part in development of English law and there is much common law on contractual rights and obligations which is largely applicable regardless of the context in, or the purposes for which, a contract has been formed. But, in addition to this general law a number of specific rules have developed to govern that particular kind of contract known as a contract of employment.

It is important at the outset to distinguish a contract of employment from other contractual relationships, including other kinds of contracts for the performance of work, because both common law and statutes have distinguished the employee, i.e. the worker who has a contract of employment, and given such workers and their employers rights and duties which are at the core of employment law, and which distinguish this branch of law from other commercial arrangements, like those for the provision of services or the sale of goods.

An employer who requires work to be performed such as painting the outside of a building, may negotiate in one of two ways for the performance of this work. He may either indicate the work to be done and ask another to quote a price for doing the job, or alternatively he may ask someone to come and work for a certain wage until the task has been completed. In this simple example the law might well regard a contract arising out of the first arrangement as a 'contract for services' because the parties to the contract might be regarded as contracting as separate business enterprises, so that the worker would be an independent contractor: in the second arrangement there would most probably be deemed to be a 'contract of service', that is to say the worker would be deemed to have become the employee of the employer and the relationship formed would be regarded as a contract of employment. The position in the first example would be unambiguous if the person offering to undertake the task were an employer of labour or a person who had a large capital investment in plant whose use would significantly contribute to the performance of the task undertaken. Difficulties might arise in both the situations described if the worker engaged had only labour to offer but wished to be treated as a 'self-employed' business person with an organisation separate from that of the employer with whom the contract for work was to be formed. In such circumstances the law, rather than the contracting parties, would determine the nature of the worker's contract and would tend to classify the arrangement as a contract of service, weighing the intention of the parties as only one of a number of factors to be taken into account.

No single perfect test has been devised by the courts for the identification of the distinction between the two types of contract, in spite of the many test cases which have been heard. One of the major reasons for the difficulties experienced by the judges is that they have had to try to identify a test which may be applied for whatsoever reason the contract is under scrutiny. Thus the distinction is relevant not only to determine the rights and duties which the employer and employee owe to one another, but also to determine the extent of the employer's liability to third parties for injuries caused to them by the employee, and it also determines the basis of the employee's assessment for income tax. In recent years the difficulties created by using the identification of a contract of employment as the determinant of rights and liabilities have been recognised by the Inland Revenue, and in some marginal situations regulations have set out arrangements for payment of income tax independently of consideration as to the type of contract under which the work was performed. This approach by the Inland Revenue may have had the effect of taking away one of the worker's incentives for claiming to be self-employed.

For their part the courts have always taken the view that the more the employer is able to exercise control over the activities of the worker the more likely that worker is to be deemed an employee. However it has also had to be recognised that there are many circumstances in which it is inappropriate for an employer to attempt to exercise any real control over a worker while at work, even though there ought to be no dispute that that worker is so 'integrated' into the employer's organisation as rightly to be held to be an employee (servant). The courts now therefore regard the 'control test' as only one factor in determining whether the contract is one of employment. The situation was analysed thus by MacKenna, J. in *Ready Mixed Concrete (South East) Ltd* v *Minister of Pensions and National Insurance* [1968] 2 Q.B. 497:

> 'a contract of service exists if the following three conditions are fulfilled: (i) the servant agrees that in consideration of a wage or other remuneration he will provide his own work and skill in the performance of some service for his master (ii) he agrees, expressly or impliedly, that in the performance of that service he will be subject to the other's control in a sufficient degree to make that other master (iii) the other provisions of the contract are consistent with its being a contract of service'.

The contractual provisions will not be consistent with there being a contract of employment if the worker is taking the chance of making a profit and running the risk of making a loss out of the sale of labour rather than offering personal service for a regular wage to be paid whether or not the labour is profitably employed.

Now that it has been recorded that there may be an initial problem of determining whether a worker is working under a contract of employment, what follows will be concerned with the attributes of the contract of employment, since it remains the principal employment relationship. In particular, modern statutory regulation of employment, such as social security law and unfair dismissal law, is primarily concerned with the protection of the employee rather than the self-employed person.

Formation, content and termination of the contract of employment

A contract is a legally binding agreement. A contractual relationship is a relationship which can only come about through agreement, and which, while it exists, imposes rights and duties on the parties to it, and which, in due course, is terminated; normally by performance of the obligations contained in it.

Formation

No person (whether employer or worker) in the UK is under any legal obligation to enter into a contract of employment: in a free society there is neither a right nor a duty to work, and similarly there is neither a right nor a duty to employ labour. However, parties who elect to make contracts enter into obligations that they will normally be bound by law to honour, and they will be liable for breach of contract if they fail to do so. Thus if persons enter contracts which promise employment 'starting 1st of next month', but learn on or before that date that they are not required, they may sue for breach of contract, even though they have not actually earned their pay by doing the work. (*Hochster* v *De la Tour* [1853] 2 E and B 678). On the other hand, if a person performs a task without previously entering an agreement under which the other party expressly promised to pay for the work, no claim for payment will be possible unless it can be shown that there was an implied promise to pay. (*Lampleigh* v *Braithwait* (1616) 80 ER 155). It will, however, be unlawful discrimination to refuse to contract with a person only on grounds of race or sex.

There are certain situations in which, though the parties have made an agreement, they will not have entered into a legally binding contract:

1   *There is no intention to create legal relations*   Where parties are negotiating in a commercial environment the courts will presume an intention to make a contract unless they have expressly said that they are not so doing, or that they are not may be implied from their conduct. The rule is not significant in regard to the contract of employment but does explain why in the UK industrial relations system there is no litigation between employer and trade union for enforcement of the collective bargain; the customary rule that the collective bargain is presumed not to be intended to be legally binding (see *Ford* vs *Amalgamated Union of Engineering and Foundry Workers* [1969] 2QB 303) is now enacted in the Trade Union and Labour Relations Act 1974, s.18.

2   *The parties lack the legal capacity to make a binding contract*   Certain persons are not permitted by law to incur normal legal obligations. For example persons under the age of 18 have only a limited contractual capacity and can only be bound by contracts of employment which are beneficial to them. In former days, when minors were more frequently employed and employment conditions were harsher, this rule was important. There are few constraints on capacity which are of importance in the employment context today: for example, although it is doubtful whether the Crown may bind itself contractually, the significance of this is reduced because civil servants have the same right as other employees to bring a complaint against their employer if they are unfairly dismissed (Employment Protection (Consolidation) Act 1978, s.138).

3 *The agreement is tainted by illegality* The courts will not assist in the enforcement of an agreement which is tainted by illegality. It would be exhaustively difficult to classify the situations in which a contract of employment might become unenforceable in the courts because of some illegality which is associated with its formation or performance. It is only possible to give examples here. Contracts in restraint of trade, that is contracts which unreasonably restrict the freedom of the employee to sell his labour to another employer, are often deemed illegal: such restraints are more likely to be considered unreasonable if they are to continue after the termination of the contract. Similarly unenforceable, because unlawful, are contracts aiming at the evasion of income tax by classifying part of wages as expenses (see *Napier* v *National Business Agency Ltd.* [1951] 2 All ER 264).

Normally the courts refuse to assist a party to enforce any of his contractual rights where the contract is tainted by illegality, but in employment contracts sometimes the courts will sever the illegal aspects of the contract and enforce the remainder.

4 *There is no consideration* The courts will not enforce an agreement in which there are not mutual obligations; each party must have agreed to make payment for what the other party is promising. The courts will not normally concern themselves with the adequacy of the bargain, however: therefore an employee will not usually be able lawfully to repudiate an agreement to work on the ground that the agreed wage is below the 'going rate' for the job, unless there is a special vitiating factor such as duress, misrepresentation, or a statutory requirement as to the wage rate.

Advantage of writing

There is no legal requirement that a contract of employment be made in writing, but the advantage of committing it to writing is that the resulting document is valuable evidence of what was agreed. The disadvantage is that such a document is itself constraining, for it is difficult to persuade a court that more was actually expressly agreed than is in the document. A court would not, for example, be sympathetic towards the argument that, while the document referred to a 50 hour week, it was verbally agreed that a further 10 hours a week overtime were to be worked as a contractual obligation (See *Gascol Conversions Ltd* v *Mercer* [1974] ICR 420.) The importance of having a clear understanding of what is intended by the agreement cannot be too much stressed: the courts are not generally concerned with the technicalities of whether a contract has been formed, if it is obvious that a working relationship has been created, but they are all too frequently required to discover the terms of the agreement.

The terms of the contract

Terms may be incorporated into a contract in one of three ways: by express agreement of the parties, by statute and by implication.

1 *Express terms*   The common law allows the parties a wide freedom to determine the terms on which they will form the contract, and the courts will not require them to observe terms which they have not expressly or impliedly incorporated into their contract, unless such terms are required by Act of Parliament. An agreement between employer and union as to the terms of a contract of employment will not become part of an individual's contract of employment unless the collective agreement can be seen to have been incorporated into the contract of employment by act of the parties (See *National Coal Board* v *Galley* [1958] 1 WLR 16).

In the past employment law contracts tended to be rather terse and the parties had a regrettable tendency not to make express provision for many of the eventualities which might reasonably be expected to occur in the course of employment. This problem is now to some extent alleviated by ss.1 and 2 of the Employment Protection (Consolidation) Act 1978, which require the employer to give all employees who will normally work 16 hours a week, certain *written particulars* of their terms of employment. Each employee must receive the statutory statement not later than 13 weeks after the beginning of that employee's period of employment.

The statute requires that the statement provided shall:

(a)   identify the parties;

(b)   specify the date when the employment began;

(c)   specify the date on which the employee's period of continuous employment began (taking into account any employment with a previous employer which counts towards that period).

The statement also has (subject to special qualifications in certain circumstances) to contain the following particulars of the terms of employment as at a specified date not more than one week before the statement is given:

(a)   the scale of remuneration, or the method of calculating remuneration,

(b)   the intervals at which remuneration is paid (that is, whether weekly or monthly or by some other period),

(c)   any terms and conditions relating to hours of work (including any terms and conditions relating to normal working hours),

(d)   any terms and conditions relating to –

    (i)   entitlement to holidays, including public holidays, and holiday pay (the particulars given being sufficient to enable the employee's entitlement, including any entitlement to accrued holiday pay on the termination of employment, to be precisely calculated),

   (ii)   incapacity for work due to sickness or injury, including any provision for sick pay,

 (iii)   pensions and pension schemes,

(e)   the length of notice which the employee is obliged to give and entitled to receive to determine his contract of employment, and

(f)   the title of the job which the employee is employed to do.

If there are no particulars to be entered under any of the heads of (d) this must be stated.

The statement is also required to include (except in small firms) a note specifying any disciplinary rules applicable to the employee or referring to a document which specifies such rules. It must also identify a person to whom the employee can apply if dissatisfied with any disciplinary decision relating to him and a person to whom he can apply for the purpose of seeking redress of any grievance relating to his employment, the manner in which any such application should be made, and what, if any, further steps are consequent upon any such application.

There is a further obligation on the employer (s.4) to ensure that amended particulars are issued if the relevant contractual particulars are changed during the course of the employment.

An employer may comply with the requirements of the law by referring the employee to a document which the employee has reasonable opportunities of reading in the course of employment.

There is no penalty for failing to provide these particulars but an employee who has not received a statement in the terms which the law requires may complain to an industrial tribunal (s.11; see also *Mears* v *Safecar Security Ltd* [1982] IRLR 183).

Useful as these statutory requirements are in identifying contractual terms, compliance with the statute ought not to be confused with the provision of a written contract of employment. The Act does not affect the common law rule that a contract of employment may be validly created orally, and care should be taken to ensure that a document which is given with the intention of achieving a minimal compliance with the Act is not unintentionally elevated to the status of a written contract. An employer could give the statutory statement this status by giving it to an employee with the directive that it was that employee's contract of employment (See *Gascol Conversions Ltd* v *Mercer*). An employer who has reduced the contractual terms to writing is not required to supply a statutory statement if the written contract covers all the statutory requirements (s.5).

2   *Statutory terms*   Statutory provisions provide a floor of rights for many employees: that is rights below which the parties to the employment relationship may not contract. Many of these rights are found in the Employment Protection (Consolidation) Act 1978 and are redressable in an industrial tribunal on the complaint of the affected employee: the normal remedy being an award of compensation to the aggrieved employee. The majority of these rights only accrue to employees with a specified length (how much varies) of 'continuous employment'.

S.151 of the Act provides that references made in the Act to continuous employment are references to a period computed in accordance with Schedule 13 of the Act. The Schedule is complex but the basic rule is that every week in which an employee has worked for 16 or more hours counts: some weeks in which no, or insufficient, work has been done (e.g. where the employee has been on strike), may not count but nevertheless may not break the continuity of employment. The weeks during which a woman is on statutory maternity leave count. However it may well be controversial whether two periods of employment may be linked (e.g. if the employee does seasonal work) to maintain continuity (see *Ford* v *Warwickshire County Council* [1983] ICR 273). Continuity of employment may be retained, in some circumstances, even though there is a change of employer (see in particular The Transfer of Undertakings (Protection of Employment) Regulations 1981). An employee who works between 8 and 16 hours per week for more than 5 years, is deemed to have continuous employment. For the purpose of the relevant statutory provisions continuous employment is calculated in months or years, beginning with the day on which the employee started work.

(a)   *Itemised pay statement*   The employer is required to supply at or before the time at which wages are paid, a written statement containing particulars of the gross amount of wages, the amount of deductions and the purposes for which they are made, the net amount of wages payable and where different parts of the net amount are paid in different ways, the amount and method of payment of each part payment (ss.8, 9 and 11).

(b)   *Guarantee payments*   An employee who has been continuously employed for at least one month, but has no contractual right to receive full wages when laid off because there is no work for that employee to do, must be paid according to the provisions of the statute. A guarantee payment is not due where the absence from work is the consequence of a trade dispute involving any employee of the employer or associated employer (as defined in s.153 i.e. where two companies are subject to the same control). Nor will an employee who has refused suitable alternative work offered by the employer or has failed to comply with reasonable requirements imposed by the employer be entitled to payment. The amounts payable are relatively small and it is unlikely that the employee will obtain normal wages (ss.12–18). These provisions are not relevant to salaried employees because they are contractually entitled to receive their full pay, even though there is no work for them to do.

(c) *Suspension from work on medical grounds* An employee who has to be suspended from his normal work by his employer on medical grounds by reason of a statutory provision (and the employer is unable to offer suitable alternative employment) may not be dismissed; and is entitled, while so suspended, to be paid by the employer for a period not exceeding 26 weeks. These provisions apply to a small number of situations where over-exposure of an employee to a harmful substance, such as lead, could cause illness: the provisions do not apply if the employee is in fact ill, and therefore entitled to sickness related payments (ss.19–22).

(d) *Trade union membership and activities* An employee has the right not to suffer action short of dismissal as an individual for the purpose of:

   (i)   preventing or deterring him from being or seeking to become a member of an independent trade union, or penalising him for doing so; or

   (ii) preventing or deterring him from taking part in the activities of an independent trade union at any appropriate time, or penalising him for doing so; or

   (iii) compelling him to be or become a member of any trade union or of a particular trade union or of one of a number of particular unions.

   Nor may an employee be penalised for not complying with a requirement to make a payment in lieu of trade union membership (normally this payment would be likely to be a contribution, equivalent to a trade union membership subscription, to charity).

'Appropriate time' used here, and in similar provisions within the 1978 Act, means time outside working hours or time within working hours at which, in accordance with arrangements with, or consent given by the employer, it is permissible to take part in trade union activities (ss.23–26). Taking part in a strike or other industrial action is not a protected 'trade union activity' for the purposes of s.23.

(e) *Time off work*   An employee who is an official of an independent trade union recognised by the employer is entitled to take paid time off during his working hours to enable him:

   (i)   to carry out those duties of his as such an official which are concerned with industrial relations between his employer and any associated employer, and their employees;

   (ii) to undergo training in aspects of industrial relations which is relevant to those duties; and approved by the Trades Union Congress or by the independent trade union in which he is an official.

There is a Code of Practice concerning the amount of time an employee should be permitted to take off (s.27).

An employer is also required to permit an employee who is a member of an appropriate trade union to take time off during the employee's working hours for the purpose of taking part in trade union activities (s.28).

(f) *Time off for public duties*   An employee who performs certain specified public duties, such as being a justice of the peace, is entitled, subject to certain provisos, to take time off during his working hours for the purpose of performing those duties (ss.29–30).

(g) *Time off to look for work or training*   An employee who has been given notice of dismissal by reason of redundancy is entitled to reasonable time off from work to look for new employment or make arrangements for training for future employment (s.31).

(h) *Time off for ante-natal care*   An employee who is pregnant is entitled to time off for ante-natal care (s.31A).

(i) *Pregnancy and confinement*   The general principle is that an employee with two years' continuous employment is entitled to be absent from work because of pregnancy from the 29th week of the pregnancy and is entitled to return to work not later than 29 weeks after the birth of the child. This right is subject to giving the employer the notifications to which he is entitled (s.33 and 45–48).

(j) *Payment of wages* The Wages Act 1986 repealed earlier legislation which had restricted the employer's right to pay wages other than in cash. Now the actual mode of payment is a matter for agreement between employer and employee. Of relevance here, however, is that the 1986 Act restricts the employer's power to make deductions from wages. Broadly the employer may make only deductions where these are required by statute (e.g. PAYE) or if there is an actual agreement between employer and employee (either in the contract itself or in a special written authority given by the employee in advance of the deduction). S.2 of the Act provides special protection for those in retail employment: deductions for cash shortages must not exceed 10% of the gross wages payable when the deduction falls to be made, though the deficit may be carried forward to the following pay day, and when the employment ends there is no limit to the amount the employer may deduct or demand. Disputes under this Act are also within the jurisdiction of the industrial tribunal. However the Act does not permit an employer to make a deduction for over payment of wages: if the employer's right to recover such money is in dispute the matter must go before a county court.

3 *Implied terms* The courts are prepared to imply a term into a contract because this term is necessary to give business efficacy to that contract, or because it is obvious to a bystander that it was the intention of the parties to include such a term. In addition they will imply a term into an employment contract because it is usual for such term to be implied in employment contracts generally, or because the term is one which it is customary to include in an employment contract with the particular employer or in the particular industry. A term which is completely contrary to what the parties have actually said, or may by their conduct be deemed to have intended, will never be implied. As a result of case law it is now recognised that the following are among duties which are generally to be implied in a contract of employment:

(a) *Duties of employer*
  (i) to pay the agreed wages when they have been earned. In the case of an employee who is unable to work because of illness the employer will be statutorily bound under the Social Security and Housing Benefits Act 1982, to make payment of such sums as are due to

the employee under the Social Security Act 1985 during the first 28 weeks of absence (the employer may recover these sums from the State). There may well remain a dispute as to the employee's right to contractual pay (see *Mears* v *Safecar Security Ltd, (supra)*). In the case of a salaried employee there is, in the last instance, an implied term that wages will be paid during illness until such time as the contract is terminated (*Orman* vs *Saville Sportswear* [1960] 1 WLR 1055);

(ii)   to provide the opportunity to work if the wage depends on the provision of work (*Turner* v *Goldsmith* [1891] 1 QB 544); the usual view is that the employer is entitled to retain a worker on full pay without provision of work (*Collier* v *Sunday Referee Publishing Co Ltd* [1940] 2 KB 647) but this was judicially doubted by Lord Denning in *Langston* v *Amalgamated Union of Engineering Workers* [1974] ICR 180;

(iii)   to reimburse the employee for expenditure properly incurred by the employee in the course of his employment;

(iv)   to take reasonable care to provide the employee with a safe system of work so that he does not suffer personal injury or incur disease during his employment by reason of the employer's negligence.

There is no duty on an employer to provide an employee with a reference unless he has expressly or by conduct impliedly agreed to do so. An employer who does provide a reference must take care that he gives an accurate one or he may incur liability to pay damages to the employee (if the reference is defamatory) or to the recipient of the reference (see *Hedley Byrne & Co.* v *Heller & Partners Ltd* [1964] AC 465). He might also incur liability to compensate the employee if reference is made to 'spent' criminal offences (see Rehabilitation of Offenders Act 1974).

(b)   *Duties of employee*
  (i)   to perform his contractual duties personally; he may not delegate them to another;

  (ii)   to obey reasonable orders; but a single act of disobedience is unlikely to be serious enough to warrant dismissal (*Laws* v *London Chronicle Ltd* [1959] 1 WLR 698);

  (iii)   to account to the employer for money received for the employer (*Reading* v *Att. G* [1951] Ac 507);

    (iv)   to indemnify the employer for loss caused to the employer by his incompetent performance of his contractual obligations, e.g. by negligence (*Lister* v *Romford Ice & Cold Storage Ltd* [1957] AC 555). As a result of a gentlemen's agreement between insurance companies this duty is unlikely to be generally enforced (but see *Janata Bank* v *Ahmed* [1981] IRLR 457);

    (v)   to respect his employer's trade secrets.

Breach of any of these implied terms may lead to an action in a common law court for damages for breach of contract; in practice they are more likely to be used as evidence in either wrongful or unfair dismissal proceedings in order to justify or dispute the termination of the contractual relationship.

Termination of the contract

At common law a contract is most usually terminated by *performance*; each party carries out his contractual obligations without recourse to law and the relationship between the parties is ended. It has always been exceptional for a contract of employment to be terminated by performance though it is possible to create a contract of employment of this description by employing a person on the agreement, preferably recorded in writing for clarification of statutory rights, that the contract is for a *fixed term* (see Employment Protection (Consolidation) Act 1978, s.142) or for a specific task.

The great majority of employment contracts are made for an indefinite period and are, at common law, terminated by *variation*, *notice*, *breach* or *frustration*.

    (a)   *Variation*   The parties may agree to alter the terms of the original contract (thus terminating the old contract) and make a new one to have immediate effect: this is a negotiation of no practical importance in the present context since the law will regard the total employment period as having occurred under one continuous contract (Employment Protection (Consolidation) Act 1978, s.152). It used to be thought that if either of the parties did not agree to accept a contractual variation which the other sought to impose unilaterally, the contract would be terminated. Recent case law has indicated that it may be possible for the aggrieved party to resist the variation (see e.g. *Rigby* v *Ferodo Ltd* [1988] ICR 29) but this may not be of great assistance in saving the contract on its original terms, in the long run, since the other party could respond by giving notice to terminate the contract (see *infra* notice and also unfair dismissal).

(b)   *Notice*   The contract will be terminated if one of the parties gives notice to the other that he wishes to terminate the contract and that notice duly expires; alternatively the employment may be terminated forthwith by the employer giving wages in lieu of notice. It is now necessary to give at least the statutory period of notice. The employee who has been continuously employed for 1 month or more is required to give the employer 1 week's notice. The employee's entitlement to receive notice varies in length in accordance with the period for which that employee has been continuously employed by that employer:

Employment of over 1 month and under 2 years	1 week's notice
Employment of over 2 years and under 12 years	1 week's notice for every year of service
Employment of over 12 years	at least 12 weeks' notice

Now that an employee has statutory rights in relation to redundancy and unfair dismissal it is unusual for an employer to be able to terminate by notice the contract of an employee with two or more years' continuous employment and incur no further statutory liability.

(c)   *Breach*   The contract will be terminated if one of the parties breaks his contractual obligations and the other party elects to demonstrate that he regards this repudiatory conduct as a termination of the contract (see *London Transport Executive* v *Clarke* [1981] ICR 355). The withdrawal of labour by a striker is likely to be a breach of contract, certainly if no, or insufficient, notice of intention to strike has been given: however, it has been suggested a strike after notice may merely *suspend* the contract (*Morgan* v *Fry* [1968] 2 QB 710, but see also *Simmons* v *Hoover Ltd* [1977] ICR 61). If the wrongful act is sufficiently serious for the injured party to be released from contractual obligations that party has no need to give notice to terminate the contract (Employment Protection (Consolidation) Act 1978, s.49(5)).

The common law will not issue an order (i.e. specific performance) to require the parties to continue an employment contract when one of them has indicated that he wishes to sever the relationship and the statutory provisions relating to unfair dismissal also stop short of compelling an employer to reinstate or re-engage an employee whom he has dismissed. However, occasionally the common law courts will grant an injunction to prevent an employer carrying out an intention to terminate the contract, particularly if the employee concerned has had long and satisfactory service with that employer (*Hill* v *CA Parsons & Co Ltd* [1972] Ch 305).

(d) *Frustration* In certain rare circumstances a contract will be deemed to have terminated by operation of law because an event has occurred, beyond the control of the parties, which makes further performance of the contract impossible or futile, always providing that this event is not one expressly provided for in the contract. Occasionally contracts of employment have been deemed to have been frustrated by outbreak of war, more frequently because of a long incapacitating illness (see *Condor* vs *Barron Knights Ltd* [1966] 1 WLR 87) suffered by, or a prison sentence (See *Hare* v *Murphy Bros. Ltd* [1974] ICR 603) served by, the employee. The occurrence of the frustrating event immediately releases both parties from further contractual obligations. If an employee suffered a serious incapacitating accident it would seem that the relationship would be severed from the moment of the accident, but in the case of prolonged illness or imprisonment, the courts have not identified the exact time at which the relationship has ended and have in the past been content to hold that the contract has ceased to exist by the time that the employee seeks to return to work. More recently there has been reluctance to see a case put outside the rules of unfair dismissal by an employer establishing that the contractual relationship was ended by frustration rather than by dismissal. From time to time the view has been judicially expressed that if the contract is to be fairly terminated the employer ought in every case to note what has happened by formally dismissing the employee (see *London Transport Executive* v *Clarke (supra)*).

Rights and remedies

At common law if one of the parties suffers loss because the contract of employment is either broken or wrongfully terminated he may bring an action for damages in either a county court or the High Court. A common law action for wrongful dismissal may be attractive to the senior manager with an exceptional contractual entitlement to notice (who is unable to mitigate his loss by obtaining other similarly attractive employment see *Yetton* vs *Eastwood Froy Ltd* [1967] 1WLR 104); but for most employees, since dismissal with notice is lawful, and any damages, the only remedy, will be limited to the sum, if any, due to compensate for an inadequate period of notice, the common law provides little satisfaction (see *Addis* v *Gramophone Co* [1909] AC 488).

The unsatisfactory common law led to statutory reforms in the 1960s and 70s to give employees, if not assurance of security of tenure of employment, at least the prospect of receiving more adequate compensation in the event of their employment being terminated unfairly or by reason of redundancy. However in the 1980s the adequacy of these statutory remedies has in turn been questioned: they are dependent on the employee concerned having two years continuous employment before dismissal, and they are of little satisfaction in times of depression when alternative employment is hard to find. For these reasons there has been something of a revival of the use of common law courts both as a means of establishing contractual rights (e.g. *R* v *BBC., ex p Lavelle* [1983] IRLR 404) and as a means of preventing or postponing dismissal (*Hill* vs *Parsons (supra)*).

Unfair dismissal

Statutory provisions (now contained in the Employment Protection (Consolidation) Act 1978 ss.54–80) give most employees the right not to be unfairly dismissed by their employers; the principal exceptions are that any employee who has not achieved two years' continuous employment at the time of the effective date of termination of his contract, or who, at the time of his dismissal is over retirement age, is not qualified to claim the statutory rights.

There are no moral connotations in the term 'unfair dismissal'; it has a strict statutory meaning and a qualified employee is entitled to the statutory remedies if he has, according to the statutory rules, been dismissed, and that dismissal was unfair, even though his case is without merit. The complainant without merit may, however, be denied any compensation (see *Devis & Sons Ltd* v *Atkins* [1977] AC 931).

The employee who considers that he has been unfairly dismissed may present a complaint to an industrial tribunal within three months of the effective date of termination of his employment, that is within three months of the last day on which the employment relationship subsisted (e.g. for an employee who is working out notice, the date on which the notice to terminate expires). The general rules concerning effective date of termination might lead to hard cases (see *Dixon* v *Stenor Ltd* [1973] ICR 157), as for example where an employee is paid wages in lieu of notice and thus required to leave immediately and so reduce his qualifying period of service – in such cases the employee is treated for the purpose of service as if he had worked out his notice.

The burden is on the employee to satisfy the tribunal that he has been dismissed, the burden then shifts to the employer to establish that the dismissal was for one of the reasons permitted by the statute.

The statute provides that an employee shall be treated as dismissed if, but only if:

(a) the contract under which he is employed is terminated by the employer, whether it is terminated by notice or without notice, or

(b) where under the contract he is employed for a fixed term, that term expires without being renewed under the same contract, or

(c) the employee terminates that contract, with or without notice, in circumstances such that he is entitled to terminate it without notice by reason of the employer's conduct.

Failure to permit a woman to exercise her right to return to work after confinement is also treated as dismissal.

The Transfer of Undertakings (Protection of Employment) Regulations 1981 provide (subject to exceptions related to economic, technical or organisational reasons) that a transfer of an employing undertaking from one person to another shall not operate so as to terminate the contract of employment of any person employed by the transferor immediately before the transfer. Any person whose contract is terminated (or terms unilaterally altered) has a right to bring a claim of unfair dismissal against the transferee.

An employee claiming that the employer's conduct was such that he has been 'constructively dismissed' (c above) will only succeed in his claim if he can show that the employer's conduct was in breach of the contract: thus an employer is entitled to behave unreasonably if the contract gives him an express right to do so e.g. withhold pay as a disciplinary penalty (*Western Excavating (ECC) Ltd* v *Sharp* [1978] QB 761). An employee might claim to have been constructively dismissed if the employer attempted unilaterally to change the terms of the contract e.g. reduce the wages.

From this it may be seen that there are a number of circumstances in which a contract of employment may come to an end without there being a *dismissal* within the statutory definition: for example, if a contract is terminated by a frustrating event, or because the employee gives notice to take up an appointment elsewhere.

Grounds for dismissal

In order to establish that a dismissal was fair the employer must satisfy the tribunal that the reason for the dismissal was one of the permitted statutory reasons or some *other substantial reason* of a kind such as to justify the dismissal of an employee holding the position which that employee held. The tribunal must also be satisfied that, having regard to equity and the substantial merits of the case, the employer acted reasonably in treating it as a sufficient reason for dismissing the employee.

The specific reasons enumerated are:

(a)   related to the capacity or qualifications of the employee for performing work of the kind which he was employed to do, or

(b)   related to the conduct of the employee, or

(c)   that the employee was redundant, or

(d)   that the employee could not continue to work in the position which he held without contravention (either on his part or on that of his employer) of a duty or restriction imposed by or under an enactment.

It is further stipulated that it is unfair to dismiss an employee with continuous employment merely because she is pregnant, provided that her pregnancy does not interfere with her capacity to do adequately the work for which she is employed and that it would not be a contravention of statute to retain her in that job.

Dismissal will also be regarded as unfair if the reason for it was that the employee

(a)   was, or proposed to become, a member of an independent trade union, or

(b)   had taken part, or proposed to take part, in the activities of an independent trade union, at an appropriate time, or

(c)   was not a member of any trade union, or of a particular trade union, or of one of a number of particular trade unions, or had refused or proposed to refuse to become or remain a member.

A dismissal in respect of trade union membership is a dismissal for an 'inadmissible reason', and a complaint may be made by an employee who claims to have been dismissed on these grounds even though he has not the continuous employment which is the normal pre-requisite of a right to bring a claim for unfair dismissal.

The hearing of unfair dismissal cases is a large part of the workload of industrial tribunals and many decisions have been published. While such decisions, unlike those given on appeal, are not precedents which have to be followed in subsequent cases, tribunal decisions have been frequently appealed and, as a result, the statutory provisions have been much interpreted by the courts.

The catch clause 'other substantial reason' has been interpreted fairly generously in favour of the employer; there have been cases allowed as fair under this rubric dismissals in the interests of the business, as for example where the employee was unacceptable to a major customer (*Scott Packaging & Warehousing Co Ltd* v *Paterson* [1978] IRLR 166) or the employee was unable to secure a fidelity bond (*Moody* v *Telefusion Ltd* [1978] IRLR 311).

An employer is unlikely to be able, except in misconduct cases, to be able to justify a dismissal if he has not considered finding alternative employment for the employee. Thus if an employee is incapable by reason of sickness or incompetence, the employer would do well to consider, before resorting to dismissal, whether he can, within the organisation, find less exacting employment for this person (see *Spencer* v *Paragon Wallpapers Ltd* [1977] ICR 301); similarly, if the employee can no longer lawfully be employed in his present occupation, as might be the case where a driver became disqualified as a result of a road traffic offence, the employer would be well advised to consider whether he might employ that person's services about the employer's premises rather than on the road (see also *Sutcliffe & Eaton Ltd* v *Pinney* [1977] IRLR 349). A dismissal for redundancy may be unfair, for example where an employee does not observe his own (or any) procedure for selection for redundancy (*Polkey* v *A E Dayton Services Ltd* [1987] IRLR 503).

Polkey's case came as a salutory reminder that in dismissal cases the employer must have regard to the procedure by which he carries out the dismissal, giving proper warnings, carrying out necessary consultation and, in most instances, terminating with notice. In the case of dismissals for misconduct the employer must take particular care to satisfy himself that he has ascertained the full facts of the situation, giving the employee the opportunity to tell his side of the story before dismissal (see *Earl* v *Slater and Wheeler (Airlyne) Ltd* [1973] 1 All ER 145). The employer would be well advised to have regard to the ACAS Code of Practice on Disciplinary Practices and Procedures in Employment, for it gives valuable guidance on how to establish and enforce disciplinary procedures within the workplace and any organisation not observing it has to persuade a tribunal that it operates a satisfactory alternative system.

It is only in relatively rare cases of gross misconduct that a single act of misconduct will warrant dismissal and even in those cases the employer ought initially to suspend the employee on full pay (unless the contract expressly allows suspension without pay: *Western Excavating (ECC) Ltd* v *Sharp*) and dismiss only if an investigation confirms that there has been misconduct sufficient to warrant dismissal. In less serious cases the wrongdoer should initially be warned, given the opportunity to mend his ways and dismissed only for repeated offences.

An employee will have no claim if he has been dismissed while the employer was conducting a lock-out or the employee was taking part in a strike or other industrial action, unless the employer has discriminated between employees in failing to dismiss (or by re-engaging) other employees in like position to the claimant (Employment Protection (Consolidation) Act, s.62).

Remedies

When an industrial tribunal considers that a complaint of unfair dismissal is well-founded it must explain to the complainant what order for reinstatement or re-engagement may be made and ask him whether he wishes the tribunal to make such an order. An order for reinstatement is an order that the employer is to treat the complainant in all respects as if he had not been dismissed; an order for re-engagement is an order that the complainant be engaged by the employer in employment comparable to that from which he was dismissed and the tribunal in making such an order is required specifically to state the terms on which re-engagement is to be effected.

In cases where reinstatement or re-engagement is not ordered (the vast majority) the complainant (who is not above the age of retirement) will receive a monetary award.

There are three elements in an award:

1 *Basic Award*   This is calculated by reference to the claimant's age, length of service (up to 20 years) and weekly wage (up to the current allowable maximum of £172), which provides an entitlement calculated

   (a)   one and a half weeks' pay for each years of employment in which the employee was not below the age of 41;

   (b)   one week's pay for each year of employment between the ages of 41 and 22;

   (c)   half a week's pay for each year of employment when the employee was aged less than 22.

   Where the dismissal was for an inadmissible reason the basic award (before reductions) must not be less than £2,520 (*NB*: this and other monetary awards are subject to annual review). An employee's award will be reduced if he was between the ages of 64 and 65 at the time of dismissal and it will also be reduced (and may be denied entirely) if the tribunal finds that the dismissal was to any extent caused or contributed to by the action of the complainant, by such amount as the tribunal considers just and equitable. The award will also be reduced by the amount of any redundancy awarded by the tribunal.

2 *Compensatory Award* The tribunal is required to make such compensatory award as it considers just and equitable having regard to the loss sustained by the complainant in consequence of the dismissal in so far as that loss is attributable to the employer – the loss to be taken to include any expenses reasonably incurred by the claimant in consequence of his dismissal, and any benefit which he might reasonably be expected to have had but for the dismissal. The award may not exceed £8,925 and in making the award the tribunal may take into account whether the complainant might have taken steps to mitigate his loss and also whether his actions have caused or contributed to his dismissal.

3 *Special Awards* Where the employer has failed to comply with an order to reinstate or re-engage and cannot satisfy the tribunal that it was not practicable for him to comply with it, the tribunal must make an additional penal award against him in favour of the complainant. This will normally be not less than 13 nor more than 26 weeks pay, but if the dismissal was unfair because it was contrary to the laws on sex descrimination or race relations then the award must not be less than 26 nor more than 52 weeks' pay. Where the dismissal was in violation of the protection given to trade union membership and activities, and any order for reinstatement or re-engagement has not been complied with, the special award may amount to £18,795 or more.

In cases where a complaint is made by an employee that he has been unfairly dismissed for becoming a member of, or taking part in, trade union activities, he may apply to the tribunal, within seven days of dismissal, for interim relief pending the hearing of his complaint. The tribunal will give an early hearing to his application and if it appears to be well-grounded, ask the employer to reinstate or re-engage the employee pending the hearing of the complaint: if the employer is not prepared to assist then the tribunal must make an order for the continuation of the employee's contract of employment until the full hearing.

Redundancy

The Redundancy Payments Act 1965 made provision for severance payments to be made to employees who were dismissed as redundant. The Act gave no security of employment but merely provided for compensation, but it did make a considerable improvement in the entitlement of many employees who would have had little redress from the common law. Subsequently the wider and more generous provisions in respect of unfair dismissal, have tended to overshadow the redundancy scheme, for the person who is made redundant is normally only entitled to the basic award outlined above. The statutory provisions of the 1965 Act are now set out in the Employment Protection (Consolidation) Act 1978. The Employment Protection Act 1975, ss.99–107 makes provision for consultation with recognised trade unions about redundancies.

Entitlement

An employee is entitled to a redundancy payment if he has been continuously employed by his employer for two years since he reached the age of 18 and he is dimissed by that employer by reason of redundancy or is laid off kept on short time. An employee who has reached retirement age or who might lawfully be dismissed for misconduct or other reasons (e.g. taking part in a strike or other industrial action) is not entitled to a redundancy payment.

The legislation defines a person as being dismissed by reason of redundancy when the dismissal is attributable wholly or mainly to:

(a)   the fact that his employer has ceased, or intends to cease, to carry on the business for the purposes for which the employee was employed by him, or has ceased, or intends to cease, to carry on that business in the place where the employee was so employed, or

(b)   the fact that the requirements of that business for employees to carry out work of a particular kind, or for employees to carry out work of a particular kind in the place where he was so employed, have ceased or diminished or are expected to cease or diminish.

For the purposes of this definition, the business of the employer and associated employers are treated as one.

The definition of dismissal is set out in the same words as are used in the context of unfair dismissal.

An employee is not entitled to a redundancy payment if his employer has made him an offer (before the ending of his contract) to renew his contract of employment, or to re-engage him under a new contract to take effect either immediately on the ending of his employment under the previous contract or after an interval of not more than four weeks thereafter. If the employer makes such an offer and the employer's proposals, to the capacity and place in which he would be employed, and as to the other terms and conditions of his employment, would not differ from the corresponding provisions of the previous contract, or, though the terms do differ, the offer constitutes an offer of suitable employment, then if the employee unreasonably refuses that offer he is not entitled to a redundancy payment. Where the new contract differs from the previous one there is, however, in addition to any contractual entitlement, a trial period of four weeks beginning with the date on which the employee starts work under the contract as renewed, and if the new contract is terminated within this period the employee will retain such rights to redundancy as he had under the earlier contract. The statutory trial period is in addition to any contractual trial period.

Case law which has developed under this legislation demonstrates that the entitlement of the employee to a redundancy payment often depends on a very careful interpretation of the terms of the contract under which he has been employed, in order to determine how much flexibility that contract gives to the employer to change the circumstances of the employment in a redundancy situation without changing the terms of the contract. There is no more right under statute than at common law for a party to make unilateral changes in the terms of the contract and in this context such changes will amount to dismissal (*Marriott* v *Oxford and District Co-operative Society* [1970] 1 QB 186). In some contracts it may not be possible to require the employee to move from one building to another in the same neighbourhood, or to work at the same place at a different time of day see *Lesney Products & Co Ltd* v *Nolan* [1977] ICR 235) while in others it may be possible to require him to work in another part of the country (see *O'Brien* v *Associated Fire Alarms Ltd* [1969] 1 All ER 93), or to transfer from the day to the night shift without varying the terms of the contract of employment. It must, however, be remembered that variation of contractual terms and redundancy are not by any means identical concepts: thus to ask an employee to change working hours may be a variation of that worker's contractual terms, but if the same number of employees are needed to carry out the same amount of work there will be no redundancy situation, though there might well be an unfair dismissal.

In these days of rapidly changing technology it may frequently be necessary for an employer to consider, when planning introduction of new plant and equipment, the extent to which the employer is entitled, within the contractual terms, to require the employee to change his work methods (*North Riding Garages* vs *Butterwick* [1967] 2 QB 56) but courts do expect employees to adapt to change (*Cresswell* v *Board of Inland Revenue* [1984] IRLR 190).

Consultation

Where there is a trade union recognised by the employer as representing employees of the description of any employee whom the employer proposes to make redundant, the employer is required to consult with representatives of that trade union about the proposed dismissal

(Employment Protection Act 1975, ss.99–107). This consultation is required even though there is only contemplated the dismissal of one employee and that particular employee is neither a member of the union nor of sufficiently long service to be entitled to a redundancy award. The consultation must take place prior to the dismissal and the length of the statutory consultation period depends on the number of employees involved and the time scale over which the dismissals will be effected: where it is proposed to dismiss 100 or more employees at one establishment within 90 days or less, consultation must begin at least 90 days before the first dismissal takes effect and where 10 or more are to be dismissed within a period of 30 days, then consultation must begin at least 30 days before the first dismissal.

For the purposes of consultation the employer must disclose in writing to trade union representatives

(a)   the reasons for his proposals;

(b)   the numbers and descriptions of employees whom it is proposed to dismiss as redundant;

(c)   the total number of employees of any such description employed by the employer at the establishment in question;

(d)   the proposed method of selecting the employees who may be dismissed; and

(e)   the proposed method of carrying out the dismissals, with due regard to any agreed procedure, including the period over which the dismissals are to take effect.

In the course of consultation the employer is required to consider any representations made by the trade union representatives and reply to those representations and, if he rejects any of them, state the reasons for so doing.

If an employer fails to comply with these requirements an appropriate trade union may present a complaint to an industrial tribunal. The employer may, however, escape a sanction if he can satisfy the tribunal that there were special circumstances which rendered it not reasonably practicable for him to comply with the statutory provisions and that he had taken all such steps towards compliance as were reasonably practicable in those circumstances. Where the tribunal finds a complaint well-founded it is required to make a declaration to that effect and may also make a protective award. This is an award that the employer shall pay remuneration for a protected period to those employees described in the award, being employees who have been dismissed or whom it is proposed to dismiss as redundant. The award will be for a period specified by the tribunal but may in no case exceed 90 days.

A complaint must normally be presented to the tribunal before the dismissal takes effect or before the end of the period of three months beginning with the date on which the dismissal takes effect.

An employee may present a complaint to a tribunal on the ground that he is an employee of a description to which a protective award relates and that his employer has failed wholly or in part to pay him remuneration under that award.

Safe systems and equal opportunities

There are two other matters which are not related exclusively either to individual or collective labour law which must be considered as part of the legal framework of employment; namely occupational health and safety and equality of opportunity.

Occupational health and safety

The law has two concerns in respect of occupational health and safety: it provides compensation for victims of industrial accidents and diseases and it provides operational standards with the objective of eliminating from the working environment the hazards which may cause accidents and ill-health.

Compensation   An injured person may bring an action for damages, claiming both for loss of income and for 'non pecuniary' loss such as pain and suffering. This is equally true whether the accident occurs at the workplace or elsewhere, even in the victim's home. However, workers who suffer injury while at work are in practice more likely to succeed in their claims than are other categories of litigants; this is especially so if the victim is an employee and the defendant is an employer. That it is socially desirable that employers should provide compensation for injuries to their employees, where the employer is legally responsible, is recognised by the Employers' Liability (Compulsory Insurance) Act 1969: it requires the employer to carry insurance cover to meet liability for such accidents if they arise out of and in the course of the employee's employment. However while the statutory requirement for insurance relates only to injuries to employees the standard of care expected of the organisation is still likely to be high whether the victim is one of its own employees, some other worker or a member of the public. Nevertheless the law of compensation for personal injury is regarded as somewhat capricious in its operation and many would argue that more generous and certain provision ought to be available for those who suffer injury at a workplace.

To succeed, the plaintiff (victim) must prove either that the defendant has committed the tort of negligence or that he has broken a statutory duty.

(a) *Negligence*   To succeed in a claim for negligence the plaintiff must prove that the defendant owed the plaintiff a duty; that the defendant broke that duty by negligent conduct; and that this breach of duty caused the plaintiff's injury.

The courts today take a liberal view as to the relationships which create duty situations and few workplace claims would be likely to fail because the plaintiff was unable to establish the duty. Similarly it is not usually difficult to establish that an accident suffered by the negligence of the defendant has caused the plaintiff's injury. In these circumstances the plaintiff's decision as to who to sue is largely determined by considerations as to which of a range of possible defendants is likely to be able to pay any damages which the court may award, and what evidence there is of negligent conduct. The employer is likely to be the most attractive defendant, both because of the insurance requirement and because the courts expect employers to take especial care to provide their employees with a safe system of work, including safe plant and equipment, a safe working place and instruction and training. However, where the employer is a small sub-contractor, the plaintiff may prefer to sue a more substantial organisation, such as a head contractor, in the justifiable belief that the courts would expect from the larger organisation a standard of care very similar to that expected of the employer.

(b) *Breach of statutory duty*   Sometimes a plaintiff is able to identify a statutory duty imposed upon a person (usually an employer) for the protection of persons such as the plaintiff and to show further that this duty has been broken and its breach has caused the plaintiff to suffer the injury in dispute. The rules governing entitlement to bring such claims are complex and even if there is a right to bring an action the plaintiff will not succeed unless he is able to relate his claim precisely to the duty imposed by the statute. However many industrial injury claims based on breach of statutory duty have succeeded; this has been especially so where the duty was created under older protective legislation such as the Factories Act 1961.

Vicarious liability   An employer is also liable (regardless of whether or not that employer is personally at fault) for the injuries caused by the wrongful acts of his employees in the course of their employment. So if one worker injuries another (or indeed a member of the public) by negligent conduct the victim may claim damages from the employer (see *Mersey Docks & Harbour Board* v *Coggins & Griffiths (Liverpool) Ltd and McFarlane* [1947] AC 1).

Prevention   It is recognised that it is better to avoid industrial accidents and work related ill-health than to compensate for them; so statutory codes have established standards for the workplace and special inspectors have been appointed with powers to enter premises to investigate whether these standards are being observed. The duties imposed by these codes are enforced in the criminal courts. There were by 1970 more than 30 statutes concerned with safety at the workplace, perhaps the best known of which was the Factories Act 1961; in addition there were more than 500 regulations made under them. The legislative coverage at that time was nevertheless inadequate: offences were tried summarily and so penalties were small; millions of people worked in circumstances where there were no statutory standards; such coverage as existed was piecemeal; the safety of the public was not provided for; enforcement methods were not entirely satisfactory.

The Health and Safety at Work etc. Act 1974 was intended as a reforming Act. It was an enabling, or framework Act, with the objectives of securing the health, safety and welfare of all persons at work and of protecting the public against risk arising out of the activities of persons at work. It did not immediately repeal the earlier statutory provisions but the ultimate intention is that the earlier codes will be reviewed and revised and this work is now well advanced.

Under the Act the Health and Safety Commission was set up and given a general responsibility for occupational health and safety. The task of inspecting and enforcing occupational health and safety laws was entrusted to the Health and Safety Executive and the earlier inspectorates were brought under the control of the Executive. Offences became subject in many cases to trial upon indictment, and, in addition, the inspectorate was given new powers of enforcement – in the form of improvement and prohibition notices. The *improvement* notice is an order from an inspector requiring the person upon whom it is served to carry out some specific task in order to comply with the duties imposed upon that person by the Act. A *prohibition* notice is an order that a certain activity shall cease, on the grounds that it involves a risk of personal injury. It is a criminal offence to fail to comply with an order but the validity of the requirements in an order may be disputed in an industrial tribunal.

General duties   The general duties contained in the 1974 Act (ss.2–9) apply to all persons at work, whether or not such persons are also protected by the provisions of earlier legislation. They aim to establish safe systems of work, and for this purpose they identify, and impose duties upon, those involved in the work activity. These duties are very broad but are of a high standard, since for the most part they impose liability for unsafe situations unless the accused can prove that it was not reasonably practicable for him to do more than he has done to remove the hazard.

Regulations may be made to create specific standards in respect of specific situations but it seems unlikely that the general duty will ever be fully discharged by observing all the relevant regulations, since it encompasses the total system of work.

The importance of the earlier statutes decreases as new regulations are brought into force; and for the most part these new regulations, like the 1974 Act, and unlike the other statutes, apply to all work activities. However until the earlier statutes are entirely repealed their provisions must still be complied with, as well as the general duties and new regulations, in the premises and situations to which they apply. Indeed the standards required by the earlier Acts in respect of such matters as cleanliness, heating, lighting, ventilation, overcrowding, sanitary facilities, and guarding of machinery, ought also to be observed in all employment wherever it is reasonably practicable to do so, since if standards lower than these are tolerated there may be difficulty in persuading a court that the general duties are being complied with.

It is fundamental to compliance with the 1974 Act that safety be seen as a matter of safe systems and related to the proper management of people. The principal responsibility for safety at the workplace in practice falls mainly upon the employer and the Act requires him to do all that is reasonably practicable to ensure the health, safety and welfare at work of all his employees. The burden is placed upon the employer not only to provide a safe environment but also to ensure that his employees appreciate the need for and understand the method of achieving safety at the workplace. As supplementary to, and, to an extent, in explanation of, the general duty imposed on the employer in s.2(1) of the Act, s.2(2) requires:

(a) the provision and maintenance of plant and systems of work that are, so far as is reasonably practicable, safe and without risks to health;

(b) arrangements for ensuring, so far as is reasonably practicable, safety and absence of risks to health in connection with the use, handling, storage and transport of articles and substances;

(c) the provision of such information, instruction, training and supervision as is necessary to ensure, so far as is reasonably practicable, the health and safety at work of his employees;

(d) so far as is reasonably practicable as regards any place of work under the employer's control, the maintenance of it in a condition that is safe and without risks to health and the provision and maintenance of means of access to and egress from it that are safe and without such risks;

(e)   the provision and maintenance of a working environment for his employees that is, so far as is reasonably practicable, safe, without risks to health, and adequate as regards facilities and arrangements for their welfare at work.

As part of his duty the employer is also required to provide a written statement of his safety policy, and the organisation and arrangements for the time being in force for carrying out that policy and to bring this statement and any revision of it to the notice of all his employees.

A defect in the earlier legislation was deemed to be its failure to involve the work force in making and maintenance of arrangements to enable promotion and development of measures to ensure safety. It is now part of the employer's general duty to consult for this purpose with safety representatives who have been appointed by unions which he recognises. The Safety Representatives and Safety Committees Regulations 1977 set out the functions of such representatives and the ways in which the employer is required to co-operate with them in order to assist them in the performance of their task. Their principal functions are to carry out regular inspections of the workplace, to consult with the employer, to represent their constituents, to inspect documents, and to receive information both from the employer and the inspectorate. They are also entitled to investigate accidents. If two safety representatives request that the employer set up a safety committee he is required to do so, but there are no statutory provisions as to the constitution and functions of such a committee. The regulations and the accompanying code of practice and guidance notes are not mandatory (employer and trade union may negotiate a different system of representation); but they do represent a floor of rights with which the employer who has a recognised trade union may be required by the union to comply in default of any alternative arrangements.

The 'systems' approach to safety is emphasised by s.3 which requires the employer to conduct his undertaking in such a way as to ensure, so far as is reasonably practicable, that persons not in his employment who may be affected thereby are not exposed to risk to their health and safety. Under this duty the employer must have regard for the safety of persons at work and also for that of the general public. Self-employed persons are also required to have regard for both their own safety and the safety of others. The Court of Appeal, Criminal Division has held that s.2(2)(c) obliged an employer to provide information to sub-contractors' men so that they did not endanger his own employees, and s.3(1) required him to provide information to the visiting workers for their own safety (*R* v *Swan Hunter Shipbuilders and Telemeter Installations Ltd* [1981] ICR 831).

Under s.4 controllers of premises are placed under a duty in respect of persons who come on to their premises to work there or to use plant or substances provided for their use there.

S.6 imposes a duty on designers, manufacturers, importers and suppliers to ensure that articles and substances for use by persons at work are as safe as it is reasonably practicable to make them. The section specifically requires that such commodities be tested and examined to ensure their suitability and also it must be ensured that there is available, in connection with their use at work, adequate information about the use for which they have been designed and tested.

S.7 imposes a broad duty upon every employee while at work to take reasonable care for the health and safety of himself and of other persons who may be affected by his acts or omissions at work and to co-operate with his employer and other persons to enable them to discharge their statutory obligations in respect of health and safety.

These general duties may not be used in civil actions for compensation and they are enforceable in the criminal courts only by the inspectorate. Employers, the performance of whose duties to provide safe systems will often depend on the conduct of others, will need to rely on contractual arrangements to ensure that safety is maintained by these other people: under the contract of employment the employee whose conduct is unsafe may be disciplined; commercial contracts with other organisations may give the employer rights to monitor the conduct of these contractors and their workers; and purchase contracts may relate to the safety of the products to be supplied.

Equality of opportunity

The common law rules of contract are based on the assumption that the contractual parties have equality of bargaining power; they therefore proved unhelpful to minority groups whose bargaining power was weak. Women and racial minorities are particularly vulnerable and it has proved necessary to legislate to make it unlawful to discriminate against a person on sexual (Equal Pay Act 1970 and Sex Discrimination Acts 1975 and 1986) or racial grounds (Race Relations Act 1976). The legislation, which is not confined to employment issues, has the positive objective of achieving equal opportunities, and the sex discrimination legislation, while predominantly concerned with eliminating discrimination against women, also outlaws discrimination against men. The sex discrimination statutes are intended to implement the Treaty of Rome's requirement for equal opportunities.

It remains lawful to discriminate against a person on grounds other than sex or race (or trade union membership as outlined above): so it is not, for example, unlawful to stipulate the age, or the colour of the hair, of persons to whom work will be offered unless such stipulations can be shown to amount to sexual or racial discrimination (See *Price* vs *Civil Service Commission* [1978] ICR 27).

The nature of discrimination Discrimination may be direct or indirect. *Direct* discrimination is treating a person less favourably than another on grounds of sex or race. *Indirect* discrimination occurs when a person applies to one person the same requirement or condition which he applied to another but

(a) which is such that the proportion of women (persons of the racial group) who can comply with it is considerably smaller than the proportion of men (persons not of that racial group) who can comply with it and

(b) which he cannot show to be justified irrespective of the sex (colour, race, nationality or ethnic or national origins) of the person to whom it is applied and

(c) which is to (her) detriment because (she) cannot comply with it.

Direct discrimination is easily recognised but indirect discrimination sometimes occurs through practices which are so deeply embedded in culture and tradition that their discriminatory character is hard to recognise. It might, of example, be indirect discrimination to offer employment or promotion opportunities only to persons with a record of continuous full time employment if it were established that only white men could comply with this requirement (see *Price*). However the person alleged to have discriminated may be able to justify his action by showing, for example, that the work concerned could only be performed by someone with the disputed attributes, but the courts are not sympathetic to explanations related merely to matters of practice or convenience (see *Steel* v *Union of Post Office Workers* [1978] ICR 181).

Discrimination in employment The legislation makes discrimination unlawful in a number of specific situations related to the formation and execution of the contract of employment. It is unlawful for an employer to discriminate in the arrangements which he makes for the purpose of determining who should be offered employment. This is a very wide provision and could, for example, cover placing and wording of advertisements, the contents of application forms, and the procedure of selecting for interview.

It is unlawful to discriminate in the terms on which employment is offered or by refusing or deliberately omitting to offer the employment. It is also unlawful to discriminate in respect of access to opportunities for promotion, transfer or training, or to any other benefits, facilities or services, or by refusing, or deliberately omitting to afford access to them. It is unlawful to discriminate by dismissing or subjecting a person to any other detriment.

Discrimination in the matters outlined may be lawful if sex or race, as the case may be, is a 'genuine occupational qualification'. Each Act includes a list of circumstances in which exceptionally discrimination may be allowed, as, for example, where the job involves participation in a dramatic performance and a particular type of person is required for reasons of authenticity.

It is also unlawful to discriminate in relation to pay. The Equal Pay Act 1970 had the broad objective that where men and women were doing the same work they should receive equal pay, but the enactment of a statutory formula to achieve this objective has proved difficult and the original Act has been revised.

Under the present law the terms of a woman's contract are deemed to include an 'equality clause' which relates to both pay and other contractual terms so that it is not, for example, lawful to require a woman to work longer hours for the same pay as her male colleagues receive. The equality clause applies:

(a)   where the woman is employed on like work with a man in the same employment;

(b)   where the woman is employed on work rated as equivalent with that of a man in the same employment; and

(c)   where a woman is employed on work which, not being work in relation to which (a) or (b) applies is, in terms of the demands made on her (for instance under such headings as effort, skill and decision), of equal value to that of a man in the same employment.

In spite of the restriction in (c) the House of Lords has allowed an equal value claim to be made even though there was a man employed on like work: in the view of the House to have decided otherwise would have defeated the objectives of the Treaty of Rome (*Pickstone* v *Freemans PLC* [1988] IRLR 357). Certainly any other decision would have invited employers to suppress wage rates by ensuring that there was at least a minimal representation of both sexes on the pay roll.

An employer may avoid the requirements of the equality clause if he can prove that the variation is genuinely due to a material factor which is not the difference of sex. It is controversial how far 'market forces' can be used in this context. (See *Rainey* v *Greater Glasgow Health Board* [1987] AC 224).

Equal pay claims are presented (as indeed are other claims alleging sex or race discrimination in employment) by way of complaint to an industrial tribunal. 'Equal value' claims are subject to a complex procedure within the tribunal, under which an independent expert is appointed to investigate the claim. Hearings therefore tend to be protracted, but interesting comparisons are being pursued (see e.g. *Hayward* v *Cammell Laird Shipbuilders Ltd* [1988] IRLR 257 – comparison between a female cook and male shipyard workers). The impact of the Act generally is limited in that there is no provision for class actions, so claims are made only for individual, rather than groups of, workers. However where the provisions of a collective agreement stipulate different contractual terms for employees according to sex, either party to the agreement may refer it to the CAC which has powers to direct that the agreement may be suitably amended.

Discriminatory rates of pay are prohibited in race cases, by the Race Relations Act.

Both the Race Relations and the Sex Discrimination Acts contain provisions making it unlawful for bodies other than the employer to discriminate; in particular it is made unlawful for a trade union to discriminate in relation to membership.

The Commissions   Under each principal Act there is established a commission which is charged with working towards the elimination of discrimination; for this purpose it is empowered to investigate where discriminatory practices appear to exist and to serve a 'non-discrimination notice' on any person whom the Commission is satisfied is committing, or has committed, unlawful discrimination. The notice requires the person on whom it is served to refrain from the discrimination and may require him to take positive steps to rectify the situation. If the notice is not complied with, the Commission may apply to a county court for an injunction: breach of such a court order would be contempt of court and could result, in the last resort, in imprisonment. The Commissions may also issue codes of practice and codes relevant to employers have been published.

Enforcement   The major responsibility for ensuring that unlawful discrimination is subjected to the legal process rests with the individuals who have suffered discrimination. It is frequently difficult for a complainant to obtain the information on which to base a complaint so the legislation has authorised a form by which the aggrieved person may question the respondent on his reasons for acting as he is alleged to have done. Not only will the answers received to these questions help to determine whether a complaint should be made, but the document may constitute evidence at the hearing of a complaint. The Commission may assist a claimant to fight his case, if that case is complex or involves an important matter of principle.

Positive discrimination and quotas   UK law does not generally favour positive discrimination and has little sympathy for quotas. It does not permit a person to refute an allegation that he has discriminated merely by demonstrating that he operated a 'quota system', but the production of employment records which showed a reasonable distribution of men and women and of racial groups in employment might be evidence of lack of intention to discriminate in a particular case. Such evidence might be valuable in cases of indirect discrimination. These records are also likely to be valuable aids to management in monitoring its performance and evaluating its policies (see recommendations of Equal Opportunities Commission's Code of Practice).

Conclusion

Anyone who has followed the analysis in this chapter will appreciate the warning in its first paragraph as to the complexity of the law of employment; nevertheless the chapter does no more than attempt to fulfil its promise to present the law in outline, as understood by the author at the time of going to press. It is hoped that the manager will bear in mind that cases often hinge on interpretations of statutory provisions too fine to be discussed here and also that Parliament and the judges are constantly introducing new rules.

General References

(Care should be taken to ensure that the latest editions of textbooks are used: the editions given below are correct at the time of going to press.)

Benedictus, R. and Bercusson, B., *Labour Law Cases and Materials*, Sweet and Maxwell (1987).
Grunfeld, C., *The Law of Redundancy*, Sweet and Maxwell (1989).
Howells, R. and Barrett, B., *The Health and Safety at Work Act: A Guide for Managers*, IPM (1982).
Kahn-Freund, O., *Labour and the Law*, Stevens (1977).
Rideout, R., *Principles of Labour Law*, Sweet and Maxwell (1989).
Selwyn, N., *Employment Law*, Butterworths (1988).
Smith, I. T. and Wood, J. C., *Industrial Law*, Butterworths (1989).
Sweet and Maxwell's, *Employment Law Manual*.
Wedderburn, Lord, *The Worker and the Law*, Penguin (1986).

Government reports
Bullock, *Committee of enquiry on industrial democracy*, HMSO, Cmnd 6706, (1977).
Donovan, *Royal commission on trade unions and employers' associations*, HMSO, Cmnd 3623, (1965–8).
Robens, *The report of the select committee on safety and health at work*, HMSO, Cmnd 5034, (1972).

Journals
Industrial Law Journal, Sweet and Maxwell.
Industrial Relations Review and Report, Industrial Relations Services.

12

Manpower planning, information and control

To be successful all organisations require strategies, plans and controls. These in turn require information. In this final chapter we focus on manpower planning. The term 'manpower planning' is preferred to 'human resources planning' because the latter includes aspects of strategic planning covered in the opening chapter.

Manpower planning provides the link between human resources strategy and the day to day operational activities examined in this book. It features as the final chapter because it provides a framework for feedback and control, ensuring that operational activities support the purposes of the organisation. Manpower planning involves line management. Indeed, it is a tool for line managers use. One of the big mistakes made in the early 1970s by some organisations setting up manpower planning departments, was to give the impression that manpower planning was the exclusive concern of a small number of highly numerate planners, who alone were capable of drawing up quantifiable models of stocks and flows of manpower using operational research techniques. Experts should of course be 'on tap' but not 'on top'. Line managers are accountable for results; they should be planning their own human resources, working in partnership with the personnel specialist. This chapter provides a framework for manpower planning as a shared activity between line managers and staff specialists.

Manpower planning defined

Manpower planning is a systematic approach designed to ensure that the right people will be in the right place at the right time. It has been described by David Bell as '. . . the systematic analysis of the company's resources, the construction of a forecast of its future manpower requirements from this base, with special concentration on the efficient use of manpower at both these stages, and the planning necessary to ensure that the manpower supply will match the forecast requirements'[1]. In the US manpower planning – now frequently termed 'human resources planning' – is usually associated with the recruitment process. According to Walker 'effective human resources planning is a process of analysing an organisation's human resource needs under changing conditions and developing the activities necessary to satisfy those needs'[2]. In the UK there is a trend away from defining manpower planning as a system towards defining it as a managerial activity. 'The manpower planning system' says Bennison 'must be replaced by manpower management . . . it is much more important, given the impossibility of forecasting the future to know which way to turn when circumstances change'[3]. Manpower planning helps managers to know 'which way to turn' at a time when skill shortages are becoming acute and labour costs more critical.

The framework for manpower planning

Manpower planning is a subsystem of corporate strategy and provides a sensible framework for management action in areas such as recruitment, training, pay and rewards and employee relations. This is illustrated in Figure 12.1 showing the links with corporate strategy on the one hand, and specific programmes on the other. To a large degree manpower planning is concerned with the reconciliation of supply and demand – the supply of human resources available internally and externally, and the demand for employees with the right skills and attitudes. The illustration provides a framework for the remainder of this chapter. Note the importance of 'feedback' or information flows from operational areas back into the manpower plans and corporate plans, to ensure plans are kept up to date.

Forecasting the demand for manpower

Demand for manpower can only be forecast with any degree of accuracy in the very short term. Most managers are aware of what their current requirements are (or should be!) and have a reasonably good idea some months into the future. After that matters become more problematical. Bennison comments that 'the notion that it is possible to estimate future manpower needs, with the precision necessary to match policies of supply, is quite fallacious. Demand is particularly susceptible to changes in the outside world: wars, commodity prices are just two examples; foreign exchange difficulties too can cause problems in managing economies which in turn can affect the growth rate of organisations'[4].

Some forecasting is however necessary even if it is less than precise. The art of management is to make the best decisions possible in situations of uncertainty. The contribution of manpower planning to this process is to investigate what useful information is available to assist the manager with these tasks. The starting point is with the

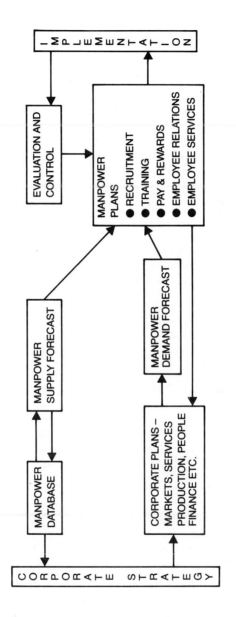

Figure 12.1 Manpower planning, information, and control

organisation's corporate plans to give a broad indication of the human resources required.

Factors to be considered when deriving the likely demand for manpower from corporate plans include the following list, (adapted from Purkiss)[5].

1 the introduction of new products;
2 future output expectations;
3 expansion/contraction plans;
4 changes in technology;
5 anticipated organisational changes: rationalisation, decentralisation;
6 manpower or financial ceilings;
7 manpower agreements and personnel policy.

Only a very brave or foolish manager would claim the ability to make accurate predictions under all these headings for up to five years ahead. However, the very exercise of considering these factors and making forecasts in which assumptions have been clearly stated usually pays dividends. It also facilitates rapid reassessment of the situation should a major crisis occur such as the oil crisis of the early 1970s.

Demand forecasting can be approached from two different angles, either by *'analysis of performance'* or *'analysis of productivity'*. The first is an analysis of the change in manpower demand arising from changes in productivity levels which alter overtime.

Four ways of tackling this are executive judgement, statistical techniques, productivity indices and work study.

1 *Executive judgement* is the simplest method. Individual managers state their estimated manpower requirements for some future date and the results are then pieced together and assessed for the whole unit or enterprise. This can be processed from the bottom upwards, starting first with junior managers and moving up through the organisation; when board level is reached a composite picture should emerge. Alternatively, top management can pass down a discussion document to be revised and commented upon by lower levels of management. The principal advantage of this approach, apart from its simplicity, is that operating managers will feel a sense of involvement in the planning process which can lead to greater commitment. The chief weakness of this method, if used by itself, is that a major plan is built up on nothing better than well-informed 'guesstimates'. Therefore the other three approaches should also be attempted.

2 *Statistical analysis* can establish whether significant quantitative relationships have operated in the recent history of the organisation between manpower and other factors of production. These

can be tabulated, and projected into the future in order to provide a forecast. Factors which have been found to vary in relation to numbers employed include sales, level of production, power consumed, wages, and the general level of economic activity. An example of this approach is provided in Figure 12.2 which features a forecast of the number of immigration officers required by the Civil Service. In the first graph, a statistical projection exercise has been undertaken based on the trend line established over a ten year period. The second graph, shows the relationship which has been established between the number of inward passengers and the number of officers in employment.

3 Simple projections of historical trends are likely to ignore the important influence of changes in *productivity*. Improved productivity may lead to a decline in the demand for manpower. Productivity itself expresses the relationship between volume of production and manpower used. It is a dynamic variable influenced principally by technological change and manpower utilisation. The Department of Employment guide considers that 'manpower forecasting using productivity measurement is satisfactory so long as the two variables, output and input, are fairly easy to quantify, and the rate of change in productivity over a forecast period can be predicted with some confidence[7]. However, measurement can pose serious problems, as those managers who have been involved with productivity bargaining will be only too aware. Purkiss warns[8] us that 'to talk in terms of tons produced each manshift, sales turnover per employee, or value added per operative, gives us a feeling of great objectivity'. Productivity depends on the will to work and to operate new machinery and procedures just as much as it does on new capital investment, and these must also be taken into account.

4 *Work study* represents a more traditional approach to estimating the demand for labour. Work study contributes two major techniques. The first of these, method study, checks on and aims to improve methods of work. The second, work measurement, makes use of time study, synthesis and analytical estimating to make an estimate of the standard time required for each job and hence the number of man hours required for each class of labour. Provided accurate sales and production forecasts are available, which can be converted into detailed production schedules, the demand for manpower can then be calculated in terms of 'man hours' and 'man days'. Complications arise in dealing with 'indirect' workers whose work cannot be so easily measured, or where new technology and work methods are needed. Work study is particularly suitable for production line work and short term estimates, and it has the added

advantage that many firms already possess well established systems of cost and work measurement.

Forecasting the supply of manpower

The supply of manpower is provided firstly by the existing stock of human resources and secondly by replenishment from the external labour market. This was first examined in the opening chapter on strategy; now we consider ways of auditing and forecasting the internal stock of human resources. We are moving into an area of greater certainty than was the case with manpower demand, because our starting point is a known quantity: existing employees. Naturally these can in a free economy choose to leave to work elsewhere, but managers in their turn, can influence these decisions and predict their occurrence with some degree of confidence.

Manpower information

A manpower information system is built up from data about individual employees. It is normally the responsibility of the personnel department to maintain up to date records containing relevant information about each employee, including personal particulars, position in the organisation, place of work, pay, qualifications, skills and career history. The objective is to create a system which is confidential and secure, but which will allow line management direct and immediate access to data concerning their own subordinates. Duplication of personal records should be avoided where possible. In order to keep this information accurate and up to date it is sensible to provide employees with an opportunity to examine what is recorded against their name at regular intervals. The Data Protection Act in UK and similar legislation in other countries protects this right of access to data stored on computer[9].

Any organisation with more than 50 employees should seriously consider computerising its personnel record system[10], although a computerised system can never fully replace manual records. Documents which need to be kept in their original form include application forms, contracts of employment, medical certificates, appraisal forms and accident reports. A central data base will cut duplication. Computers enable the core data to be passed on to other systems such as word-processing packages, payroll and pension systems. A good system will update automatically throughout. A computerised system will give fast analysis and retrieval of information about employees. A specific analysis by department or function can be provided in a wide variety of reporting formats and will include the use of graphics and spreadsheet packages.

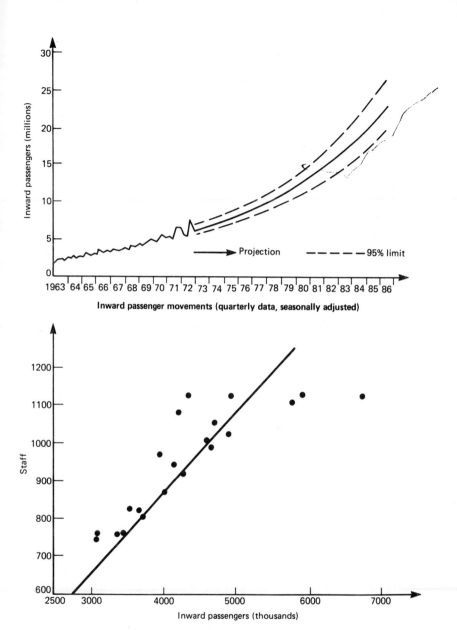

Relationship between numbers of inward passenger movements (seasonally adjusted) and numbers of permanent staff. Based on quarterly data from 1.4.68 to 1.10.72

Figure 12.2 Manpower demand forecasts using (A) projection of manpower data and (B) relationship between manpower and work load (Reproduced from an article by Bartholomew, Hopes and Smith in *Personnel Review*, Vol. **5**, 1976, Teakfield Press[7])

Modern computerised personnel information systems work at two main levels[11]. They can reduce the personnel department's workload by automating systems. They can also provide a most useful management information system although many line managers do not yet make full use of them. A line manager, for example, may wish to increase productivity by reducing manpower and improving manpower budgeting processes, and therefore needs access to current information concerning staff analysed by type, age, and length of service. Historical attrition rates should also be available. By using the enquiry language of a typical CPIS* system, manpower costing information can also be accessed. The financial effects of introducing a voluntary severance scheme for a particular group of staff for example could then be quickly explored. A good CPIS system can provide an analysis of manpower flows (turnover, promotion, recruitment, transfer in, transfer out, secondment and any other losses) which have occurred. This will help the line manager to take more informed decisions concerning likely vacancies or resulting promotion opportunities. Computerisation can also enable companies to analyse absenteeism by departments, keep training records up to date, assist with salary reviews involving complex calculations and recalculations taking into account many considerations and generate word processing packages which include a range of offers of employment letters to candidates.

An example of a CPIS system in use is provided by Nissan Motors Manufacturing (UK) Ltd[12]. Personnel systems are under the overall control of the personnel manager while specific responsibility for maintaining the manpower data base lies with a personnel systems expert. Departmental management determines the nature of the output required. This system provides:

- Manpower stocktakes – analyses of age distributions, length of service, stocks of skills and qualifications, monthly headcounts, analyses of current performance and future potential relevant to succession planning.

- Manpower forecasts – forecasts from senior managers of their future manpower requirements are fed into spreadsheet, analysed by department and occupational group, produced in summary report with bar and pie charts and line graphics, and compared with forecasts.

- Adjustments – detailed plans for recruitment, training, management development, promotion and organisational change are developed jointly by the personnel department and line management. Modern computerised personnel information systems are moving towards further integration with other management

---

* Computerised personnel information system

information systems. 'My vision', comments Don Beattie, Personnel Director, STC Ltd 'of a fully functional personnel information system is that it should whilst maintaining all the confidentiality criteria which we professionals would require of it, interact and integrate with the other management information systems used to run the enterprise'[13].

Age profile analysis

A practical example of manpower supply forecasting using personnel records is provided by age profile analysis. An age profile of a section of the labour force, such as all employees in a particular department, or all those doing the same job, can indicate in dramatic fashion how many people are about to retire and will require replacement, or whether career prospects and morale are being jeopardised by the existing distribution of age groups. This is illustrated by the three profiles in Figure 12.3.

In the first profile it is obvious that a large number of employees are soon going to retire and require replacing. Heavy recruitment may be called for. However new young employees may not mix easily with the predominantly older labour force which may lead to further wastage. In the second situation with a predominantly middle-aged labour force dissatisfaction with promotion prospects is likely to occur as well as

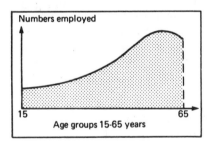

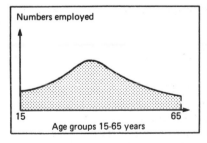

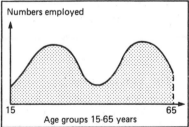

Figure 12.3 Age profiles – some examples

leading eventually to a replication of the first age profile. The third profile can arise because of over-reaction to the first situation and create further problems. This simple type of exercise greatly facilitates the planning of recruitment and training.

Labour wastage

Labour wastage takes a major toll of the existing stock of manpower, and is a major consideration if manpower planning is to be effective. It has concerned management for many years because of the ensuing cost and inconvenience. Labour wastage was reckoned to cost the electronics industry in Britain well over ten million pounds some years ago while the cost of recruiting and training skilled workers in the clothing industry was calculated to be as much as twelve hundred pounds per head[14]. In spite of this, few organisations give sufficient consideration to their labour wastage. This may be because managers become fatalistic, are too busy, or may not feel personally concerned because such costs are 'hidden' costs and therefore not directly attributable to them. The recruitment and selection of new employees invariably attracts greater attention and status. However prevention is undoubtedly better than cure. Of course, limited wastage is useful in many organisations, permitting the run down of a labour force or to introduce fresh blood and new ideas.

Measuring labour wastage is a necessary prelude to planning and remedial action. The most popular method is by an annual labour turnover index. Indeed, labour wastage is frequently referred to as labour turnover, although strictly speaking labour turnover is but one way of looking at the wastage of labour. The most commonly found index of labour turnover (sometimes referred to as the 'BIM Index') uses the following formula:

$$\frac{\text{total number of leavers in the past year}}{\text{average number employed in the past year}} \times 100$$

Thus assuming an average of 1000 employees and 290 leavers during the year in question, we have:

$$\frac{290}{1000} \times 100 = 29\% \text{ labour turnover}$$

This index has the advantage of being easily calculated using data that is readily available, and giving some indication as to whether losses are high or low. However, it suffers from a number of weaknesses, and should not be used on its own or where numbers employed are subject to fluctuation. It does not tell us, for example, whether leavers are distributed over a range of jobs, or concentrated in just one or two. In the example above, the 290 leavers might have come from 290 different jobs, or just conceivably have all been employed in the same job, with no worker staying more than a few hours! Nor does it tell us the length of service of the leavers, or the stability of the bulk of the labour force.

A simple *stability index* does provide complementary data concerning stability and is normally calculated as follows:

$$\frac{\text{Number of employees with more than one year's service}}{\text{Average number employed}}$$

But, this still gives too limited a picture and suffers from statistical weakness. A better method is provided by an analysis of the completed length of service of leavers. This can be portrayed as a *completed length of service distribution* (with leavers expressed as a percentage of the average number employed in each occupation). Two distributions are illustrated in Figure 12.4.

In this example taken from a large light engineering plant, we have a fairly typical profile for male process workers, but an unusual and perturbing one for maintenance fitters[15]. During the year concerned a large number of maintenance fitters with long service have left the firm, suggesting that something is amiss, and urgent action required.

Studies of labour wastage by the Tavistock Institute of Human Relations in London, UK, have provided a valuable insight into the processes manifest in labour wastage. Based on methods developed by

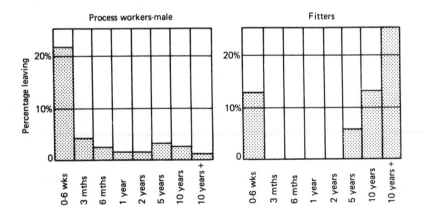

Figure 12.4   Completed length of service distributions

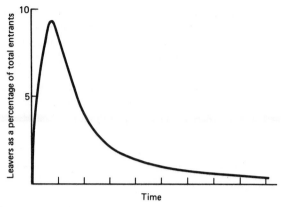

Figure 12.5   A survival curve

Rice, Hill and Trist[16] the survival patterns of 'cohorts' of new starters in a number of industries have been analysed. The wastage pattern illustrated in Figure 12.5 above was found to be typical. (The 'survival curve' represents the length of time new employees 'survive' or remain with their employer. A 'cohort' is a group of employees who commence their employment in a new firm at the same time.)

Most wastage takes place during the initial period of employment, and then falls away as the remaining new starters begin to settle down. Rice, Hill and Trist described this as a 'social process' with three distinct phases. The first phase they labelled 'the period of induction crisis' during which labour wastage quickly reaches a peak. This is followed by a 'period of differential transit' during which wastage declines, and leads to a 'period of settled connection' when those still remaining become 'quasi permanent' employees.

Management should be aware of wastage patterns within their own organisations; such information can indicate the size of the problem, the time when new employees are most likely to leave, and when positive action should be taken to reduce the problem. For manpower planning purposes, it is important to know the rate at which employees are likely to leave and require replacement. The completed length of service distribution described above has distinct advantages over the survival curve of new cohorts as a method of analysis. Many organisations do not take on large cohorts of homogeneous groups of new employees and in any case, long service employees merit as much or more attention. It is also important to distinguish between different occupations when analysing labour wastage.

Considerable debate still exists on the principal reasons for labour wastage. Silcock[17] concluded that the existing evidence shows that labour turnover varies widely between firms, the amount of wastage decreases as the length of service increases, wastage is higher among females than males, and wastage decreases as the amount of skill exercised increases. Common sense suggests however that job satisfaction, local unemployment levels and other considerations as well as pay also exercise considerable influence, and there is some evidence to support this[18]. When account is taken of the fact that women are excluded from many skilled and interesting occupations, their labour stability may be found to be as good or better than men. The lack of conclusive evidence underlines the need for management to carry out its own wastage analysis and then to exchange information with other local employers in order to establish standards of comparison.

Quantitative analysis of a human situation is rarely sufficient. Remedial action concerning labour wastage requires information about the motivation of employees. Traditionally the emphasis in labour wastage prevention has been laid on finding out the reasons given for leaving. This can be carried out by questionnaire or 'exit' interview. Unfortunately, the reasons given frequently fail to reflect the real reasons for leaving, and require careful interpretation. There is much to be said for reversing the direction of enquiry by investigating why employees stay rather than leave and what creates good morale and job satisfaction. This places the emphasis fairly and squarely on the effective management of people and on measures designed to integrate new employees into the work force.

'Employers have been uttering cries of despair about skill shortages, but when the question is examined in detail, we find more often than not, that a greater underlying problem is their failure to retain good workers' commented Stephen Bevan in *The Sunday Times* (12 February 1989). Research at the Institute of Manpower Studies and elsewhere points to the beneficial effect on retention rates of well designed jobs, high quality line management and realistic recruitment procedures[19]. Similar emphases will emerge in the next section on absenteeism.

Absenteeism

In a typical year more than 250 million working days are lost in UK through absenteeism – a figure fifty times higher than the number of days lost through strikes. Absenteeism is a major problem in all industrialised countries costing employers and governments substantial sums of money[20]. Yet the time and attention devoted to analysing and controlling it is far less than that devoted to industrial disputes. We consider it here alongside manpower planning and control because it should feature in any cost-effective system of manpower planning. It also has an affinity with problems of labour wastage and attrition. Most absenteeism is attributable to sickness. Relevant aspects of this have already been considered in the chapter on welfare and counselling. Here we are concerned chiefly with measurement and control.

At company level information on absenteeism can be gathered from attendance sheets, clock cards, medical records, personal files and return to work interview forms. Computerised data bases can be built up to monitor overall absence levels, or attendance records of individual employees. The most common formula for measuring absenteeism calculates the percentage of the total time available in a specified period which has been lost because of absence for any reason:

$$\frac{\text{Total absence (days/hours) in period}}{\text{Total possible time (days/hours)}} \times 100$$

As absenteeism will vary between departments as well as category of employee, indices must be maintained for relevant groups. These may then be compared with national industrial and regional norms to estimate the extent of the problem. The national daily absenteeism rate in UK for full time workers is just under 5% per annum varying regionally from less than 4% (South East) to over 5% (North West). Workers in heavy industry record the highest figures; workers in agriculture, forestry, fishing, banking, insurance and finance record the lowest. Managers in small enterprises had the lowest rate overall (under 3%). Skilled manual workers record more than double this level. There is significant correlation between the nature of the job and absenteeism, pointing to job satisfaction as an important component[21].

Control starts with the keeping of adequate records. Improved selection plays a major part too as can joint management-union committees, 'return to work' interviews, attendance bonuses, disciplinary action, counselling and target-setting. Working time can be reorganised as with flexi-time or 'annual hours' working agreements. The key figure in absence control is the supervisor. Good supervisors enjoy relatively low absenteeism in their departments.

Manpower models

Quantitative models are now a feature of all business forecasting and manpower planning is no exception. Manpower planning models generally attempt a representation of the stock of manpower in an organisation and aim to demonstrate the likely consequences of major decisions in such areas as recruitment, training and promotion policy. Developing large complex models is a job for the expert, although the principles and conclusions need to be designed in a way that makes sense to line management.

The basis for a typical manpower model is illustrated by the simple 'stationary population model' shown in Figure 12.6. This is a kind of 'snapshot' of a graded staff structure at a moment in time. Recruitment in this example is confined to young persons who enter a training grade. At subsequent stages in their employment some are promoted, some remain in their present grade, and some leave. Even such a simple model carries important implications for organisational decision making and manpower planning concerning recruitment, promotion and retirement.

No organisation is, of course, stationary, and a good manpower model must reflect the dynamics of the situation. First and foremost it

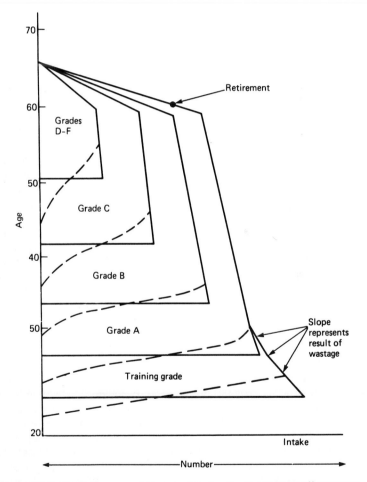

Figure 12.6   Stationary population model of a simple graded staff structure (Horizontal lines represent average ages of entry and promotion. Dotted lines represent spreads of ages.)

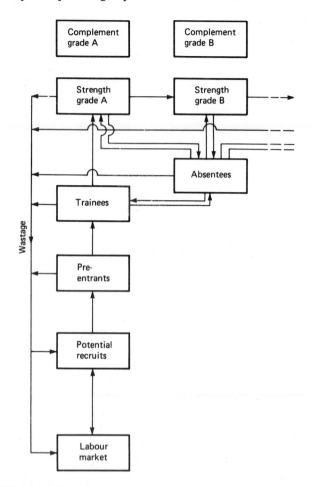

Figure 12.7 Manpower flow system

must reflect the flow of personnel through the system and attempt to quantify the process depicted in Figure 12.7, above.

The manpower flow system shown here helps to illustrate the flow of new recruits into the organisation from the labour market. Any forecast of recruitment needs to take account of likely wastage at all stages between attracting potential recruits until the new recruits are trained and settled into their respective departments. This type of forecast was formerly very difficult because of the difficulty of 'capturing' an essentially dynamic situation. Analysing this process has been assisted in recent years by developments in mathematics using Markov

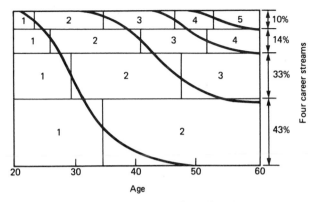

Figure 12.8 Career stream diagram using 'Camel' model

chain models and Renewal Theory[22]. An example of this is provided by the so called 'Camel' model, developed for career planning in a hierarchical organisation[23]. Figure 12.8 illustrates the results of an analysis using this model for a five grade hierarchy. On the vertical axis showing four 'career systems' there is one for each possible final grade at retirement age. The *vertical* lines show the typical ages of promotion for staff in each stream. The *curved* lines represent the results of the exercise. Given data concerning existing ages and grades of the work force, an estimate of promotion prospects has been calculated and is shown as appropriately 'smoothed' curves on the diagram.

Evaluation and control

Evaluation and control complete the manpower planning cycle. Manpower planning provides a framework for implementation in relevant functional areas: recruitment, training, pay and rewards and employee services. Targets may be set for numbers to be recruited in different skill categories as well as for training and development programmes. Pay and reward systems may then be reviewed and modified to stimulate motivation, retention and productivity. Each chapter in the book has indicated appropriate criteria for the major areas of human resource management.

Information is the key to evaluation and control. Modern manpower planning has become increasingly a process of well-informed decision making, feedback and control. 'Data must be at least as good as data presented in other areas such as marketing and finance' is the advice of David Bell[24]. 'One of the most potent sources of information is the manpower planning process itself . . . Monitoring actual data against the plan can clarify what is happening and why'. Evaluation and control bring together line management and personnel specialists. Line managers are expected to achieve their operational goals and will protest loudly when manpower targets in recruitment and training for example are not being met. Personnel specialists now have the tools and techniques to manage professionally and have a powerful incentive to monitor the achievement of targets in key result areas.

References

1   Bell, D., *Planning Corporate Manpower*, Longman, 1974.
2   Walker, J. W., *Human Resource Planning*, McGraw Hill, 1980.
3   Bennison, M., *The Manpower Planning Handbook*, McGraw Hill, 1983.
4   Bennison, M., *opus cit.*, p. 5.
5   Purkiss, C., 'Estimating the demand for manpower', paper presented to Manpower Society Annual Conference, 1972.
6   Bartholomew, D. J., Hopes, R. F. A. and Smith, A. C., 'Manpower planning in the face of uncertainty', *Personnel Review*, **5**, no. 3, 1976.
7   Department of Employment, *Company Manpower Planning*, HMSO, 1972.
8   Purkiss, C., *opus cit.*
9   Bell, D. J., 'Practical implications of the Data Protection Act', *Personnel Management*, June 1984.
10 'Personnel Record Systems', *Personnel Management* Factsheet no. 2, Feb. 1983.
11 Richards-Carpenter, C., 'Making managers into manpower planners', *Personnel Management*, Oct. 1988.
12 Carolin, B. and Evans, A., 'Computers as a strategic personnel tool', *Personnel Management*, July 1988.
13 Beattie, D., 'Better decisions through Information Technology', paper presented to 'Computers in Personnel' Conference (IPM/IMS), June 1987.
14 'Labour Turnover in the clothing industry', National Economic Development Organisation, HMSO, 1967.
15 Cowling, A. G., 'Pay and wastage in a local labour market', unpublished Ph.D thesis, The City University, 1977.
16 Rice, A. K., Hill, J. M. M. and Trist, E. I., 'The representation of labour turnover as a social process', *Human Relations Journal*, **11**, no. 2.
17 Silcock, H., 'The phenomenon of labour turnover', *Journal of the Royal Statistical Society*, 1954.
18 Bowey, A. M., *A Guide to Manpower Planning*, MacMillan 1974.
19 Bevan, S., The Management of Labour Turnover, *IMS Report* no. 136, Institute of Manpower Studies.
20 'Absence Control', *IDS Study*, no. 403, Feb. 1988. Incomes Data Services.
21 'Absence from Work', Industrial Society, Dec. 1985.
22 Bartholomew, D. J. (ed.), *Manpower Planning: Selected readings*, Penguin, 1976.
23 Keeney, G. A., Morgan, R. A. and Ray, K. H., 'The Camel Model: a model for career planning in a hierarchy', *Personnel Review*, **6**, no. 4, 1977.
24 Bell, D. J., 'Why manpower planning is back in vogue'. *Personnel Management*, July 1989.

Index